# Genesis Understood

## LANCE THOMAS WYNN

authorHOUSE

*AuthorHouse™*
*1663 Liberty Drive*
*Bloomington, IN 47403*
*www.authorhouse.com*
*Phone: 1 (800) 839-8640*

*Scripture quotations marked KJV are from the Holy Bible, King James Version (Authorized Version). First published in 1611. Quoted from the KJV Classic Reference Bible, Copyright © 1983 by The <u>Zondervan</u> Corporation.*

*Published by AuthorHouse 08/24/2017*

*ISBN: 978-1-5246-2411-8 (sc)*

*Library of Congress Control Number: 2016913072*

*Print information available on the last page.*

*Any people depicted in stock imagery provided by Thinkstock are models, and such images are being used for illustrative purposes only. Certain stock imagery © Thinkstock.*

*This book is printed on acid-free paper.*

# Contents

Contents

# Chapter 1

## From darkness comes light

## God is born

## What is Gravity?

"In the beginning"… well, actually there was no beginning. Before God there was nothing. Well, that is not exactly true either. At this time, we would all assume there is nothing, just darkness. I have asked myself this one question since I was a young boy. "How can something come from nothing?" My answer has always been the same, "Something cannot come from nothing." So how can there be a God? How can there be anything? If the big bang theory is true, how did it create itself from nothing?

I have thought about this all my life and the answer came to me in the month of September 2008, at 2:00 am while sleeping. I woke up from a dream two nights in a row. I do not remember the two dreams, but I had an answer to two of my questions, how was God created, and what was gravity. Yes, before God there was something. In my galactic astronomy class in high school, my teacher taught Einstein's theory of relativity. As a boy, I had trouble understanding how God created himself from nothing, and then as a teenager, I could not accept this theory of relativity.

When there is nothing in the universe, we are guaranteed darkness, and the result from darkness is dryness and coldness. All three are conditions, but they are not concrete. However, we have reaction, when it is cold outside, the air is dry, and grabbing the doorknob can cause a static shock, which is electricity.

Two conditions dry and cold have a reaction, the result creates static electricity, and the small particles are formed by conditions not made by God. Without something, there would be no God, no universe, and no us. Can you imagine darkness forever, without God, stars, galaxies, and people?

Darkness is something! It covers every cubic inch of space going out in every direction forever and ever. The small particles in a neutral state under a constant pressure have been created by the conditions of cold and dry. The particles are round, pressure causes them to bump, and some spinning right, and some left. The right spin is positive, and the left spin is negative. Positive and negative particles attract each other creating electricity. Everything in the universe will come from opposite spinning particles.

Two positive or two negative particles will push away from each other, because they are going in opposite directions while bumping. Positive and negative particles are going in the same direction while bumping which cause attraction and creates reaction.

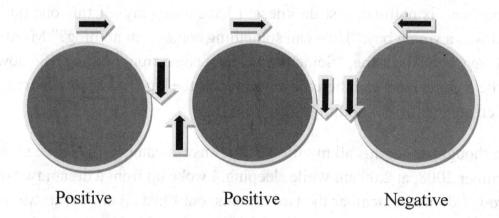

Positive          Positive          Negative

*Out of Darkness comes Light*

*JEHOVAH, I AM THAT I AM IS BORN*

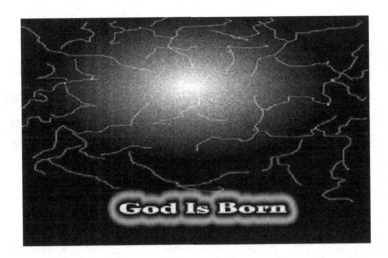

Two like spinning particles repel from each other, and soon finding an opposite spinning particle, they attract rubbing against each other causing friction and heat. This is our first heat, light, and electricity. Trillions and trillions of opposite particles come together producing an arc light from electricity and heat. From electricity comes intelligence, the light that shines in total darkness is the first Entity. God is the light, "I Am That I Am."

It can be hard to understand how this all came about, but we know it did because we are here living on a planet surrounded by billions of stars. We cannot have all the things we see, feel, smell, and taste without an intelligent designer, architect, and engineer. Many people believe all this has been created by chance, if that it so, how was the eye created. Even Charles Darwin had trouble with knowing the chances were a thousand trillion to one shot.

Nothing can come from chance! Ask a smart scientist that does not believe in God, if he or she is smarter than an atom, and I am sure he or she will say yes. Then ask this person if he or she can create a human. Again, I am sure the scientist will say no. Since the scientist believe atoms and molecules created the animals and people by chance, and they are smarter than an atom, why can they not create a human?

Do you really think a bunch of atoms came together, met at a Starbucks, and one said to the other, "hey man why don't we create a human?" "Okay man," and the others asked, "What is a human... man?" Scientist are so smart, yet they believe everything was created by chance, without an entity to design it. It is not possible!

From the very small round, spinning particles comes heat, light, and electricity. From electricity comes intelligence, and an entity is born. God is born, and he now owns the dark expanse, and how did this come about, by chance possibly.

*Electricity is the result from one particle spinning*
*Right and one spinning left*
*The electricity arc's and there is Light*

## I AM THAT I AM

## God Creates the Universe

God is alone in forever darkness, so can you imagine no other entity to love or to love you back. God does not want to be alone; He must learn how to create. At this time, there is no protons and no neutrons; he has only very small particles to work with. Can you imagine there is nothing but darkness and his arc light? How in the world can God create everything we see today from particles so small we are not able to see them with the strongest microscope? How does a computer today create an image, by using two maneuvers zero and one? God's advantage is He can see the particles we cannot.

God has to make something much larger, He has three things to work with, and that is positive, negative, and neutral.

*Positive + Negative = Neutral*
*Positive + Positive + Negative = Positive*
*Negative + Negative + Positive = Negative*

God had to learn and experiment just as we have in the flesh earth today. He did just as Edison, experimenting with the light bulb. Edison thought it would be easy, but it turned out to be very time consuming trying every substance he could think of. God created the proton with the perfect amount of negative and positive particles with one more positive particle to have a positive charge. Even though He has increased, the size by over 1834 times, it can still travel through our bodies without touching an atom. All the different charges that scientist have named consisting of positrons, electrons, hadrons, and quarks make up the proton. Quarks have one-third charge made up of three charged particles. Without the quarks, there would be nothing today. Nevertheless, like Edison finally getting the right substance to make the light bulb work, God has created the first proton, getting the perfect size and charges to create the first element.

The weather is a good example of how these particles work right here on the earth. Our weather system has a high and low-pressure system. The high-pressure system rotates to the right producing sinking air, which gives us calm winds, dryer air, and plenty of sunshine. The low-pressure system rotates to the left producing lift, which gives us windy and rainy conditions all due to rotation. Turn a screw to the right, and it drives in; turn a screw to the left, and it backs out. To produce power or electricity today we have generators, gas engines, electric motors, and all must spin. Even the water wheel used thousands of years ago has to rotate to produce power. Our earth, the moon, the sun, and all the planets spin. The planets orbit the sun, and the stars orbit the black holes. Without spin, nothing would exist.

God creates the positron, adds an electron, and puts it in orbit around the positron creating a proton. The electron orbits the positron like our planets orbit the sun, except it probably travels the speed of light, and travels a different orbit each time, creating a shell, which makes the area of the proton much larger. We never see the proton, what we see and touch is the electron shell.

God created the proton and added an electron, and we have our first element hydrogen. The universe is made up of 90% hydrogen, the most common element, and lightest element in the universe. It is also a very unstable element, which will create something very valuable for the creation of stars and humans.

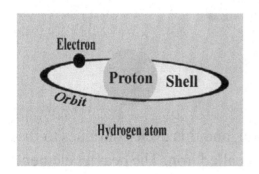

Hydrogen = one proton and one electron

Darkness is made up of these small little particles, and God has a never-ending supply. God creates protons by the billions and trillions, and he has a ball the size of our earth. God still just has one element, so he continues to create hydrogen, and now the ball is the size of Jupiter. Pressure from gravity push has become much greater and the core of this giant ball has become very hot. God continues to create more hydrogen and the ball is now the size of our sun.

The pressure has become so great in the core of this ball the electrons have left the protons. The protons are now all positive and do not attract, but the pressure is so great the positive protons are forced together and this causes hydrogen fusion. The whole ball is lit up like a candle and our first star is born.

## The Neutron is born

## The second element Helium

From the fusion of two positive protons comes a miracle, a neutron is created, and our second element (helium) has been created. Helium is a heavier element made up of two protons and two neutrons with two electrons orbiting the core creating the electromagnetic shell.

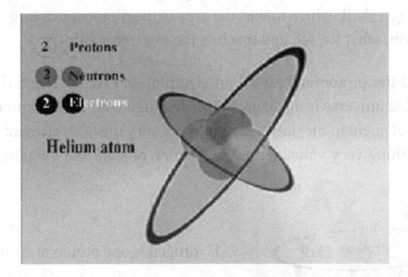

Hydrogen fuses into helium, helium into lithium, and this cycle continues to fuse heavier elements all the way to our 26th element called iron. The heavier elements will not be created for millions of years, when the light elements are used up. The core builds up with iron, the most stable nuclei of all atomic nuclei. Because iron is stable, it does not release energy to counteract gravity force. Something has to give, and the core collapses, and the result is a major rebound explosion, which we call a nova, or supernova. To explain this collapse, the iron reaches its maximum density, and the gravity force is very great. The outer layers are pushing on the iron core, and something has to give. Say you have a balloon filled with water, and you step on it. The water shoots out to the right and left side of your foot. This is what happens to the iron core. The core collapses, and a rebound explosion creates all other heavy elements, like gold, zinc, titanium, and nickel sending them into outer space, where other stars and planets can catch them. Red giant stars produce the majority of our heavy elements.

God continues to create galaxies of different types, and many planets orbit the stars. God is still lonely. It is time to create man and animals. However, before this, we need to understand why the pressure of a star became greater, the larger the hydrogen ball became.

## What is Gravity?

God did not create gravity, when God created the proton gravity was a natural phenomenon or result of it. The size of the proton created gravity.

In my galactic astronomy class, I learned about Albert Einstein theory of relativity. I never believed the theory that curvature of space and time creates gravity. Another theory of Einstein is, if two space ships back to back go in opposite directions at the speed of light; the gap will not open twice the speed of light. He says the gap cannot open faster than the speed of light. The gap is nothing, and it will open twice the speed of light.

This is a dream, the gap is not concrete, and the curvature of space and time are not concrete. Can love or peace create gravity? No love and peace are not concrete. Gravity can only be created by something concrete. Einstein says light bends, I do not believe light bends, it distorts and reflects, but it does not bend. If light does bend, it would not cause gravity push towards the radius or center of the earth. Why? Because, the light will bend around the earth, and continue in a straight line. If the light were traveling in one direction, stars or planets would not form. The earth has gravity push toward the center or radius, and that means the push is coming from all directions. How can space-time, which is nothing, create gravity? A warped universe, no way!

In the eleventh grade, I could not understand how scientist could fall for this dream or great imagination. When I was in high school, the scientist could not understand relativity. Yet they followed it like dumb sheep. Today they claim to understand relativity, and are adding to the of Einstein dream, like Parallel universes, and wormholes. I guess the scientist with the greatest imagination wins the prize.

Gravity, what is it? When God created the proton, which is 1830 times larger than the electron, its size displaced darkness creating gravity force. If the proton did not create gravity, then God would still be alone today. No stars or planets could form without gravity. What makes them round? The gravity force from all directions is pushing against the stars holding them together, and the pressure is pointing to the median of the star or planet.

When big rocks and little rock come together, they first have awkward shapes. As they collect more rocks the gravity force becomes stronger and points to the median of that mass. Once it gets large enough the gravity increases and the awkward formation of rocks become round. Because of gravity push, planets and moons are created. The core of planets become molten iron, which helps the planets to become round.

Since darkness goes on forever these particles are contained and have a weight, just like sand in a box has weight. When God created the protons and neutrons it displaces the darkness, like a boat displaces water, and it floats.

To explain how it works. Let us say we have a two-foot cube box full of air that we can say is darkness, and say the air pressure is at 10 pounds. Without letting the air out of the containment, we put a baseball in the box, and we really cannot measure much difference, but there is a difference. Then we put in a basketball and the pressure increases enough to measure. Let us say we now have 20 pounds of pressure on the basketball. The air pressure is pushing to the core or radius of the ball. Therefore, if you have a beetle sitting on the ball, the beetle now weighs twice as much.

# However, it is not that simple.

The sun is one million times bigger than the earth. If a 200-pound man were standing on the sun, he should weigh 200 million pounds. This would not be the case. The earth is made up of heavy elements with lots of protons and neutrons that have displaced more darkness per cubic foot. The sun is made mostly of hydrogen and helium with far less protons and neutrons displacing the darkness per cubic foot. Therefore, a 200-pound man would weigh 5414 pounds standing on the sun not 200 million pounds.

Gravity works two ways: #1. Our sun feels a gravity push, like a boat that displaces the water, and the water pushes at the boat trying to take back the area displaced. The particles in the darkness are pushing back at the sun trying to fill the displaced area. The heavier the boat is loaded, the more water is displaced, and the more weight pressing against the boat. The bigger the star, the more displacement, and a greater gravity push.

The second way: #2. The second way is gravity pull. The sun pulls on the earth, the earth pulls on the Sun and moon, the moon pulls on the earth, and all three have gravity push. The pull from the moon gives us two high tides, and two low tides, and this is proof that stars and planets pull on each other.

Darkness must be something, if it is not, there would be nothing forever and ever. So, before God there was something, but not an intelligent entity. God created the proton, and gravity was born. Without gravity, the stars and planets would not form, and our first element would not fuse and create the second element helium, that created the neutron, which is needed to create all the other elements in the universe.

God is the electricity, and the light; the everlasting light and his intelligentsia and memory, have no bounds. God is the creator of all the mass in the universe. He created the stars and planets so his children and creatures could have a home.

 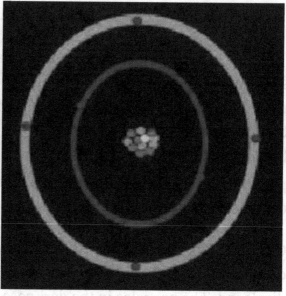

Iron Atom: Atomic # 26
Protons 26, Neutrons 30

Carbon Atom: Atomic # 6
Protons 6, Neutrons 6

Iron has more protons and neutrons displacing more darkness giving it more weight. Carbon has less area displaced and less gravity push.

# The Light

### Exodus 3:2 (King James Version)

*²And the angel of the LORD appeared unto him in a flame of fire out of the midst of a bush: and he looked, and, behold, the bush burned with fire, and the bush was not consumed.*

*The bush did not burn, because it was the arc light of God.*
*The light from a modern arc welder is similar.*
*The fire of God is the light of God.*
*Electricity and light = God.*

The flame of fire was the arc light of God, and that is the reason why the bush did not burn. Therefore flesh man cannot look upon God.

*Isaiah 60:19-20 (King James Version)*

[19]*The sun shall be no more thy light by day; neither for brightness shall the moon give light unto thee: but the LORD shall be unto thee an everlasting light, and thy God thy glory.*

[20]*Thy sun shall no more go down; neither shall thy moon withdraw itself: for the LORD shall be thine everlasting light, and the days of thy mourning shall be ended.*

*Ezekiel 1:13 (King James Version)*

[13]*As for the likeness of the living creatures, their appearance was like burning coals of fire, and like the appearance of lamps: it went up and down among the living creatures; and the fire was bright, and out of the fire went forth lightning.*

*Matthew 28:3 (King James Version)*

[3]*His countenance was like lightning, and his raiment white as snow:*

*Again, the arc light*

*He is dressed in light*

*John 3:20-21 (King James Version)*

[20]*For every one that doeth evil hateth the light, neither cometh to the light, lest his deeds should be reproved.*

*21But he that doeth truth cometh to the light, that his deeds may be made manifest, that they are wrought in God.*

*John 8:12 (King James Version)*

[12]*Then spake Jesus again unto them, saying, I am the light of the world: he that followeth me shall not walk in darkness, but shall have the light of life.*

### Acts 9:3 *(King James Version)*

*³And as he journeyed, he came near Damascus: and suddenly there shined round about him a light from heaven:*

### Acts 9:8-9 *(King James Version)*

*⁸And Saul arose from the earth; and when his eyes were opened, he saw no man: but they led him by the hand, and brought him into Damascus.*

*⁹And he was **three days without sight**, and neither did eat nor drink.*

The light Paul experienced, which was the light of Christ, is much like the light of the arc welder of today. When Paul looked at the light, the arc light burned his retina, and the result was blindness for three days. (My father lost his eyesight for three days from looking at the ark welder too long.) I believe when we return in our spirit bodies we can look at Gods light without any consequences.

Our computers compute by using zero and one, and by using the zero and one it can produce a beautiful mountain image on our screen. God uses positive and negative particles to create all that is, in the universe.

### One Chronicles 13:10 *(King James Version)*

*¹⁰And the anger of the LORD was kindled against Uzza, and he smote him, because he put his hand to the ark: and there he died before God.*

*Uzza I believe died of electrical shock, from the arc of electricity*

*Some Bible Scholars today believe the ark had a magnetic field surrounding it*

God is our light that came out of darkness; we are here today because of this great light. If you believe in God, you are a child of light. During judgment time, the fire of God will quench the children that followed Christ, and will burn to ashes the followers of Satan.

# Why did God create all these galaxies?

In the beginning, God was all alone; he had no one to talk to, no one to love, and no one to love him back. He created the stars and planets for one reason, and that reason is for his pleasure.

**Revelation 4:11**

*[11]Thou art worthy, O Lord, to receive glory and honour and power: for thou hast created all things, and for thy pleasure they are and were created.*

God has been building galaxies made up of billions of stars for many more years than we can imagine. Moreover, out there, as far as we can see there are billions of galaxies. Every once in a while, a planet the perfect size for human existence, the right distance from the sun, and the perfect size star, and we have an earth like ours able to sustain human and animal life. God loves his creations, the mountains, oceans, rivers, trees, flowers, animals, and most of all his children, created in his likeness.

Nebula with clusters of blue and red stars.    Nebula giving birth to newly formed blue stars

**Deuteronomy 10:22 (King James Version)**

*[22]Thy fathers went down into Egypt with threescore and ten persons; and now the LORD thy God hath made thee as the stars of heaven for multitude.*

### 1 Chronicles 27:23 (King James Version)

[23]*But David took not the number of them from twenty years old and under: because the LORD had said, he would increase Israel like to the stars of the heavens.*

### Psalm 147:4 (King James Version)

[4]*He telleth the number of **the stars**; he calleth them all by their names.*

*The stars = Gods children*

*We may have a star out there with our name on it*

### Revelation 6:13 (King James Version)

[13]*And the **stars of heaven** fell unto the earth, even as a fig tree casteth her untimely figs, when she is shaken of a mighty wind.*

*Stars of heaven = Gods children in heaven*

### Revelation 9

[1]*And the fifth angel sounded, and I saw a **star** fall from heaven unto the earth: and to **him** was given the key of the bottomless pit.*

*Star = him*

For Gods pleasure, he created everything, so we humans can enjoy the stars, planets, and all the beautiful creations here on earth. God created billions of galaxies, and trillions of stars. Are we so arrogant to think we are the only humans to exist in the universe? I think most of us agree that there are many earths out there like ours.

What we can see today with the Hubble and other telescopes is very limited to what is actually out there. In one small speck of space, we can see thousands of galaxies, so can you imagine how big the universe really is. How long has God been creating galaxies and placing people just like us on the planets created by these stars?

Along with these billions of stars, planets are formed from red giant stars. The larger the star, the shorter the life span. The star explodes, and other stars and planets in their galaxy capture the remnants of that star. I believe there are more planets than stars, but now, we really do not know.

Why did God create so many galaxies? God never runs out of space, darkness goes on forever. He loves the beauty of his galaxies, and everyone is different like a snowflake. The stars, in each galaxy, have many planets. Very few planets like our earth exist in each galaxy. God loves his entire creation, but most of all he likes his children made in his likeness. Many Earths are being newly formed, so God can give new homes to his newly created children.

## Why can we not see spirit bodies, bodies in a different dimension?

The hydrogen atom is made up of 99.9% darkness, and all other atoms are at least 99% darkness. This small (–) dash would take 20 million protons to fill it. Our bodies contain 1% mass and 99% darkness. This is hard to believe, but true. The electron shell is very important, the area is far larger than the proton, allowing us to see and touch it while in flesh bodies.

### 20:26 (King James Version)

[26] *And after eight days again his disciples were within, and Thomas with them: then came Jesus, the doors being shut, and stood in the midst, and said, Peace be unto you.*

When Jesus was resurrected, he was in a different dimension. No longer did he have electrons circling the atoms in his body. The electron shells were gone, and Jesus could walk through walls. The reason the disciples could see him, he was transfigured where the flesh men could see him.

To explain this more without trying to bore you. The electromagnetic shell created by the electrons orbiting the protons and neutrons is far larger than the atom nucleus. The reason we can see and touch people is that the shell is many times larger. Once the shell is removed, the atom nucleus is so small it can travel through concrete. To understand how this can be possible is to look at the very large galaxies. When two large galaxies with 300 billion stars each are on a head on collision, (from the earth,) it looks like they will destroy each other. However, they do not, the two galaxies travel through each other without one collision. Why you ask, the stars are millions of miles apart, the chances are slim that two stars will meet, but by chance, it can happen. The same is true with the protons and neutrons. They are so small the distance is great between them and having a collision is slim. You look up at the stars, and you see how large our galaxy is, and then try to imagine how very small the fundamental particles are. They are just as small as our galaxy is large. We need both the small particles and large galaxies to sustain life for animals and humans.

Another example is when Peter was in prison under King Herod, and the king set 16 soldiers to guard him. Two guards were chained to Peter, and while they slept, the Angel of the Lord spoke to Peter. A light shined down on Peter, the Lord told him to get up quickly, Peter stood, and the chains fell off from his hands. How did this happen? God removed the electron shells from the atoms of Peter's body, and the shackles fell to the ground. This is the second time God had transfigured Peter's body, the first time was when he walked on the water.

### Mark 9:2-5 (King James Version)

*2And after six days Jesus taketh with him Peter, and James, and John, and leadeth them up into a high mountain apart by themselves: and he was **transfigured** before them.*

*Jesus was changed into a spirit body*

*3And his raiment became shining, exceeding white as snow; so as no fuller on earth can white them.*

*This shining is Gods light*

*4And there appeared unto them Elias with Moses: and they were talking with Jesus.*

*5And Peter answered and said to Jesus, Master, it is good for us to be here: and let us make three tabernacles; one for thee, and one for Moses, and one for Elias.*

*Moses and Elijah are still in their flesh bodies, and can be seen by the Apostles*

Three men of God are still in flesh bodies, Enoch, Moses, and Elijah. Two of them, I believe, will be the two witnesses during Satan's hour. I believe the third could possibly be Pastor Arnold Murray who taught the elect for many years, and passed away February 12, 2014. I first thought for many years Pastor Arnold Murray was Elijah, but I now believe he is Enoch. Pastor Murray may not be any of the three, however he was a great man in the first earth age, and was chosen by God to teach the elect during the fifth trump.

The reason is Moses and Elijah both used the fire of God, and the two witnesses that will come down just before Satan will use the power from God against Satan during his hour. Yes, Elijah was the great teacher, and Pastor Murray was the teacher of the elect at the end times, but Enoch was a great teacher also. This leaves only two men who both died thousands of years ago, and they are still in their flesh bodies today.

I do not believe they are in flesh bodies here on the earth, but they are both in heaven waiting to come down from heaven to use the fire of God against Satan and his angels. Most people on the earth will hate the two witnesses, which I believe are Moses and Elijah. The reason Satan can kill the two witnesses is that they are in the flesh, which is why Moses, Elijah, and Enoch had to remain in flesh bodies. Three great men of God and I am so lucky to have met Pastor Arnold Murray and sat on his seat where he taught God's elect.

# God works in threes

## Before God, there were three conditions

*Darkness/coldness/dryness = 3*

## The result of the three conditions

*Positive/negative/neutral = 3*

*Earth is the third planet from the Sun*

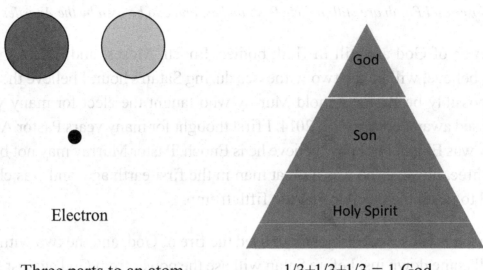

Electron

Three parts to an atom                    1/3+1/3+1/3 = 1 God

2/3 = .666 Satan's number

1/3 = .333 Father, Son, and Holy Spirit

Quarks come in 3s, 1/3 charges (positive or negative)

### Ezekiel 5:12

*[12]A third part of thee shall die with the pestilence, and with famine shall they be consumed in the midst of thee: and a third part shall fall by the sword round about thee; and I will scatter a third part into all the winds, and I will draw out a sword after them.*

*One third of God's children follow Satan*

*One third of God's children take no stand*

*One third of God's children follow God*

*1/3 + 1/3 = 2/3 = .666*

*Two thirds of God's children are lost*

*One third of the children on this earth today are Christian*

## *Zechariah 13:8-9 (King James Version)*

*⁸And it shall come to pass, that in all the land, saith the LORD, two parts therein shall be cut off and die; but the third shall be left therein.*

Two thirds of Gods children chose not to follow God, and they will be considered dead during the millennium. They will be taught for a thousand years, and at the end of that thousand years they will have a choice, choose Christ or Satan. Unfortunately, many will follow Satan to the lake of fire.

*⁹And I will bring the third part through the fire, and will refine them as silver is refined, and will try them as gold is tried: they shall call on my name, and I will hear them: I will say, It is my people: and they shall say, The LORD is my God.*

*The third part that is refined through the fire is the people
that stood up for God in the first earth age.*

*Two thirds of God's children that did not make a stand for God are liable
to die in the lake of fire, if they do not have a change of heart.*

*The third part will walk through the fire unharmed (everlasting life.)*

## Revelation 8:12

*¹²And the fourth angel sounded, and the third part of the sun was smitten, and the third part of the moon, and the third part of the stars; so as the third part of them was darkened, and the day shone not for a third part of it, and the night likewise.*

## *Revelation 12:4 (King James Version)*

*⁴And his tail drew the third part of the stars of heaven, and did cast them to the earth: and the dragon stood before the woman which was ready to be delivered, for to devour her child as soon as it was born.*

*Stars = Gods children*

*The third part of Gods children that followed Satan was cast to the earth*

*Dragon = Satan*

## The universe works in threes.

*Positive charge*

*Negative charge*

*Neutral*

## God works in threes

*Father (Godhead)*

*Son (Christ)*

*Holy Spirit (Gods spirit)*

## God created three races

*Mongolian*

*Black*

*White*

*We humans work in threes*

## The government works in threes

*Legislative*

*Executive*

*Judicial*

## Politics works in threes

*Conservative (right)*

*Moderate (neutral)*

*Liberal (left)*

### Revelation 3:15-16

*[15]I know thy works, that thou art neither cold nor hot: I would thou wert cold or hot.*

*[16]So then because thou art lukewarm, and neither cold nor hot, I will spue thee out of my mouth.*

*Are you one that straddles the fence, never taking a stand?*

*Hot, lukewarm, Cold = 3*

*God gives us three selections*

*Follow Christ = Everlasting life*

*Follow Satan= Lake of fire*

*Take no stand = Life or death*

*Taking a stand, even if it is against God is better than no stand at all.*

People who do not take a stand will have very little blessings from God during their life while in their flesh bodies. Do you think it makes God Happy to watch people not caring who wins, God or Satan?

*[40]For as Jonas was three days and three nights in the whale's belly; so shall the Son of man be three days and three nights in the heart of the earth.*

Everyone born in the flesh will die, and all will go back to heaven. Nevertheless, not all will be with Christ. There is a division called the gulf, and people who pleased God are with Abraham. People that did not please God are on the other side of the gulf wondering what their future will bring. Jesus dies on the cross, and for three days, he teaches the people on the wrong side of the gulf. Many believed in Him and were instantly standing on the side of Christ.

### John 2:19 (King James Version)

*[19]Jesus answered and said unto them, destroy this temple, and in three days, I will raise it up.*

Christ is the temple, He dies on the cross, in three days he is resurrected, and the temple is with us. Christ is our church.

### Exodus 10:23 (King James Version)

*23They saw not one another, neither rose any from his place for three days: but all the children of Israel had light in their dwellings.*

### Genesis 9:19 (King James Version)

*19These are the three sons of Noah: and of them was the whole earth overspread.*

### 1 John 5:7 (King James Version)

*7For there are three that bear record in heaven, the Father, the Word, and the Holy Ghost: and these three are one.*

*Father = Godhead*

*The word = Jesus Christ*

*Holy Ghost = Holy Spirit*

### Mark 15:33 (King James Version)

*33And when the sixth hour was come, there was darkness over the whole land until the ninth hour.*

*Three hours of darkness*

### Luke 2:46 (King James Version)

*46And it came to pass, that after three days they found him in the temple, sitting in the midst of the doctors, both hearing them, and asking them questions.*

*Jesus was twelve years old at the time*

*The number three is divine it means completeness*

*How can we build without using the triangle?*

The number three is miraculous. Without it, there is no fundamental particles, and without fundamental particles, there is no God and no universe.

Instead of holding up, two fingers for peace hold up three fingers for life.

## We have three earth ages

In the first earth age, we walked with the dinosaurs in our spirit bodies. During this earth age our personality, traits, and beliefs were formed. At the end of this first earth age, one third of God's children are deceived by Lucifer/Satan. One-third follow God and the other third sit on the fence.

In the second earth age, we are born of woman, and we are tested in our flesh bodies on earth. Unfortunately, because one third of God's children chose to worship Lucifer, and another one third chose neither God nor Lucifer, the children that fought for God will be tested also. The ones that followed God are far from being perfect, they need to learn to. It is unfortunate many of the people who followed God in the first earth age will change over to Satan in the flesh age, and some that followed Satan will end up following God in the flesh age. This is the reason why we are going through the flesh to give people a better chance. God could have destroyed the ones that followed Satan in the first earth age, but he loves his children, he is the great redeemer.

The third earth age begins at the end of the millennium after God's judgment. The people, who refuse to follow Christ at the end of the Millennium, will lose their soul in the lake of fire.

### Mark 14:58 (King James Version)

[58]*We heard him say, I will destroy this **temple** that is made with hands, and within **three days** I will build another made without hands.*

*Christ is the temple, and all his children are the congregation.*

*Three days he taught on the other side of the gulf.*

*Many people from the other side of the gulf believed upon him and now are in the bosom of Abraham.*

During the time of Jesus' death to his resurrection, He went to the people that had passed on. People of this time knew not of Jesus, and today many people still have not known him. He gave the people that had passed on the opportunity to except Christ as their Savior. Everyone that is born in the flesh will get a fair chance during the millennium to follow either Christ or Satan. Many people worry about their loved ones, that have passed on, wondering if they made it to heaven or not. Everyone that dies goes back to the father, which is heaven, some on the good side of Abraham, and the majority unfortunately, are on the wrong side. Do not worry they will be taught during the one thousand years, many will choose everlasting life.

Remember God will refine his children through the fire like silver taking all the bad out. Do we really want these evil troublemakers living with us forever?

# Chapter 2

## *Understanding Genesis*

## *The first seven days before Adam and Eve*

Before we get started, I would like to say, without pastor Arnold Murray's teachings, I would not be writing this book today. Pastor Arnold Murray is the teacher chosen by God to teach the elect, and very elect, at the end times. I have met him, and have never met a man with such a great spirit, and he has been my mentor from day one. Not everyone likes Pastor Arnold Murray's teaching; many cannot give up the way they are taught by their church doctrine. It seems, as if the church going people today do not want to hear God's truth, and would rather follow the traditions of man. If you are one of the elect, you will have a desire to learn the truth. The churchgoers that refuse to learn are not prepared for the sixth trump, and Satan the wolf in sheep's clothing will deceive them.

### *Romans 11:8 (King James Version)*

*[8](According as it is written, God hath given them the spirit of **slumber**, eyes that they should not see, and ears that they should not hear;) unto this day.*

*Slumber = Spirit of stupor, Drowsy, not with it.*

*God protects his children, by causing them to be in a slumber.*

God knows his children, he knows who can handle the truth and the ones that cannot. Let us say you are not one of the elect, you are taught the truth, and you are no longer ignorant. Then Satan is thrown out of heaven, and is standing on Mount Zion claiming to be the messiah. You are deceived, and the consequences are not good for you. Therefore, God protects his children by making them to slumber. If you are one of the elect, you will definitely know, for your appetite for God's truth will not cease as long as you live. Once all the elect on this earth today are taught, Michael the archangel will kick Satan out of heaven onto the earth. Then Mr. Satan will deceive all of God's children.

Therefore, Jesus spoke in parables. Not everyone is to know all the truth. Even the apostles had a hard time understanding Jesus' parables. During the millennium, the elect will teach the people who followed Satan; because of ignorance, they still have a chance to overcome Satan and to receive everlasting life.

## They say ignorance is bliss

## Does God forgive sin committed by Ignorance?

### Numbers 15:24-28 (King James Version)

*24Then it shall be, if ought be committed by **ignorance** without the knowledge of the congregation, that all the congregation shall offer one young bullock for a burnt offering, for a sweet savour unto the LORD, with his meat offering, and his drink offering, according to the manner, and one kid of the goats for a sin offering.*

*Ignorance = Not knowing (unwittingly)*

*Everyone on earth is ignorant of something, but to remain ignorant of God's word is not something to be proud of*

*Give it some effort and your reward will be in heaven*

*25And the priest shall make an atonement for all the congregation of the children of Israel, and it shall be forgiven them; for it is ignorance: and they shall bring their offering, a sacrifice made by fire unto the LORD, and their sin offering before the LORD, for their ignorance:*

*26And it shall be forgiven all the congregation of the children of Israel, and the stranger that sojourneth among them; seeing all the people were in ignorance.*

*27And if any soul sin through ignorance, then he shall bring a she goat of the first year for a sin offering.*

*²⁸And the priest shall make an atonement for the soul that sinneth ignorantly, when he sinneth by ignorance before the LORD, to make an atonement for him; and it shall be forgiven him.*

Since the time of Christ, billions of people have been taught of his resurrection, and today there are two billion believers. Yet billions of people, since the time of Christ resurrection to present, have not had the opportunity to know Jesus personally as their savior. Will God judge them to the lake of fire without them having an opportunity to learn the sacrifice of Jesus Christ? Because of ignorance, every child of God, that did not make it, will be taught for one thousand years, including Christians that will be deceived by Satan during his five-month reign over the world.

## Genesis the beginning

### Genesis 1

*¹In the beginning God created the heaven and the earth.*

The first verse in God's word covers a period of time that expands over trillions of years and probably much more. God created galaxy after galaxy, all made up of stars and planets. The super nova explosion of stars created many planets, and by chance, some were the right size, the right gravity weight, the right distance from the star, and the right size star. This verse covers the time between the creations of God, to Satan's overthrow in the first Earth age.

God created people just like us on each earth for his pleasure. Are there people from other planets visiting us? I do not think so! The distance is much too far away. Who knows, maybe when we are in spirit bodies we will be allowed to visit other earths like ours. I hope so!

Our galaxy is billions of years old, and our own earth is estimated to be 4.5 billion years old. Our galaxy, the sun, moon, earth, the animals, and we the children of God, were all created before the second verse of Genesis.

There are three earth ages in the bible. The first verse, in Genesis is the first earth age. We lived on this earth, in spirit, (different dimension) up to the second verse. The second verse is Satan's overthrow, and the beginning of the second earth age. The second earth age will last until all of God's children have been born of woman, and then one thousand years of learning in our spirit bodies called the millennium. The third earth age begins after God's judgment at the end of the seventh day. The third earth age begins on the eighth day, called the new beginning. We all want to live to this eighth day, so why not start learning now, come out of ignorance, and have peace of mind.

## The first earth age

In the first earth age, we walked on this earth for hundreds of millions of years. Yes, I believe we walked on this earth before the first dinosaurs were created. We had a wonderful life, a life without pain, worry, aggravation, aging, and so much more. We experienced the divisions of the continents. Can you imagine walking with the dinosaurs, then seeing that age destroyed, and then God creating new animals for a new age. We saw many ice ages come and go, and the Colorado River slowly carving out the Grand Canyon. We lived in cities at this time, but in a different dimension that we would not be able to see in our flesh bodies today. In a spirit dimension, we were protected from meteorites, volcanoes, earthquakes, and the sun's rays. All these had no effect on our spirit bodies.

During the millions and millions of years, our personalities, and traits emerged as they are today. Today we are living in the second earth age in flesh bodies, and we have no remembrance of the first earth age. During this first earth age, we all had free will, just as we do today. There is something God cannot do, and that is force his children to love him.

## We all have good and bad traits

It took millions of years to form our personalities, our mannerisms, and good and bad traits. We all have many different traits good and bad. What kind of world would it be if we all have the same personality and traits? Over this long period during the first earth age, God gave us free will to build our very own personality. Pick out the traits you have between your sister and brother, you will be surprised at the difference.

## Good Traits

Ambitious, determined, easygoing, efficient, active, honest, brave, giving, confident, humble, lively, imaginative, loyal, funny, determined, compassionate, independent, honest, giving, loving, and many more.

## Bad Traits

Arrogant, lazy, mean, crafty, doubtful, angry, obnoxious, impolite, bossy, foolish, disrespectful, domineering, mischievous, cold-hearted and many more.

### Ecclesiastes 1:9-11 (King James Version)

*⁹The thing that hath been, it is that which shall be; and that which is done is that which shall be done: and there is no new thing under the sun.*

*What we have accomplished today is nothing compared to the first earth age.*

*¹⁰Is there anything whereof it may be said, See, this is new?* **It hath been already of old time, which was before us.**

*We have lights, television, cars, airplanes, computers, cell phones, and much more, but all this we had in the first earth age millions of years ago.*

*¹¹There is no remembrance of former things; neither shall there be any remembrance of things that are to come with those that shall come after.*

*When we became flesh, God took our remembrance away.*

*When we die, we give up our flesh bodies, but our spirit body remains and our remembrance is restored.*

There is nothing we have today, that can come close to what we had during the first earth age. We think we are so modern and high tech today; what more can heaven add to it, wait and see. Fossil fuels were not needed for transportation, and heat and cold had no effect on our spirit bodies. We had flying vehicles and transportations that would put us to shame today. Communication was far beyond what we have now. Cell phones, television, I-pads, and computers were not needed. Even though we had no pain, or sickness, and did not age, we did have plenty of emotions that caused mental pain and stress. How can we live in a perfect world when God gives us all free will? How boring a place if we all were exactly alike, a bunch of clones, and having very little difference in personalities. Even in heaven, we cannot reach one hundred percent utopia, and would we want that.

## *Did we exist on this earth before dinosaurs?*

Is there any proof of us living with the dinosaurs? I believe so. In two states, New Mexico and Texas, human footprints have been found. The footprint found in Mexico is older than the first dinosaurs on earth. Footprints of humans and dinosaurs are found in a riverbed in Texas, and both were formed at the same time over sixty million years ago.

Photos taken at the Creation Evidence Museum located at Glen Rose Texas

Human footprints discovered by Archaeologist Alvis Delk in July 2000. Human footprints found walking among the Dinosaurs. CT scan verified Dino and human footprint. In the first earth age, we humans, in a different dimension, (not flesh) were walking the earth before the dinosaurs and during the dinosaur age. No human bones have ever been found during the dinosaur period, because humans were in a spirit dimension, which did not die. In this dimension, people still had the same weight we have today. Remember we have the same amount of protons and Neutrons, except we did not have the electron shells, which makes us flesh today. Spirit bodies do have weight, and we walked among the dinosaurs without harm and our footprints prove it. **Go on You Tube type in: <u>Footprints in stone,</u>** and make up your mind if you believe it or not. Visit the Creation Evidence Museum on the Paluxy River near Glen Rose Texas.

During the dinosaur period, humans were in spirit bodies. We lived in the Great City, and walked on the earth enjoying all of Gods creations. The creationist versus the evolutionist will never come to an agreement because of their ideology. If these footprints have been faked, it will in no way take away my belief that humankind lived on the earth during the time of the dinosaur, and before.

They did prove the footprints were real. The dinosaur and human prints ended where a lime rock shelf at a higher elevation was above the prints. They decided to dig into the rocky shelf to see if the human footprints continued with the dinosaur prints. When the excavation was done, the results were that the human footprints continued with the dinosaur prints. This proved the footprints were not carved into the rock. Still, this did not persuade the Darwin evolutionist. They destroyed the prints in the park, and many of the excavated footprints where bought up and destroyed. Why does the evolutionist hate God so much?

We have been living on this earth for hundreds of millions of years, and right now, we have no remembrance of our past life, however our remembrance will be restored when we go back to our spirit bodies.

Why would they choose no God, over a loving God that promises everlasting life? Why are they so adamant about not believing in God? My belief offers me life eternal; their belief offers nothing. I have no understanding of people who think this way.

*Satan deceives Gods children*

*The end of the first earth age*

*God floods the earth the beginning of the second earth age*

### Genesis 1:2 (King James Version)

*²And the earth was without form, and void; and darkness was upon the face of the deep. In addition, the Spirit of God moved upon the face of the waters.*

This is the Great overthrow, in the Greek; it is (Katabole) meaning disruption and ruin of the world. In this second verse, God floods the earth; the earth has no geography, and is void of any living thing on earth. The earth has no form because it is underwater. Did God create the earth void and without form? Let us find out.

### Isaiah 45:18

*¹⁸For thus saith the LORD that created the heavens; God himself that formed the earth and made it; he hath established it, he created it not in vain, he formed it to be inhabited: I am the LORD; and there is none else.*

Whoops! What do we have here? It looks like the Bible has a contradiction, and we are only in the second verse. How can this be? In Genesis, 1:2 it says the earth is void and without form, and in Isaiah, chapter forty-five, and verse eighteen it says God created it to be inhabited. Let us do a little work, which God expects from all his children who love Him.

### 2 Peter 3:5-6 (King James Version)

*⁵For this they willingly are ignorant of, that by the word of God the **heavens were of old**, and the earth standing out of the water and in the water:*

> *When I was young, many people believed the earth was only 6000 years old*

> *The earth is billions of years old, and the universe trillions of years old*

*⁶Whereby the world that then was being overflowed with water, perished:*

The world that was in the first earth age, the age when Satan deceived one third of God's children. God destroyed the earth with a great flood, and the first earth age ended. God dried up the waters, and the second earth age began. In the first earth age, we are in a different dimension. In the second earth age, we are still in spirit bodies until we are born in the flesh. After we die, we go back to spirit bodies of a different dimension once again.

### *Jeremiah 4:22-28 (King James Version*

*²²For my people is foolish, they have not known me; they are **sottish** children, and they have none understanding: they are wise to do evil, but to do good they have no knowledge.*

*Ish (Hebrew) = man*

*Sot (Celtic) = stupid*

*Sottish = Stupid man*

*²³I beheld the earth, and, lo, it was without form, and void; and the heavens, and they had no light.*

*The Earth was completely flooded; it had no form (no geography)*

*Void = waste, empty, and no living thing left on earth*

*Standing on the Earth looking into the heavens there is no light*

*The clouds and water in the heavens blocked out the light*

*²⁴I beheld the mountains, and, lo, they trembled, and all the hills moved lightly.*

*²⁵I beheld, and, lo, there was no man, and all the birds of the heavens were fled.*

*All living things on the face of the earth are gone*

*This is not the flood of Noah, Noah's family and the animals he placed on the ark all survived*

*²⁶I beheld, and, lo, the fruitful place was a wilderness, and all the cities thereof were broken down at the presence of the LORD, and by his fierce anger.*

*Yes, we lived in cities during the first earth age, but in a different dimension*

*Satan deceived Gods children, and God destroyed our stuff because of his fierce anger*

*God did not destroy us; he placed us in the great city over Jerusalem*

²⁷*For thus hath the LORD said, the whole land shall be desolate; yet will I not make a full end.*

*Desolate = void of anything living (the land is waste)*

*God does not destroy humankind, but we will pay the price of our sin by living on this earth in flesh bodies*

²⁸*For this shall the earth mourn, and the heavens above be black; because I have spoken it, I have purposed it, and will not repent; neither will I turn back from it.*

*God removes his light from the face of the earth, and this is one dark day for God and his children*

*God purposed it, he thought it out, and he planned it. He destroyed the earth and He will not repent*

## We can look at verse two in Genesis two different ways.

Way # 1

The interpreters made a mistake.

"Was without form"_should have been interpreted_became waste.

In Hebrew (Tohu-va-bohu) = Became waste

The verse should read like this.

In addition, the earth became waste, and void; and darkness was upon the face of the deep. Moreover, the Spirit of God moved upon the face of the waters.

*God created the earth to be inhabited*

*God destroyed the earth, and it became waste*

Way # 2

The interpreters did make a mistake saying the earth was without form, and it should have been interpreted became waste. Even if the verse was interpreted right, it still works. The second verse could have come after Gods overthrow describing the earth after he destroyed it. The bible does not contradict itself; it actually explains and gives us understanding of the three earth ages. God's desire is for us to seek out, and work for His truth.

## Why did God destroy the earth?

One little tiny thing caused God to destroy the earth. That little thing is free will. God cannot force someone to love him. Because of free will, two thirds of God's children turned their backs on Him. After millions of years, one third of God's children chose to follow Lucifer/Satan. One third of God's children took no stand, sitting on the fence waiting on the wind to make its decision that can change from day to day. One third of God's children followed and stood up for God. Eight billion souls did not follow God, but four billion did. How would that go over with you, if two out of three of your children decided not to love you anymore? I need not say more. I believe there are probably twelve billion souls altogether created for this earth, and only one third followed God. I would like to add one thing, one third of God's children are Christians living on the earth today. All five races are part of this two billion plus people today.

*Two thirds of God's children are no longer on Gods side = .666 Satan's number*

*One third of God's children follow God = .333 Gods number*

## The Reason for the great overthrow

## Satan the evil archangel deceives God's children

### Ezekiel 27

*[1]The word of the LORD came again unto me, saying,*

*[2]Now, thou son of man, take up a lamentation for Tyrus;*

*Tyrus Symbolizes Lucifer*

³*And say unto Tyrus, O thou that art situate at the entry of the sea, which art a merchant of the people for many isles, Thus saith the Lord GOD; O Tyrus, thou hast said, I am of perfect beauty.*

*People followed him for his good looks, and his wealth.*

⁴Thy borders are in the midst of the seas; thy builders have perfected thy beauty.

*Tyrus the city on the rock, the great city of merchants.*

*Lucifer is the great merchant.*

*We thank of Satan being an ugly man with a pitchfork, not so he is perfect in beauty.*

## Satan's pride

*Satan desires to sit in the seat of Christ*

*Unfortunately, he deceives many and takes away one third of God's children.*

### Ezekiel 28

¹*The word of the LORD came again unto me, saying,*

²*Son of man, say unto the* **prince of Tyrus**, *Thus saith the Lord GOD; Because thine heart is lifted up, and thou hast said, I am a God, I sit in the seat of God, in the midst of the seas; yet thou art a man, and not God, though thou set thine heart as the heart of God:*

*The Prince of Tyrus = Satan*

*His pride gets the better of him*

*Satan desires to be God sitting in the center of the people*

*Seas = people*

*Satan believes he can overthrow God*

*Satan is a narcissist*

³Behold, thou art wiser than Daniel; there is no secret that they can hide from thee:

*He is so wise; he will deceive the world once he arrives on mount Zion*

*Gods elect will overcome*

⁴*With thy wisdom and with thine understanding thou hast gotten thee riches, and hast gotten gold and silver into thy treasures:*

*Satan the great merchant*

⁵*By thy great wisdom and by thy traffick hast thou increased thy riches, and thine heart is lifted up because of thy riches:*

*Traffic = Trade/Merchandise*

*His riches increased his pride*

*Satan is on an ego trip*

⁶*Therefore thus saith the Lord GOD, because thou hast set thine heart as the heart of God.*

*Lucifer/ Satan in his heart desires to be God*

⁷*Behold, therefore I will bring strangers upon thee, the terrible of the nations: and they shall draw their swords against the beauty of thy wisdom, and they shall defile thy brightness.*

*God's awesome children will cause Satan to tremble*

*His splendor will be no more*

⁸*They shall bring thee down to the pit, and thou shalt die the deaths of them that are slain in the midst of the seas.*

*Satan gets the death sentence; he will die in the lake of fire*

⁹*Wilt thou yet say before him that slayeth thee, I am God? But thou shalt be a man, and no God, in the hand of him that slayeth thee.*

*The fire of God will slay Satan at the end of the Millennium*

*¹⁰Thou shalt die the deaths of the uncircumcised by the hand of strangers: for I have spoken it, saith the Lord GOD.*

*Uncircumcised, people that refuse Jesus Christ, will be cast into the lake of fire*

*Not physical circumcision, but spiritual*

*¹¹Moreover the word of the LORD came unto me, saying,*

*¹²Son of man, take up a lamentation upon the king of Tyrus, and say unto him, Thus saith the Lord GOD; Thou sealest up the sum, full of wisdom, and perfect in beauty.*

*King of Tyrus = Satan*

### Ezekiel 28:13

*¹³Thou hast been in Eden the garden of God; every precious stone was thy covering, the sardius, topaz, and the diamond, the beryl, the onyx, and the jasper, the sapphire, the emerald, and the carbuncle, and gold: the workmanship of thy tabrets and of thy pipes was prepared in thee in the day that thou wast created.*

*The tree of good and evil in the midst of the Garden of Eden is Satan himself*

*Satan loves his precious stones and metals*

*Tabrets = Tambourine*

*Pipes = Jeweler's work (to set precious stones)*

*¹⁴Thou art the anointed cherub that covereth; and I have set thee so: thou wast upon the holy mountain of God; thou hast walked up and down in the midst of the stones of fire.*

*The archangel (Satan) was anointed by God to protect Christ's seat in heaven*

*¹⁵Thou wast perfect in thy ways from the day that thou wast created, till iniquity was found in thee.*

*¹⁶By the multitude of thy merchandise they have filled the midst of thee with violence, and thou hast sinned: therefore I will cast thee as profane out of the mountain of God: and I will destroy thee, O covering cherub, from the midst of the stones of fire.*

*The abundance of merchandise has changed Lucifer*
*from one loving God to just loving himself.*

*He wants you to worship him, if you are not prepared in God's word you will fall.*

*O covering cherub = Satan the protector of Christ mercy seat*

*[17]Thine heart was lifted up because of thy beauty, thou hast corrupted thy wisdom by reason of thy brightness: I will cast thee to the ground, I will lay thee before kings, that they may behold thee.*

*Beauty = good looking*

*Brightness = Splendor*

*[18]Thou hast defiled thy sanctuaries by the multitude of thine iniquities, by the iniquity of thy traffick; therefore will I bring forth a fire from the midst of thee, it shall devour thee, and I will bring thee to ashes upon the earth in the sight of all them that behold thee.*

*Iniquity = Unrighteousness, wicked, to deviate from the truth*

*Traffic = Trade (the great merchant)*

*The fire of God (lake of fire) will turn Satan into ashes*

*Satan will be no more at the end of the seventh day*

*[19]All they that know thee among the people shall be astonished at thee: thou shalt be a terror, and never shalt thou be any more.*

*Terror = Destruction, Calamity*

*The great deceiver will lose his soul, in the lake of fire*

Lucifer was the man, the top dog, the protector of the mercy seat, which is the seat of Christ. He was the most beautiful and wisest man that God had created. God loved him very much, but pride and riches got in the way. Lucifer, the great merchant, do not let him sell you a bag of lies that he led you to believe was a bag of truth. Lucifer, the great deceiver, follow him and lose your soul.

Many of God's children loved Lucifer's great wisdom, his beauty, his riches, and his sales pitch. Many people became rich and powerful through ill-gotten gain; they loved Lucifer and themselves very much. One third of God's children looked up to these wicked deceivers, and fell for the lies of Lucifer. If you look around, you will see the same thing happening today. Look at that person. He or she is so smart that they have everything the world can offer, but one thing, and that is the love for God. We have a very short time on this earth; we forget about God, and we jeopardize our souls. Is this a smart person? Is it worth it to love money and power for a very short stay on this earth, and lose our chance for everlasting life?

***Matthew 6:24 (King James Version)***

*[24]No man can serve two masters: for either he will hate the one, and love the other; or else he will hold to the one, and despise the other. Ye cannot serve God and mammon*

*Mammon = Money*

***Matthew 6:21 (King James Version)***

*[21]For where your treasure is, there will your heart be also.*

I would say it is much smarter to follow God's word than to listen to some rich person give you a great sale pitch. I am not saying everyone that is rich is evil, but we need to discern the way this person became rich. Abraham, Isaac, and Jacob, were rich, not by unrighteousness, but by hard work, and the blessings of God.

# In the first earth age (based on twelve billion souls)

Lucifer deceived 4 billion people (wrong choice)

4 billion did not make a choice (on the fence) (did not care who ruled over them God or Satan)

4 billion chose our Father, (a smart choice)

All of this occurred in the first verse of Genesis.

God tells us that we are ignorant, that the heavens are very old. Many preachers today say our earth is only six thousand years old. No wonder people believe in the monkey theory today. Europe has become secular, and more and more people in the United States are heading in that direction. When the people hear nonsense coming from these so-called men of God, we can understand why they are moving in that direction. Ye men of God, travel to the Grand Canyon, look at the many layers, and explain to all of us how it was formed in six thousand years.

## God replenishes the earth

The earth has been flooded, there are no living creatures on the earth, and the waters recede back as they were before the flood. God has already created the universe along with our earth; all of this was done in verse 1-2. God's children are no longer on the earth; they are above heaven living in a very large building. God will create new creatures more compatible for human flesh to live with.

## Understanding the first seven days of creation

### First day

**Genesis 1:3-31 (King James Version)**

*3And God said, Let there be light: and there was light.*

*The light is the light of God*

*4And God saw the light, that it was good: and God divided the light from the darkness.*

*The darkness represents Lucifer*

*Good separated from evil*

*5And God called the light Day, and the darkness he called Night. And the evening and the morning were the first day.*

Standing on the earth looking up, you would see a thick fog of water. The stars, the sun, and the moon are there, but cannot not be seen, due to the water in the atmosphere. The light is the light of God, not the light of the sun or moon. The darkness is symbolic of Lucifer the devil, and God will divide the light from darkness.

*Twelve hours of Gods light, or twelve hours of darkness (Your Choice)*

*Light = God, Darkness = Satan*

Spirit man does not need the light from the sun, but flesh man does. Without the sun, plants animals, and man cannot survive. In the near future, we will change over to spirit bodies, and will no longer need the light from the sun. God again will be our light.

### Revelation 21:23 (King James Version)

[23]*And the city had no need of the sun, neither of the moon, to shine in it: for the glory of God did lighten it, and the Lamb is the light thereof.*

*No more light from the sun or reflection from the moon*

*God is the light*

In the new earth, our light will come from God, no longer needing the light source from the sun or moon. Will the sun and moon still be with us? I believe so; but God's light will be far brighter than the sun.

## Second day

### Genesis 1:6-8 (King James Version)

[6]And God said, Let there be a firmament in the midst of the waters, and let it divide the waters from the waters.

*Firmament = Heaven*

*Waters = Gods children*

*The firmament divides spirit man from flesh man*

⁷And God made the firmament, and divided the waters which were under the firmament from the waters which were above the firmament: and it was so.

⁸And God called the firmament Heaven. And the evening and the morning were the second day.

*On the second day heaven is established*

*Heaven will divide spirit people from flesh people.*

*Spirit people on the second day are living above heaven, waiting
to be born on the earth at the beginning of the sixth day.*

*Spirit becomes flesh on the sixth day.*

## Revelation 17:15 (King James Version)

¹⁵*And he saith unto me, **The waters** which thou sawest, where the whore sitteth, are peoples, and multitudes, and nations, and tongues.*

*The waters symbolize people and nations of people.*

## Revelation 19:6 (King James Version)

⁶*And I heard as it were the voice of a great multitude, and as **the voice of many waters,** and as the voice of mighty thunderings, saying, Alleluia: for the Lord God omnipotent reigneth.*

*Waters do not have a voice*

*Waters = People*

*Voice of many people*

*Omnipotent = Almighty GOD*

Heaven is the firmament where God is. Spirit man is above the firmament, waiting to be born in the flesh. Flesh man is on the earth. When flesh man dies, he or she goes back to the firmament/heaven in the midst of the waters/peoples.

# Lazarus and the rich man

**Luke 16:19-28 (King James Version)**

<sup>19</sup>There was a certain rich man, which was clothed in purple and fine linen, and fared sumptuously every day:

<sup>20</sup>And there was a certain beggar named Lazarus, which was laid at his gate, full of sores,

<sup>21</sup>And desiring to be fed with the crumbs which fell from the rich man's table: moreover the dogs came and licked his sores.

<sup>22</sup>And it came to pass, that the beggar died, and was carried by the angels into Abraham's bosom: the rich man also died, and was buried;

<sup>23</sup>And in hell he lift up his eyes, being in torments, and seeth Abraham afar off, and Lazarus in his bosom.

*They both went to the firmament called heaven*

*The beggar went to the good side*

*The rich man, the bad side*

*Hell = Grave, and Torments = Mental anguish*

*Grave = spiritually dead*

The rich man could see Lazarus standing with Abraham, but cannot cross the gulf or divide. The rich man not suffering from pain, but is in great mental distress not knowing if he will end up in the lake of fire.

The spiritually dead will be taught for one thousand years during the millennium, and at the end, they will be judged. If they follow Christ they will receive everlasting life, if they choose Satan, they will lose their soul. It is hard to believe a child of God would choose Satan after being taught for one thousand years, learning the truth yet following Satan to the lake of fire.

*24And he cried and said, Father Abraham, have mercy on me, and send Lazarus, that he may dip the tip of his finger in water, and cool my tongue, for I am tormented in this flame.*

*Living water*

*Torment=distressed*

*Flame = the fire of God*

*25But Abraham said, Son, remember that thou in thy lifetime receivedst thy good things, and likewise Lazarus evil things: but now he is comforted, and thou art tormented.*

*26And beside all this, between us and you there is a **great gulf fixed**: so that they which would pass from hence to you cannot; neither can they pass to us that would come from thence.*

*Gulf=Separation/divide*

*27Then he said, I pray thee therefore, father, that thou wouldest send him to my father's house:*

*28For I have five brethren; that he may testify unto them, lest they also come into this place of torment.*

*Do you want to end up on the wrong side of the gulf, and be tormented for one thousand years?*

*Immortal body = everlasting life guaranteed (right side of gulf)*

*Mortal body = liable to die (lake of fire) (wrong side of gulf)*

The torment is not from God, it is not the lake of fire. It is a self-inflicted mental torment, not knowing their destiny. It is your choice, Lake of fire, or everlasting life.

When we die, there is two separate places we can end up at, the good side in the bosom of Abraham, or the bad side where you are in a mortal body for one thousand years. The place on the other side of the gulf is a place of uncertainty, not a place you want to end up. You have the opportunity while in your flesh body to guarantee your place in the bosom of Abraham. Look up John 3:16.

## *The place where I believe we go after we die*

### *The Great City*

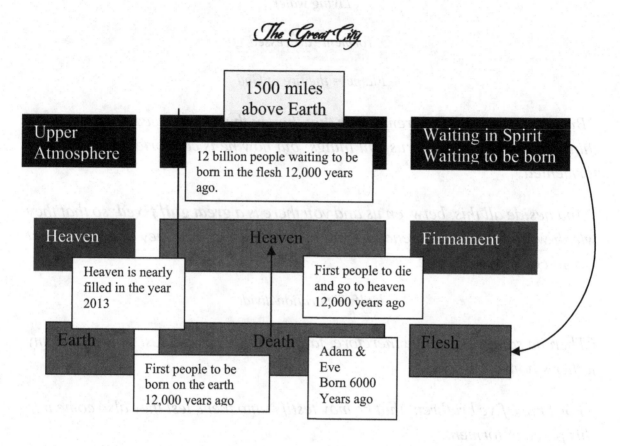

## John 3:12-13 (King James Version)

[12] *If I have told you earthly things, and ye believe not, how shall ye believe, if I tell you of heavenly things?*

[13] *And no man hath ascended up to heaven, but he that came down from heaven, even the Son of man which is in heaven.*

*If you do not understand Genesis, you will not understand these two verses*

*Second Earth age waiting in the upper floors of the great city (in spirit)*

*Spirit descends to Earth, now in the womb (flesh)*

*Flesh dies and ascends back to the great city (spirit)*

Are the people in the upper atmosphere and heaven just floating around in space like a bunch of astronauts? People in spirit bodies and flesh bodies, have equal weight when standing on the earth. The space shuttle used to fly from 200 to 240 miles above sea level, and the great city is 1500 miles high. Therefore, if the astronauts had zero gravity that must mean the people living in the great city are floating around with zero gravity. This is not the case, in the building the people are connected to the earth having floors to stop there fall, which causes weightlessness. Gravity continues into outer space and weakens as it goes. At 1500 miles the gravity force has weaken very little, so our weight would not change much.

### *Revelation 21:10-27 (King James Version)*

*[10]And he carried me away in the spirit to a great and high mountain, and shewed me that **great city**, the holy Jerusalem, descending out of heaven from God,*

*[11]Having the glory of God: and her light was like unto a stone most precious, even like a jasper stone, clear as crystal;*

*[12]And had a wall great and high, and had twelve gates, and at the gates twelve angels, and names written thereon, which are the names of the twelve tribes of the children of Israel:*

*[13]On the east three gates; on the north three gates; on the south three gates; and on the west three gates.*

*[14]And the wall of the city had twelve foundations, and in them the names of the twelve apostles of the Lamb.*

*[15]And he that talked with me had a golden reed to measure the city, and the gates thereof, and the wall thereof.*

*[16]And the city lieth foursquare, and the length is as large as the breadth: and he measured the city with the reed, **twelve thousand furlongs**. The length and the breadth and the height of it are equal.*

*One Furlong = 202 English Yards*

*One English Yard = 3.26 Feet*

*12,000 Furlongs by 202 English Yards = 2,424,000 English Yards*

*2,424,000 English Yards by 3.26 Feet = 7,902,240 Feet*

*One Mile = 5280 Feet*

*7,902,240 divided by 5280 Feet = 1497 Miles*

*This building is 1497 miles square by 1497 miles tall.*

[17]*And he measured the wall thereof, an hundred and forty and four cubits, according to the measure of a man, that is, of the angel.*

*Man = 6 Feet*

*Man with his arms stretched out = 6 Feet*

*Man from the center of his chest to the tip of his finger = 3 Feet = The Yard*

*Man from the elbow to the tip of the finger = 1.5 Feet = the Cubit*

*The fathom that we use to measure the depth of water = 6 Feet = One Man*

[8]*And the building of the wall of it was of jasper: and the city was pure gold, like unto clear glass.*

[19]*And the foundations of the wall of the city were garnished with all manner of precious stones. The first foundation was jasper; the second, sapphire; the third, a chalcedony; the fourth, an emerald;*

[20]*The fifth, sardonyx; the sixth, sardius; the seventh, chrysolyte; the eighth, beryl; the ninth, a topaz; the tenth, a chrysoprasus; the eleventh, a jacinth; the twelfth, an amethyst.*

[21]*And the twelve gates were twelve pearls: every several gate was of one pearl: and the street of the city was pure gold, as it were transparent glass.*

*Can you imagine how beautiful this place is?*

*[22]And I saw no temple therein: for the Lord God Almighty and the Lamb are the temple of it.*

*When we die in the flesh, and go back to the great city, we ask where the temple is.*

*The Answer: I AM THAT I AM (EHYEH ASHER EHYEH) (JEHOVAH) = GOD –JEHOSHUA, JOSHUA, EMMANUEL, MASTER, MESSIAH, the ANOINTED 1 = JESUS the CHRIST. The FATHER, the SON, and the HOLY SPIRIT is our temple.*

*[23]And the city had no need of the sun, neither of the moon, to shine in it: for the glory of God did lighten it, and the Lamb is the light thereof.*

*[24]And the nations of them which are saved shall walk in the light of it: and the kings of the earth do bring their glory and honour into it.*

*[25]And the gates of it shall not be shut at all by day: for there shall be no night there.*

*[26]And they shall bring the glory and honour of the nations into it.*

*[27]And there shall in no wise enter into it any thing that defileth, neither whatsoever worketh abomination, or maketh a lie: but they which are written in the Lamb's book of life.*

*No more bad people*

*Are you in the book of life?*

*Only good people who love our creator will have everlasting life in this great city*

How can 12 billion people fit in this building? Unfortunately, there will not be 12 billion souls in the great city (many will not make it)

(Based on housing 12 billion people)

*Cubic acres per person = 941,908 cubic acres*

*An average home of 2000sf with 12' ceiling will give each person 1,712,560 homes.*

*1.7 million Homes per person*

*Moreover, the earth will also be ours*

*The Animals will live on the earth*

*God will dry up the seas giving us 70% more land*

*After judgment time far less than 12 billion will be living on earth and in the great city, this will give us plenty of living space (based on 12 billion total)*

## Third Day

### Genesis 1:9-13 (King James Version)

*[9]And God said, let the waters under the heaven be gathered together unto one place, and let the dry land appear: and it was so. [10]And God called the dry land Earth; and the gathering together of the waters called he Seas: and God saw that it was good.*

*[11]And God said, Let the earth bring forth grass, the herb yielding seed, and the fruit tree yielding fruit after his kind, whose seed is in itself, upon the earth: and it was so.*

*[12]And the earth brought forth grass, and herb yielding seed after his kind, and the tree yielding fruit, whose seed was in itself, after his kind: and God saw that it was good.*

*[13]And the evening and the morning were the third day.*

The waters in verse 9-10 are actually the ocean and seas on the earth. The people now are in the great city in the upper atmosphere. God begins to replenish the earth planting grass, and trees. There is no sun light, the light of God provides for the growth of the trees and grasses. The sun, moon, and stars are there, but cannot be seen standing on the earth looking up.

## The Fourth Day

### Genesis 1:14-19

*[14]And God said, Let there be lights in the firmament of the heaven to divide the day from the night; and let them be for signs, and for seasons, and for days, and years:*

*<sup>15</sup>And let them be for lights in the firmament of the heaven to give light upon the earth: and it was so.*

*<sup>16</sup>And God made two great lights; the greater light to rule the day, and the lesser light to rule the night: he made the stars also.*

*The Sun, the moon, and stars have been in the sky for billions of years*

*On the fourth day standing on the earth, the clouds began to dry up, and the Sun, moon, and stars could be seen.*

*It does not say when God made the lights, but we know the lights were made billions of years prior.*

*<sup>17</sup>And God set them in the firmament of the heaven to give light upon the earth,*

*<sup>18</sup>And to rule over the day and over the night, and to divide the light from the darkness: and God saw that it was good.*

*<sup>19</sup>And the evening and the morning were the fourth day.*

*Divide good from evil*

## The Fifth Day

***Genesis 1:20-23***

*<sup>20</sup>And God said, Let the waters bring forth abundantly the moving creature that hath life, and fowl that may fly above the earth in the open firmament of heaven.*

*<sup>21</sup>And God created great whales, and every living creature that moveth, which the waters brought forth abundantly, after their kind, and every winged fowl after his kind: and God saw that it was good.*

*<sup>22</sup>And God blessed them, saying, Be fruitful, and multiply, and fill the waters in the seas, and let fowl multiply in the earth.*

*<sup>23</sup>And the evening and the morning were the fifth day.*

*God replenishes the seas and firmament with fowl and fishes.*

*On the fifth day, God begins to replenish the earth with living creatures*

*He fills the oceans, rivers, and lakes with fish*

*He fills the sky with birds*

## The Sixth Day

### Genesis 1:24-31

[24]*And God said, Let the earth bring forth the living creature after his kind, cattle, and creeping thing, and beast of the earth after his kind: and it was so.*

[25]*And God made the beast of the earth after his kind, and cattle after their kind, and every thing that creepeth upon the earth after his kind: and God saw that it was good.*

[26]*And God said, Let us make man in our image, after our likeness: and let them have dominion over the fish of the sea, and over the fowl of the air, and over the cattle, and over all the earth, and over every creeping thing that creepeth upon the earth.*

*God creates sixth day man, six to twelve thousand years, before Adam and Eve*

*The Black race, the Mongolian race, and the white race were created on this day*

[27]*So God created man in his own image, in the image of God created he him; male and female created he them.*

*Man = Mankind = Humankind*

*Male or man = Ish (Hebrew)*

*Female = nek-ay-baw (Hebrew)*

[28]*And God blessed them, and God said unto them, Be fruitful, and multiply, and replenish the earth, and subdue it: and have dominion over the fish of the sea, and over the fowl of the air, and over every living thing that moveth upon the earth.*

*Replenish = to fill the earth*

*God refills the earth with animals, and humankind*

*Humankind is now back on the earth, but only in flesh, not spirit*

²⁹*And God said, Behold, I have given you every herb bearing seed, which is upon the face of all the earth, and every tree, in the which is the fruit of a tree yielding seed; to you it shall be for meat.*

³⁰*And to every beast of the earth, and to every fowl of the air, and to every thing that creepeth upon the earth, wherein there is life, I have given every green herb for meat: and it was so.*

³¹*And God saw every thing that he had made, and, behold, it was very good. And the evening and the morning were the sixth day.*

The three races were created after the end of the last ice age around 10,000 BC. Humankind has been living in the flesh for at least 12,000 years. In spirit bodies, we have been living on the earth for hundreds of millions of years. Adam and Eve will not be created for another 6000 years. Adam was not the first man to live in a flesh body. How do you think Cain took a wife in the land of Nod? The sixth day races were hunter-gatherers, before Cain there was no man to till the ground.

*The fifth day God created Creatures for the sea, and creatures for the air.*

*On The sixth day, God creates creatures to walk the earth.*

*Many new species are created.*

In verse Genesis 1: 26 God said let, us make man in our image, after our likeness. We are all of God's children including thearchangel . Archangels are not born of woman they remain in spirit. Satan is an archangel, and will not become flesh. Preachers of all faiths, teach that Satan will be born of women, and many believe Satan is on the earth today waiting for his time to deceive the world. Not so! Anti-Christ/Satan will be cast down to earth in a transfigured body, a spirit body, which can be seen by flesh man.

*We are the children of God made in the likeness of Christ and his Angels.*

In 10,000 BC, 12,000 years ago, or possibly thousands of years earlier, God took spirit man from the upper atmosphere, placed him on the earth, and changed him into flesh. I am not certain there was a gender difference in the first earth age, but a new gender was needed in the second earth age, and the female was created. This means half of the first earth age people would become women, when born in the flesh. If you notice all angels are male, this is why I believe all of God's children were male in the first earth age. Does this mean women will change back to a male gender when in heaven, I do not know? I also believe it is possible that there was only one race of people in the first earth age. I believe God divided his children once they became flesh. God is still dividing his children today, you can tell where people come from by their accents, that is division.

Adam and Eve will not be created until 6000 years later, around 4004 BC. The black, Mongolian, and white races are created at this time, and the indigenous race of people living in remote areas around the world maybe a mix of the three races. All three races are hunter-gatherers; they replenish and explore the earth for six thousand years. During this age, there is no farmer to till the ground at this time. We still have hunter-gatherers today in remote parts of the Earth. Today we are fortunate to still see how the sixth day humankind lived back ten thousand years ago. Today modern man is slowly influencing ancient people living in South America and many areas around the world.

Possibly the oldest American skull found in America was the Penon Woman III near the airport in Mexico City. Her skull is estimated to be 12,700 to 13,000 years ago when she died, making her 2000 years older than Buhl woman. The woman has Caucasoid features, which means Sixth day white man was possibly in the Americas before the American Indians. The sixth day white man either died out, or mixed with people that migrated from China, Polynesia, and Australia. The Penon woman possibly came from China or Japan. Go online, type in: **edition.cnn.com/2002/TECH/science/12/03/oldest.skull/**

# Ancient mummies found in the America's proving mankind was here thousands of years, before Adam and Eve

## Spirit cave man

Discovered August 11, 1940 in Fallon Nevada

Said to be 9400 years old

Caucasoid features (sixth day white race)

## Buhl woman

Discovered in 1989 in Idaho

Said to be 10,600 years old

American Indian and East Asian (Sixth day Mongolian race)

## Luzia woman

Discovered in 1975 in Lapa Vermelha, Brazil

Said to be 11,500 years old (the oldest found in the America's)

African woman probably came over to the
Americas by Australia or New Guinea

(Sixth day black woman)

## Clovis people

Found remains in New Mexico

Lived in the America's from 11,200 years to 10,900 Years

Hunted Mammoth and Bison, and some small game

10,900 years ago, the great Mammoth and Clovis people became extinct

(Clovis people may have come from Europe)

## Migration of the sixth day man

All three races were in the America's, going back from 9000 to 11,000 years ago. Chinese history goes back 14,000 years, and that gives us a good estimate on when the sixth day humankind was created. The Chinese have kept very good records of their history and genealogy.

Remember the sixth day man were hunter - gatherers, they moved on the earth, they followed game; it was a matter of life or death. I believe all three of the races began in Mongolia, the land of the nomads. Have you ever heard of the Mongolian spot, a blue spot on the buttocks at birth? All three races of people will have this spot giving us a good idea of our sixth day man origin.

The Mongolian spot is a blue-gray or blue-black birthmark located on the buttocks. It is most prevalent among Asians, where the name originates. All three races of the sixth day humankind have this spot. The pureblooded eighth day man does not have the Mongolian spot; their origin is not from Mongolia.

## Migration of the Mongolian race

First not all Mongolians left a land God chose to plant flesh man. Some stayed on this very harsh, but beautiful land, and they live there to this day. These people were, and are a hearty tough nation of people; they have lasted for 12,000 years or maybe more. Today Mongolia is still a mostly nomadic nation still living off the land the same way they began thousands of years ago.

The Mongolians migrated towards the rising sun to the east. Some moving northeast towards Russia, and the Bering Strait, and then on to the America's. Others were moving east towards the yellow river, and yellow sea area, including North Korea and South Korea. Some settling in the Tarim basin and Tibet regions. Then others heading south to Thailand, Vietnam, and Cambodia. Mongolians mixing with whites migrated to the islands of Indonesia, Philippines, Micronesia, and Polynesians. The Polynesian people then migrated all the way to the continents of North and South America.

Mongolians migrated to the America's from the North pacific, and the South Pacific Ocean. The people from the north pacific were full blood Mongolians, the people from the south pacific were a mix of all three races, the dominate race being Mongolian. God looked down on the Mongolians, and said this is good, they have replenished a good part of the earth, and many great nations will come forth from them.

## The migrations of the Black race

The blacks took a different route; they chose to move south into India, Bangladesh, Iran, Iraq, and then Africa. A few blacks followed another route towards Southeast Asia, from there south to Papua New Guinea, Australia, and then to the America's. The Spanish, French, and English discovered black tribes in California. Yes-Black people lived in the Americas thousands of years before Christopher Columbus. God looked down on the black race and said this is good; they have replenished a good part of the earth. Many great nations were established by the black race, and today black people live in many countries around the world. The black and white races made it to the Americas thousands of years before Adam and Eve were created, where they both died out or assimilated with the Mongolian race. Thousands of years later both races, black and white will make it back to the Americas once again. God looked down on the black race, and said this is good; they have replenished a good part of the earth.

## The migration of the white race

Unlike the Mongolians, the white race followed the setting sun towards Europe, where they hunted and gathered from Norway down to Spain east to turkey, and then north through the Caucasus Mountains into Russia. Some whites did travel east; they traveled south and east to an island now called Japan. A small remnant of these people lives there today, they are called the Ainu people. The people are not full-blooded today, but were a few hundred years ago. From Japan, I believe they built boats and followed the land mass north and east to the American coastline. Several white mummies have been found in the United States dating back 9000 years. Go on you-tube: Watch the video on Ainu people of Japan.

Other whites ventured south traveling south and east by boat mixing with Mongolians, and the outcome of that became the Polynesian nation of people.

The Polynesian kept venturing farther east until they came across a large land mass now called South America. God looked down on the White race and said this is good; all three races have now replenished the earth. God is well pleased. By the way, the Ainu people of today will not have a DNA match with white people today because they are of the sixth day whites, not the Adamic whites.

*There still is no man to till the soil*

*Humankind at this time were hunter-gatherers*

*There are cities at this time, but for the most part, they are nomads*

## **The seventh day**

### *Genesis 2*

*¹Thus the heavens and the earth were finished, and all the host of them.*

*²And on the seventh day God ended his work which he had made; and he rested on the seventh day from all his work which he had made.*

*³And God blessed the seventh day, and sanctified it: because that in it he had rested from all his work which God created and made.*

On the seventh day God rest and humankind continues to replenish the earth. Man has now been on the earth for two day's 6000 years or maybe more, and we have another 6000 years to go. As you can see, the days are not 1000 years each at this time. However long it took to replenish the fish in the sea, and fowl in the air that equals one day. From the first day to the seventh day, each day got shorter. The new day, which is the eighth day, or first day, will equal 1000 years. The seventh day is the end of the week, and the next day will be a new beginning. The next seven days will last 1000 years each. We are living at the end of the sixth day, Satan's day. The millennium is the seventh day, and Christ second coming begins the millennium.

## *It's time for a new beginning*

# Chapter 3

## God forms Adam and Eve
## Eighth day man a new race of people
## The new beginning

**Genesis 2:4-7**

*⁴These are the generations of the heavens and of the earth when they were created, in the day that the LORD God made the earth and the heavens,*

*⁵And every plant of the field before it was in the earth, and every herb of the field before it grew: for the LORD God had not caused it to rain upon the earth, and there was not a man to till the ground.*

*Before Adam, men and women were hunter gatherers, and nomadic*

*The yellow man, black man, and white man*

⁶But there went up a mist from the earth, and watered the whole face of the ground.

*Before Adam there was no rain, no hurricanes, no tornadoes, no drastic temperature change, they lived in darn near perfect conditions.*

*Plenty of fruits trees and berries growing wild on the land*

*Fish, fowl, and animals galore*

*They say good things always comes to an end*

*Good times are about to end*

*⁷And the LORD God formed man of the dust of the ground, and breathed into his nostrils the breath of life; and man became a living soul.*

*God formed or created the eighth day man*

*Man = eth-ha-adham = The Adam*

*Breath=Nĕshamah = Breath of God/Spirit/Life*

*Soul = nephesh = self*

*<u>Strong's concordance</u>: Adam means to show blood in the face (ruddy complexion)*

*Adam is the first eighth day man, the beginning of a new race of people*

*Adams DNA will not match the sixth day white man*

Through Adam and Eve's genealogy, Christ will be born, and sacrificed for our sins, giving the sixth and eighth day man the opportunity to receive everlasting life.

God had destroyed all living creatures on the face of the earth, why because Lucifer/Satan had deceived Gods children. On the sixth day, he created the three races, He rested on the seventh day and on the eighth day, He created Adam. So why do our teachers of God's word teach that Adam was the first man, when clearly, he was not. The bible say's humankind was living on the earth before Adam. The bible is correct and the traditions of man are not.

When I was in third grade my mother had bought material for a dress, and my grandmother had the dress pattern at her house. Therefore, instead of leaving my brother and me home alone she took us to our grandmother's house. I was bored sitting in the living room staring at the walls. I picked up my grandparent's large bible, and started to read. I started reading Genesis chapter 1:1 and was surprised at what I had read. I was taught that Adam and Eve were created on the sixth day, by my parents, Pastor, and Sunday school teacher. Even today, Jews, Catholics, and Protestants, still teach that Adam and Eve were created on the sixth day. I was nine years old, and had a simple mind, I had just read that God had created man on the sixth day, He then rested on the seventh day, and the next day he formed

Adam and Eve. I could never understand why we were taught this way, and over the years, it would haunt me, and finally I came to the truth when I found pastor Arnold Murray on Satellite TV. I asked God for truth and he provided.

Remember God had flooded the earth in the first earth age. Sixth day man has lived in a near paradise on this earth for six thousand years, but things are about to change. At this time, the whole atmosphere was saturated with water, giving a cover for flesh man, protecting him from the suns radiation. With a thicker Ozone people lived far longer, because of less radiation.

Read Genesis 1: 31 thru 2: 1-7 Again

What do you think, was Adam created on the sixth day or the eighth day?

The bible plainly states that God rested on the seventh day,
and the next day he created Adam and Eve.

## What does the number eight mean?

### Genesis 21:4 (King James Version)

*4And Abraham circumcised his son Isaac being eight days old, as God had commanded him.*

*Why eight days? He was an eighth day man a new race of people*

*Adam and Eve were created on a Monday "a new beginning"*

*From Abraham to Jesus, the twelve tribes of Israel Would circumcise their baby boys on the eighth day.*

*After Christ death he became our circumcision, believe in Christ, and you are circumcised in your heart, whether you are sixth day man or eighth day man*

### Acts 7:8 (King James Version)

*8And he gave him the covenant of circumcision: and so Abraham begat Isaac, and circumcised him the eighth day; and Isaac begat Jacob; and Jacob begat the twelve patriarchs.*

*Covenant = Promise*

## Galatians 3:14

*14That the blessing of Abraham might come on the Gentiles through Jesus Christ; that we might receive the promise of the Spirit through faith.*

*Circumcision is the promise of everlasting life.*

*The eighth day is everlasting life.*

## 1 Samuel 17:12 (King James Version)

*12Now David was the son of that Ephrathite of Bethlehemjudah, whose name was Jesse; and he had **eight sons**: and the man went among men for an old man in the days of Saul.*

*David was the eighth son of Jesse, and became God's chosen king.*

*Saul was not God's chosen king, he was a Benjamite,
the smallest of the twelve tribes of Israel.*

*The true king of Israel can only come from Judah.*

*A new beginning for Israel (King David).*

## 1 Peter 3:20 (King James Version)

*20Which sometime were disobedient, when once the longsuffering of God waited in the days of Noah, while the ark was a preparing, wherein few, that is, **eight souls** were saved by water.*

*All but eight Adamic souls were destroyed in the flood*

*Noah with his wife, their three sons and their wives = Eight souls*

*Noah's family of eight Adamic souls will have a new beginning after the flood*

## John 20:26

*26And after **eight days** again his disciples were within, and Thomas with them: then came Jesus, the doors being shut, and stood in the midst, and said, Peace be unto you.*

*On the eighth day, all of God's children will be with Jesus*

The eighth musical note is the same as the first, back to the beginning. In other words, the eighth day is Monday. We always dread Mondays in the flesh, but this Monday will be forever and ever.

### 2 Peter 3:8 (King James Version)

*⁸But, beloved, be not ignorant of this one thing, that one day is with the Lord as a thousand years, and a thousand years as one day.*

Adam begins that first day; Satan will end the sixth day, Christ will begin the seventh day, and our Father will begin the eighth day with a new earth and new heaven (the new beginning.)

*Adam was created at the beginning of the first day 4004 BC which is Monday*

*Abraham was born in 2004 BC the end of the second day and beginning of the third day.*

*Jesus is born in 4 BC the end of the fourth day, and beginning of the fifth day*

*We are now living in the end of the sixth day, which is Saturday*

*Christ comes back to this earth at the beginning of the seventh day, which is the start of the millennium, or Sunday*

*At the end of the thousand years, it is judgment time, the end of the seventh day.*

*The people that walk-through Gods fire will enter into the eighth day, the day that will last forever (A new beginning)*

*Let me throw in something, if you are a sixth day man you have the same chance to receive everlasting life as the eighth day man*

## Follow Christ and the fire will not harm you

### Daniel 3:24-27 (King James Version)

*²⁴Then Nebuchadnezzar the king was astonished, and rose up in haste, and spake, and said unto his counsellors, Did not we cast three men bound into the midst of the fire? They answered and said unto the king, True, O king.*

*[25]He answered and said, Lo, I see four men loose, walking in the midst of the fire, and they have no hurt; and the form of the fourth is like the Son of God.*

*Jesus was with them*

*[26]Then Nebuchadnezzar came near to the mouth of the burning fiery furnace, and spake, and said, Shadrach, Meshach, and Abednego, ye servants of the most high God, come forth, and come hither. Then Shadrach, Meshach, and Abednego, came forth of the midst of the fire.*

*[27]And the princes, governors, and captains, and the king's counsellors, being gathered together, saw these men, upon whose bodies the fire had no power, nor was an hair of their head singed, neither were their coats changed, nor the smell of fire had passed on them.*

*Shadrach, Meshach, and Abednego were not harmed, Jesus was with them*

At the end of the millennium, Satan will deceive many, but the ones that Follow God will walk through the fire of God, like Shadrach, Meshach, and Abednego. The eighth day is a very important day, everlasting life. Now we have sixth day man and eighth day man on the earth, both have the opportunity to walk through Gods fire, and receive everlasting life. Unfortunately, many will choose Satan over God.

# Chapter 4

## The Garden of Eden, where is it?

## Where I believe the Garden and the four riverheads are located

**Genesis 2:8-9**

[8]*And the LORD God planted a garden **eastward in Eden**; and there he put the man whom he had formed.*

[9]*And out of the ground made the LORD God to grow every tree that is pleasant to the sight, and good for food; the tree of life also in the midst of the garden, and the tree of knowledge of good and evil*

*The first location mentioned in the Bible is Ur of Mesopotamia (Iraq)*

*God planted a garden east of Ur in the land of Eden*

*God prepares the Garden of Eden*

*The tree of life = Christ*

*The tree of Knowledge of good and evil = Satan*

Standing in Ur Iraq looking towards the east, our first country is Iran, then Afghanistan, Pakistan, Tajikistan, Turkmenistan, Uzbekistan, Kyrgyzstan, India, and China. In one of these Countries, the Garden of Eden is located.

## Genesis 2:10-14

¹⁰*And a river went out of Eden to water the garden; and from thence it was parted, and became into **four heads**.*

*Going up stream from Eden to the four River heads*

¹¹*The name of the first is **Pison**: that is it which compasseth the whole land of Havilah, where there is gold;*

*Pison = dispersive*

¹²*And the gold of that land is good: there is bdellium and the onyx stone.*

¹³*And the name of the second river is **Gihon**: the same is it that compasseth the whole land of Ethiopia.*

*Gihon = to break forth*

*Ethiopia = Cush, Kush, Black (The Hindu Kush Mountains)*

¹⁴*And the name of the third river is **Hiddekel**: that is it which goeth toward the east of Assyria. And the fourth river is **Euphrates***

*Hiddekel (Hebrew) = Tigris*

*Assyria = Asshur second son of Shem, became the Assyrians*

*Euphrates = to break forth (rushing)*

# Searching for Eden and the four rivers

If I can find the Rivers, I can locate the Garden of Eden. When I was young, I never heard anyone explain where these four Rivers were located. I want to know! Where are they?

Somewhere on this earth, four rivers come together, and these rivers must fit the descriptions of Genesis. If the rivers do not fit, we look elsewhere. I have been looking for these four rivers, off and on, for at least ten years, and all this time I have been looking in the wrong place.

Most people would assume Mesopotamia, present day Iraq, would definitely be where the Garden of Eden was located, since two Rivers are named here. However, we have a problem, only two rivers, and small feeder Rivers are in Iraq today. The Tigris and Euphrates, and no other rivers have existed before, other than feeder Rivers. People that had lived near the original two Rivers years before must have named the Euphrates and Tigris Rivers later. I have not been looking for the four Rivers in Mesopotamia, but the Pamir knot located in Tajikistan, and Afghanistan. Why there, you ask! Four great Rivers come out of the Pamir Knot, one source, four Rivers. The only place, supposedly, in the world where this happens is the Pamir Knot.

The four Rivers are, the Amu Darya, Syr Darya, Indus, and the Tarim/Kashgar Rivers, which all have their beginning in the Pamir Knot. There are three mountain ranges located in the Pamir Knot, and they are the Pamirs, Hindu Kush, and the Tian Shan mountains. The Pamir Knot region is called "the roof of the world".

Since 1988, I have believed the Garden of Eden was located in this high plateau, the Pamir Knot. I concluded that these Rivers mentioned would have never connected, even going back 6000 years. In September 2009, I gave up looking.

In the last week of February 2010, I was very sick, and I started writing on my book again trying to get my mind off how sick I was. It is amazing how God works, during the worst time of my life, I find the Garden of Eden. God works in mysterious ways.

## Can the Garden of Eden and the four Rivers be found?

Ten long years I have been searching in the Pamir plateau at elevations of 13,000 to 15,000 feet, and now I am thinking it could be in a valley. What information will lead me to the Garden of Eden?

What has led me to this geographical region is the writings, and Quotes of French Orientalist, M. Renan, Prof. S. H. Buchannan, Author of (The World and the Book), Sir Gaston Maspero director of Egyptian Antiquities, and Frederick Haberman Author of (Tracing our Ancestors) all Believe the Garden of Eden was located in the Pamir Knot. The ancient Persians, Hindu, Chinese, and the Tibetan people of China, all believe the cradle of the world (Garden of Eden or Shangri-Lawere located in the high mountains of Belurtag where the Pamirs, Hindu Kush, and Himalaya's unite.

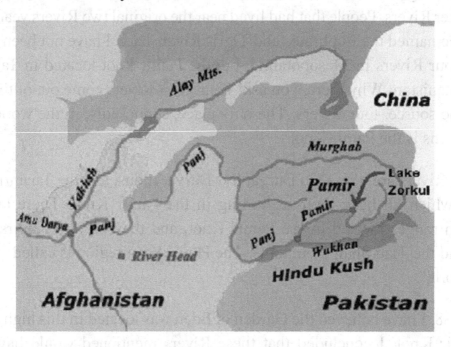

The four River Heads

For ten years, I believed the Garden was located at the head of the Pamir River on Lake Zorkul. The lake is very beautiful; it looks like a perfect place for the Garden of Eden. Following the Pamir River downstream from Lake Zorkul to the Panj River head, and then onto the Amu Darya River head. This only gives me two Riverheads not four. I cannot make it work, so I decide to follow the Rivers downstream to the Amu Darya head, and from here, I will invert my thinking. I believe I have the right rivers, but I need to find the Garden of Eden first.

I must go back to Genesis 2:11-12 for information on its location. Without these two versus the Garden could not be found, I could come very close, but not close enough to suit you or me.

*[11]The name of the first is Pison: that is it which compasseth the whole land of Havilah, where there is gold;*

*[12]And the **gold** of that land is good: there is **bdellium** and the **onyx stone**.*

*The Pison River is the first river mentioned flowing out of the Garden of Eden.*

*Our first clues, Gold, Bdellium, and Onyx stone*

Before I can find the four Rivers, I must find the Garden of Eden first. I was trying to follow the rivers to Eden, "not going to happen". How in the world am I going to find Eden without rivers, I thought to myself it cannot be done? Then this crazy idea came to me, instead of reading books that men have written, and looking at rugged mountains over twenty thousand feet high, why not try God's word. Maybe, just maybe, God left a few clues in his word, so I can finally find the location of the Garden of Eden.

Havilah is not a clue, but a location somewhere on this earth that has gold, bdellium, and the onyx stone. If I can find all three in one location, this will give me a starting point, and hopefully more clues. God gives us three clues, gold, bdellium, and the onyx stone. The three clues are very important, without them, it would be impossible to find the Gardens location.

## First Clue

### Gold

As you know, we can find Gold in many locations around the world, so how can gold be a good clue? Genesis say's the Gold is good. What does this mean? Is not all gold good? Have you ever seen someone wearing a gold nugget on his or her finger, or around his or her neck? I have not! Gold is good, because melting it down produces beautiful ornaments. In other words, it is hand made, and is pleasant to look at. Would you wear a chunk of gold around your neck? No! Would you call that gold good? No! Good means worked, Moreover, of course gold is worth much more when hand crafted.

The Greeks and Soviet Union discovered a large cache of gold in Tillia Tepe in the land of Bactria in 1979. Tillia Tepe is located sixty miles southwest of the ancient city of Balkh. The hoard of gold found on golden hill had laid there for two thousand years before Greek and Soviet Archeologist discovered it. Over 20,000 gold ornaments were found, and by far the most beautiful crafted ornaments ever found on the earth. It is said, the Anglai or Saki tribes from 600

69

BC to 50 BC probably created the gold pieces. Both tribes were Israelite tribes that had migrated to this region. The Greeks also occupied this region during the period from 300 BC to 50 BC.

The gold has been in this land of Bactria for over 6000 years, and over the years has been made into fine ornaments, including necklaces, gems, coins, crowns, and other uses.

The gold was in Bactria, the land of Havilah, and the city of Balkh, on the River Balkh, was a city of commerce where the merchants traded their goods from East to West. This was happening before Adam and Eve were formed in the Garden of Eden. Sixth day man traded and swapped as the American Indians did before the White man.

*Gold found in Bactria, the finest gold in the world.*

*Surrounded by the Pamirs to the east, and the Hindu Kush to the south, can this be the land of Havilah? (Yes, Havilah is Bactria)*

*Our first clue gives us the area in Afghanistan called the land of Bactria*

*Can this land of Bactria possibly be the land where the Garden of Eden could have been located?*

*Can we find bdellium in the land of Bactria?*

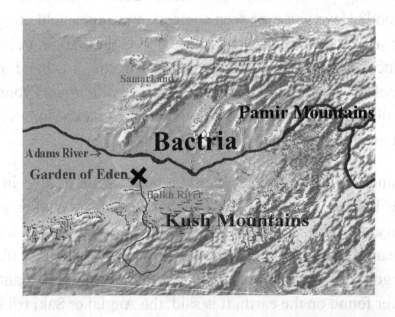

*A land fertile, and rich with gold and minerals*

*Today this land is said to have a mineral wealth of over one trillion dollars*

# Second Clue

### Bdellium

Bdellium is also in the land of Havilah. My first question is what is bdellium? I had always assumed bdellium was some type of stone, until I Googled it. To my surprise it is not a stone, it comes from a thorn tree in the land of Bactria. The thorn tree produces a resin or gum made into perfumes. In ancient times, Bdellium would be worth more than gold. Remember the thorn tree; it has a deeper meaning, relating to Satan.

Strong's Concordance: Bdellium (Gum or Resin)

Information below copied from Wikipedia:

## Bdellium

From Wikipedia, the free encyclopedia Theophrastus is perhaps the first classical author to mention it, if the report that came back from his informant in Alexander's expedition refers to *Commiphora wightii*: "In the region called Aria there is a thorn tree which produces a tear of resin, resembling myrrh in appearance and odour. It liquifies when the sun shines upon it."[6] Plautus in his play *Curculio* refers to it. Pliny the Elder describes the best bdellium coming from Bactria as a "tree black in colour, and the size of the olive tree; its leaf resembles that of the oak and its fruit the wild fig", but his descriptions[7] seem to cover a range of strongly perfumed resins.

*Aria = Sogdiana and Bactria*

The best bdellium according to Pliny comes out of Bactria not Aria, which is west of Bactria. The Chinese imported their bdellium by way of the ancient Silk Road not used today. Asia Minor and parts of Europe imported their bdellium from the Indus River south of Bactria.

The land of Bactria has the best gold, and the best bdellium. One more clue to fit in is the onyx stone.

# Onyx stone, can it be found in the land of Bactria?

## Third Clue

<u>Onyx Stone</u>

The Onyx stone is mined in the land of Bactria., Onyx Marble is mined in the Hindu Kush, and the Pamir mountains. There is white Onyx stone and many other colors found in Afghanistan. Onyx stone has been mined for over six thousand years in the ancient city of Balkh in the land of Bactria.

*The finest gold ever found is in the land of Bactria/Havilah*

*The best bdellium comes from Bactria/Havilah*

*Onyx stone has been mined in Bactra/Bactria before Adam and Eve were formed*

I believe I found the land of Havilah, the land of Gold, Bdellium, and Onyx stone. The land of Havilah is a big area, I need to pin point a location that will fit with the four rivers. There is one major river that flows east to west on the north side of Bactria, and that is the Amu Darya River. I already know this river is one of the four rivers mentioned in Genesis, I have known it for twenty-four years. The difference now is that I am looking for the Garden of Eden in the valley, not the Mountains.

*[10]And a river went out of Eden to water the garden; and from thence it was parted, and became into **four heads**.*

I believe the River that flowed out of Eden was the Balkh River, which gets its source out of the Hindu Kush Mountains. Today the River does not make it to the Amu Darya River. In Ancient times, The Balkh River flowed through the city of Balkh, and emptied into the Amu Darya River tributary.

## The Balkh River Is the River of the Garden of Eden

The land of Bactria got its name from the city of Balkh, which relied on the Balkh River for agriculture. The ancient city of Balkh is one of the oldest cities on earth, located on the ancient Silk Road passage connecting the travels of all three races. Balkh was a very important city for trade and commerce well before Adam and Eve over six thousand years ago. The city of Balkh relied on the water source from the Balkh River that travels to Balkh from the Hindu Kush Mountains. Today the city is an ancient ruin, and the river is nearly dry. Back six thousand years ago the city of Balkh was a very busy place, with a beautiful green lush landscape. Today Balkh is arid and dry yet the land is still very fertile.

## Iraq is not the location of Eden

Many people believe Iraq is the location of the Garden of Eden, because of two rivers with the biblical names Euphrates, and the Tigris (in Hebrew called the Hiddekel). The source of these two rivers is located in Turkey, and the tallest mountain is named Mount Ararat. Many people have, and are looking for Noah's Ark on Mount Ararat; (they will never find it there.) The origin of Ararat is unknown, but it possibly means the tallest Mountains. Mount Ararat is the tallest mountain in Turkey, and it is part of the source of the Euphrates River. Therefore, you can understand why they named the Tallest Mountain Mount Ararat. The flood story was well known before the offspring of Noah entered into Mesopotamia/Iraq.

One River stands out in Iraq, and it is the Balikh River. It flows south into the Euphrates River as a feeder river. The town of Haran where Abraham journeyed to from Ur is located on the upper part of this feeder river called the Balikh River. Abraham and his father Terah moved to Haran from Ur in Mesopotamia/Iraq. Isaac took a wife in Haran where their kin people still lived. Jacob took two wives and lived on this river for fourteen years. Before Abraham, Cain I believe named this River Balikh, and built a temple for the worship of the moon god, which represents Satan his Father.

We have two rivers with the same name, one in Afghanistan, and one in Iraq. In Afghanistan, the river is spelled Balkh, in Iraq the river is spelled Balikh, and I believe Cain named this River after the River in Eden, where he was born. Both

Rivers are feeder Rivers that flow into a major River. In Afghanistan, the Balkh River flows into the Amu Darya River, and in Iraq, the Balikh River flows into the Euphrates River

## Names migrate along with people

Some of the names of Dan (a tribe of Israel): The Danes, the Danai, which Homer mentioned 147 times, the Danish people, the Dan-mark/Denmark people, and the Donsk/Swedish people are all names derived from Dan.

Now the rivers: The Danube, Donetz, Danzig, Dnieper, and more, they derived their names from Dan. When the Angles, Saxons, Vikings, Jutes, Friesians, Franks, Normans, Gauls, Iberians, and more, moved into Great Britain their names moved with them. Names ending in ham, ing, stowe, sted, or ton are Saxon names. Names ending in (by) like Goolsby are Danish. Names beginning with Van like Van Orden are also Danish. Names ending in wick are Viking names. The name dale is Nordic that means valley. The Saxons, Vikings, Danish, and others migrated to Great Britain, naming their homesteads, valleys, and rivers with the names they were accustomed to.

The same thing happened in Mesopotamia, the Euphrates, Tigris, and Balikh Rivers were all named from Rivers of a distant land. Cain named these Rivers after the Rivers he grew up with while living in Afghanistan. Cain moved into Mesopotamia in 3800BC, hundreds of years before Noah's descendants migrated from China into Mesopotamia/Babylon after the great flood.

The Balkh River in the Land of Bactria is the river that flowed out of Eden and parted into four riverheads. The land of Havilah is Bactria and the ancient city of Balkh I believe is the Garden of Eden.

## The History of Balkh

The city of Balkh before Adam and Eve was the city of all cities. The land was well watered and very fertile; this was the city of trade and commerce for all three races, of the sixth day humankind. At this time, the city of Balkh was the center of the world, and today Balkh is the center point of the world's population of today. The largest populations on earth now surround the very place where

Adam and Eve were created, and this is no accident. The mysteries of God never end once you start searching for His truth.

It is no accident that the land of Bactria is the center of the world population today. This very place Where God formed Adam and Eve is now the center of the largest population. The city of balkh was the center of trade and commerce, during the time of Adam and Eve, and Satan was the master merchant and moneychanger of it. The city of Tyrus in Canaan becomes the second city of merchants, and moneychangers, and today the city of New York is the new Tyrus, the money changing capital of the world. Satan doing business in the midst of the Garden of Eden, in the center of the town of Balkh, he is the great Merchant and moneychanger doing his evil work just as he did during the first earth age.

*The City of Balkh the center of the world population*

*Easter Island the center of the least population*

Zoroaster a prophet of the tribe of Israel is said to have first started preaching in the city of Balkh. Zoroaster was of the Saki tribe in captivity south of the Caspian Sea. In 600BC, the Saki migrated to the land of Bactria, and Sogdiana. Zoroaster lived in Balkh, and began to preach to the people about the one true God, and the first Adamic man the Persians call Gayomart. Adam the first man created on the eighth day in the Garden of Eden, on the Balkh River. 3400 years later, a prophet is teaching about him in that very same spot. This is not by accident, these are the mysteries of God, and if we seek the truth, we shall find the truth. Zoroaster taught in many nations and died in Balkh where he began.

*Zoroaster = Gold Camel, or Golden Light*

After Zoroaster's death, Darius the Great Conquered Balkh, he was a believer in the Zend-Avesta, and the teachings of Zoroaster. In 329 BC, Alexander the Great took the city of Balkh, but never gained full control. Alexander met a strong resistance from the Asa/Saki People, (an Israelite Tribe that lived in Balkh at that time.) Darius III of Persia was defeated and killed by Alexander the Great, and the satrapies of Bactria lost most of their power during the Greek occupation. Alexander was married in the City of Balkh to a woman named Roxana in 327AD. She was very beautiful, and was the only women that Alexander truly loved. Her father's name was Oxyartes, and he lived in Bactria/Balkh with his daughters.

*Satrap/Satrapies = Rulers of a dominion*

Genghis Khan destroyed the city of Balkh in 1220AD, and he tore down many of the beautiful buildings and slaughtered all the inhabitants. What was Genghis Khan looking for? Was it gold? Yes, it was, and thank God, he did not find it. As we know, the Russians and Greeks would find the gold in 1979. Marco Polo Visited the city after Khan had destroyed it, and said it was a noble and great city. Everyone in the city was killed, and portions of the temples were destroyed, yet the city came back, but never to be what it once was. The Russians were unable to capture and take full control over Afghanistan. Now we the USA occupy this same area, and we do not have full control, and never will. Five races of people came from the city of Balkh, the sixth day whites, blacks, and mongoloid all lived here. The eighth day man (Adam and Eve) was created in this great city, and Cain the son of Satan was born here. I will explain why Cain is a separate race later.

The great city of Balkh is possibly the oldest city on Earth, we know it existed before Adam and Eve, and the ruins of that city still exist there today. The Arabs called it the mother of all cities, a city with unbelievable history, possibly ranging over 8000 years. The city of Balkh, was renamed Bactra by the ancient Greeks.

Balkh was a city considered rich not powerful, mainly a city of trade located on the ancient silk rout to China. We can compare it with Tyre of Canaan, before Alexander the great captured, and destroyed it. I must not leave out Buddhism as a prevalent religion that entered the city in 600AD by a Monk named Bhalika, which his name probably derived from Balkh.

*Go on-line to Google Earth and type in Balkh Afghanistan; you can see the ancient ruins of Balkh where Adam and Eve was created. The ancient city is round and Satan once stood in the center of it.*

## The four Riverheads

## If I cannot find the four heads, the city of Balkh is not the location of the Garden of Eden.

Strong's Concordance Etymology of Head #7218

Root word (Head) from an unused root meaning to shake

The shakiest place on Earth is the Pamir Knot. The Pamir Mountains are a hot bed for small and large Earthquakes. Is it not ironic, the root for head, means to shake, and these four riverheads are located in the shakiest location on Earth?

## Searching for the four river heads

Back six thousand years ago Balkh/Eden would have been a beautiful fertile land, with a small river flowing thru Eden, and its source coming from the Hindu Kush Mountains. A tributary from the Amu Darya River, which Flowed thru Balkh in ancient times giving life to this city. Today the Balkh River only has a seasonal flow, no longer a Garden of Eden.

*Four Riverheads mentioned in Genesis*
*Pison*
*Gihon*
*Hiddekel*
*Euphrates*
*All four Rivers must connect*
*Beginning of a River = Head*
*Two Rivers connecting = Head*

### First River Head
Pison River = Increase
Largest River, lowest elevation

The first River mentioned in Genesis is the Pison River, and the River I believe to be the Amu Darya River of today. Our starting point will begin at the intersection where the Balkh River in ancient times flowed into the Amu Darya tributary, and then heading east towards the Pamir mountains. In Ancient Babylon writings, Anu is the name for Adam. The locals still call the River the Oxus. The Oxus

River got its name from the Asa tribe, a mix of the ten tribes of Israel called Ephraim. They migrated into Bactria around 600BC. Their symbol was the calf, ox, and unicorn; and the Asa people renamed the river Oxus.

The indigenous people continued to call it Amu/Adams River, and the Israelites, Greeks with a mix of other tribal people who are still living in the Region today call it the Oxus. Moving upstream on the Amu Darya/Oxus River, two great Rivers coming out of the High Pamirs and Hindu Kush mountains join and become the first head named the Pison River. The two rivers that join are the Vakhsh, and Panj rivers. The Amu Darya/Pison River continues toward the west and empties in the Aral Sea.

Alexander the Great as a young boy broke a horse and named him Ox Head, in Greek (Bucephalus.) This special horse lived seventeen years with Alexander riding him through many battles. His first horse was named Ox head, and the first Riverhead of Genesis was called Oxus Head. Could it be the Oxus head was named after Alexander's horse? Maybe, but I believe it was given the name almost three hundred years earlier by the Asa tribe.

Oxus derived from Israelite tribes, and the Greeks = Ox
Amu Darya (In middle Persian) = Good River
Pison River = Amu Darya = Oxus = Ox
Darya (Hebrew word meaning River or Sea)
Darya (African word Meaning River or Sea)
Darya (Persian word meaning Sea or River)
Amu = Adam, and Darya = River,
The Amu Darya is Adam's River
Anu, Ea, Bel = Adam, Eve, and the devil (Written in ancient Babylon text)

The Balkh River which is the River flowing through Eden/Balkh flows into Adams/Amu Darya River, and the city of Balkh is where the Garden of Eden was located.

## The Second Head

The Panj River, is the second river mentioned in Genesis called the Gihon. We follow the river upstream through the Wakhan Corridor to where two rivers join together named the Pamir and Wakhan Rivers to form the Gihon/Panj head. The best evidence yet, The Panj River today, is still called the Gihon River, by the locals and the ancient peoples. The second River in Genesis was called the Gihon and the second River from Balkh is also called the Gihon. If you look up the Amu Darya River on the internet, Wikipedia and other sites, they say the Amu Darya River is called the Jayhoun River that is derived from Gihon. The Amu Darya is the Oxus, and the Panj is the Gihon.

Gihon = Jayhoun = Panj

The reasons I believe the Panj or Gihon River are the same is based on its location. In Genesis 2:13 it says the Gihon River compasseth the whole land of Ethiopia. How can that be? Ethiopia is in Africa, not Afghanistan. Look up Ethiopia in your Strong's concordance, and you will see it means Kush or black. The Amu Darya River does not flow through the Hindu Kush Mountains; it flows west along the edge of the Pamir Mountains to the north. The Panj/Gihon River flows between the Pamir and Hindu Kush Mountains dividing the Pamirs to the north and the Hindu Kush to the south. Kush is an ancient word that means black. Ethiopia is derived from Kush which also means black.

Ethiopia in Africa is called the land of Cush/Kush. The Cushite tribes of North Africa are thought to be the oldest black civilization in Africa, and they lived in Ethiopia. I believe the black race migrated from the Hindu Kush to India, then to Africa Taking the name Kush/Cush with them. From Ethiopia, they populated the entire continent of Africa. The Cushite people today live in Sudan just north of Ethiopia.

### *Strong's Concordance: Ethiopia*

*#3568 Kush=Black*

*Jayhoun (Arabic) derived from Gihon*

*Panj=Gihon*

The Panj River that is still called the Gihon by the Local people today, I believe is the Gihon of Genesis. Gihon the second River out of Eden, and the Panj, the second River out of Balkh, and the River fits.

## Third Head

The third river is the Wakhan River, which I believe to be the Hiddekel. We follow this river along the Wakhan Corridor (ancient Silk Road passage) to Lake Chakmaktin. From the Wakhan head at Lake Chakmaktin to the Panj Head the elevation starts at 13,221' and drops down to 9,180' in only 93 miles. That equates to a 4,041' drop in 93 miles, and that equals a 43' drop per mile.

*Strong's Concordance: Hiddekel = Rapid*

## Fourth Head

The forth river is the Pamir river its head is at Lake Victoria, or now called Lake Zorkul. This River connects with the Panj River at the Wakhan Corridor, and I believe this is the Euphrates River. All four rivers are connected. I believe Adam and Eve may have migrated from Balkh/Eden to Lake Zorkul, and raised their two sons on this beautiful lake. Flowing out of this lake was the Pamir/Euphrates River, and later Cain would settle in Mesopotamia naming three of the Rivers the Euphrates, Hiddekel/Tigris, and Balkh, from the Pamirs where he grew up on as a child.

Strong's Concordance: Euphrates = Fruitfulness

| Bible Names | Today's names |
|---|---|
| Pison | Amu Darya/Oxus (Vakhsh and Panj join) |
| Gihon | Panj/Gihon (Divides the Hindu Kush and Pamirs) |
| Hiddekel | Wakhan (The head starts at Lake Chakmaktin) |
| Euphrates | Pamir (The head starts at Lake Zorkul) |

The Rivers Connect and they fit; I believe they are the Rivers mentioned in Genesis. This I believe also proves the city of Balkh is the location of the Garden

All the above are reasons why I believe this location is the place where Adam and Eve sinned in the Garden of Eden shown on this map.

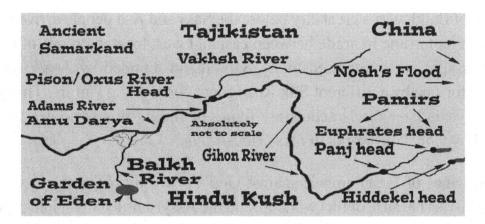

This ancient city Balkh, possibly 8000 years old, or more, is where I believe the Garden of Eden was located. Every bit of history and facts that I discovered along this long journey has led me to an ancient old city, where I believe God formed Adam and Eve. Is there a chance my location is wrong? Certainly, but it is up to you to absorb the facts, and history, and decide for yourselves.

## History of Balkh and the Israelites
## Who are these Saki and Asa People?

Over four hundred years before Alexander the Great invaded Balkh/Bactria, around 745 BC to 717 BC, the Assyrians under Tiglath–Pileser, Shalmaneser, and Sargon the 2nd took captive the ten tribes of Israel. At around 700 BC, the Samarian Empire had declined to where the Israelite tribes were free to leave their captivity in the (land of the Medes) south of the Caspian Sea.

The ten Tribes migrated in many directions, some moving through the Caucasus Mountains and back west into Europe, others migrating through Turkey, Greece, and on into Europe. Three tribes which I believe were a mix of the ten tribes traveled into Persia, and then into Afghanistan. The Three tribes were named Asa/Anglai/Engle, Getai/Guti/Catti, and the Saki/Saks tribe, which means sons of Isaac. These Three tribes settled in Sogdiana and Balkh the land of Bactria. The tribe of Asa founded the city of Samarkand north of Balkh also called Engle. God works in mysterious ways, the chosen people of God homesteaded in the land of Bactria, and lived in the city of Balkh where Adam and Eve were created.

The city of Balkh was a great city before the Saki and Asa people arrived, a city that made its fortune by trade between east and west located on one of the Silk Road passages no longer used today. Samarkand founded by Asa/Engle also made its fortune by a different Silk Road route north of the Pamirs. Thirty-four hundred years later the Israelites are living in Balkh, this is no accident, but planned by God. God works in mysterious ways.

The ten tribes of Israel sinned against God by worshipping other gods. God divorced Israel because of Idol worship, and the Assyrians led them into captivity. They migrated in different directions, but all ended up in the same place, (Great Britain.) The Asa, Saki, and Catti tribes worshipped the Golden Calf. This Golden calf is the same Calf worshipped by the Israelites while Moses was with God on Mount Sinai. Today we think of the Vikings with horns on their helmets, but this is not true, the Vikings never wore horns. The Asa tribe wore horned headdress to resemble their worship of the calf, bull, ox, and unicorn.

### Hosea 8:5 (King James Version)

*⁵Thy calf, O Samaria, hath cast thee off; mine anger is kindled against them: how long will it be ere they attain to innocency?*

*Calf = Engle*

*Samaria = Ephraim = ten tribes of Israel*

*Samarkand = New Samaria*

### Deuteronomy 33:17 (King James Version)

*¹⁷His glory is like the firstling of his bullock, and his horns are like the horns of unicorns: with them he shall push the people together to the ends of the earth: and they are the ten thousands of Ephraim, and they are the thousands of Manasseh.*

*Asa tribe = Ephraim (Represents the ten tribes of Israel)*

*Ephraim's sign = Calf, Ox, and Unicorns*

*The Oxus River I believe derived its name from the Asa tribe's worship of the Ox*

The Asa, Saki, and Getai people will migrate to the ends of the earth, and during that journey a new language will be born, and that new tongue will become an international language spoken in part by many or all nations on this earth today.

## Who Is Ephraim?

Joseph was one of the twelve tribes of Israel, sold into slavery by his jealous brothers. He became a great leader of Egypt, and only the Pharaoh did he answer too. He married a woman in Egypt, (of the Hyksos tribe) who were ruling over the Egyptians at this time. The Hyksos people were relatives of Abraham, and the name Hyksos means "Shepherd kings". The Israelites were despised by the Egyptians because they were sheepherders and wore beards. Joseph had two sons Manasseh the first-born, and Ephraim. Both Ephraim and Manasseh became tribes of Israel, and now we have thirteen tribes instead of twelve.

The United States started with thirteen original colonies, and one would represent Satan's seed. Jesus sat down with twelve disciples making the total number of thirteen at the last supper. There were thirteen altogether, one was of the devil, and he would deliver Jesus to the Pharisees. The number thirteen is a number that represents evil, rebellion, and haters of God. Thirteen is a bad number in the bible, and today thirteen is known as an unlucky number. Some buildings exclude the thirteenth floor, and Friday the 13th is known as a bad day.

## All ten tribes are known as Ephraim

The ten tribes of Israel from Great Britain will migrate to the USA, Canada, Australia, New Zealand, and South Africa. The Saki Asa, and Getai tribes would be the last tribes of Ephraim to enter into Europe, and then Great Britain. These Three tribes will be known as the Anglo Saxons.

> Asa is pronounced ace, and yes, this is where the ace in our cards are derived. You can say the Asa people were "bull headed" since they wore horns on their heads. The expression "John Bull" comes from the Asa tribe.

God has always set aside certain men to fulfill his plan. God plants them in certain geographical locations, and at very important times. Thomas Edison was chosen in the late 1800s during the invention frenzy. God knew he would invent the phonograph, light bulb, movie projector, and much more. Adolf Hitler was chosen by God to rule the people of Germany, not for the slaughter of 50 million people, but the re-birth of the state of Israel in 1948. Hitler disobeyed the word of God by uprooting the Tares. God did not choose Alexander the great to create a Greek world in Asia. Alexander's true destiny was to send the Israelites to Europe, and Great Britain, where they would meet up with the other tribes of Israel. From there they would disperse all around the world. Little did Alexander know his trying to conquer the world, would lead the people he fought so hard to subdue, to a new land that would become the richest and most powerful superpower on earth.

When Alexander the great invaded Bactria in 329 BC, the Asa, Getai, and Saki people had been living there for 270 years. The Three tribes of Israel gave Alexander much trouble, and he actually never subdued them. Herodotus claimed Cyrus was killed by the Messagetai/Getai on the Jaxartes River. Greek influence remains in Bactria to this day. Alexander had no idea of his true destiny, and Gods plan for him. Alexander was an Israelite of the tribe of Judah, but did not know this. The Asa and the Saki tribes were his relatives; they fought so hard against him not knowing they were related. He did write about the people having white skin, blue eyes and red and blond hair. Alexander in the city of Balkh, had no idea he was standing where Adam and Eve were created. God works in mysterious way's.

The Asa and Saki began their migration towards the setting sun into Europe, where their kinsmen had already settled more than two hundred years before, and much earlier. The Saki people migrated south of the Caspian Sea, and then north through the Caucasus Mountains into Russia now known as the Royal Scythes or Scythians. Around 100 AD they had reached Germany, and are at this time known as the Saxons. The Asa people moved north of the Caspian Sea into Russia and at this time were called the Angle/Anglos people.

The Anglos migrated into Germany around 300 AD. The Anglo/ Saxons are now in Europe. Not well liked, they will not stay long. In 300 AD, they settled in West Germany and south Jutland/Denmark an area where the tribe of Judah had migrated. When the Anglo people packed up and left Germany, not one person was left behind. By 446 AD to 501 AD they had left their habitation, and crossed the North Sea conquering with the sword, the land of Brutus called Great Britain. The Angles will have the greatest impact on people this world has ever known. I myself am not an Anglo Saxon; I am of the tribe of Judah descended from the line of Zarah and Pharez, however many people of German, and British descent are from these tribes out of Afghanistan. The German people make up the largest ancestry group in the United States at 17 percent, and possibly 70 percent are the Saki/Saxons from Afghanistan.

### Ezekiel 5:2-12 (King James Version)

*²Thou shalt burn with fire a third part in the midst of the city, when the days of the siege are fulfilled: and thou shalt take a third part, and smite about it with a knife: and a third part thou shalt scatter in the wind; and I will draw out a sword after them.*

*¹²A third part of thee shall die with the pestilence, and with famine shall they be consumed in the midst of thee: and a third part shall fall by the sword round about thee; and I will scatter a third part into all the winds, and I will draw out a sword after them.*

The Angles invaded Great Britain with the sword, which God had promised. "I will draw out a sword after the Israelites who worshipped Bel and other gods, and I will bring them back to me." In this case, the Angles were the pagans at that time. The British had already established a church called (the church of the Culdees,) over 350 years earlier. The Culdees founder was (Joseph of Arimathea) in Glastonbury England. Young Jesus built the first church out of wattle in Glastonbury England, the first Christian church.

## The sword actually symbolizes truth in God's word

### Jeremiah 9:16

*¹⁶I will scatter them also among the heathen, whom neither they nor their fathers have known: and **I will send a sword after them**, till I have consumed them.*

The sword of the Assyrians took captive the ten tribes of Israel starting in 745 B.C. through 677 B.C. the final deportation of the ten tribes of Israel. The sword of the Babylonians took captive the Tribe of Judah and Benjamin around 600 B.C. The sword of Alexander the great invaded Bactria and Sogdiana and caused the Israelites to move "westward ho" towards the setting sun. The sword of the Angles invaded Britain from 449 to 557 A.D. bringing in the birth right blessings of Ephraim and Manasseh. The Saxons did not enter into Britain; they remained in Germany, northern France, Switzerland, and Scandinavia where they live today. Later the great Saxons will migrate to the USA, and today they have the highest percentage of Europeans living in the United States of America by far.

### Revelation 1:16

[16]*And he had in his right hand seven stars: and out of his mouth went a sharp **two edged sword**: and his countenance was as the sun shineth in his strength.*

*The last sword will be Christ at the beginning of the millennium*

*The two edged sword will be his tongue*

*His words will shame the people that followed Satan*

# The Asa/Anglo people become the English

The Asa people worshipped the golden calf, the same calf they worshipped during the time of Moses. The Hebrew word Engle means calf, and the Asa tribe are the Engle people, or calf people. By the time, they settled Great Britain they became the English, uniting the country, and it became England. They roared into Great Britain with their swords to conquer the British, bringing with them their idol worship. In one hundred years, they succumbed to the sword of Christ word, and converted to Christianity. Because of the Angles, the holder of Joseph birthright, many nations are blessed.

*Ish (Hebrew) = Man*

*Engle (Hebrew) = Calf*

*Engle+Ish = English*

*Engle+Land= England*

*The language they spoke became English*

*This Language today is spoken worldwide (the international language)*

*All twelve tribes of Israel are now in Great Britain*

People who chose to stay in the Pamirs, and Chitral areas before Noah and after the flood still have Caucasian features proving they once came from Mongolia, and Bactria. You will notice many have fair skin, light hair, and blue eyes. These are possibly offspring of the Israelites, and Greeks. However, some of them could be direct descendants of Adam and Eve, not ever going to Israel, an indigenous people surviving the harsh mountainous regions. Yes, during the time of Noah, some of Adams offspring may have lived in the Pamirs, and survived the flood. They survived because they were above the flood waters.

The people with Caucasian features are of the tribes of Kalish, and Wakhi. The kalash people living in Chitral, (Hindu Kush) Left the area of Bactria in 200 BC after the invasion of the Greeks. The Wakhi people are still living in the Pamir Knot where Adam and Eve raised Cain and Abel.

Go on-line to (Holli's Ramblings) and look at the Indigenous people in this region of the world.

## History of the ancient tribes of Afghanistan and Persia

The Pashtun tribe in Afghanistan

The Pashtun people make up forty percent of the people living in Afghanistan. Oral tradition claims they are descended from the ten lost tribes of Israel, from the Bani Israel people who migrated to Ghor Afghanistan. They are Indo-European, possibly Greek, Israelite, Iranian, Arab, Persians, Medes, and some are indigenous people going back to Noah and Adam. They are a mixed people, like the Mediterranean people today, with light colored hair and eyes, and others dark skin and dark eyes.

Ancient Pashtun legends of their origin begins in Judea with King Saul's grandson Afghana, whom they are descended. King Saul was a Benjamite of the twelve tribes of Israel, and his grandson Afghana was raised by King David. 180 years before their release from Babylon a tribe of Judah called the Yuti or Yoti lived in

Bactria along with the Asa and Saki tribes. The Afghana Family probably knew of their location and headed towards their kinsmen. After the Afghana royal family arrived in this land, they ruled over the many tribes, and the land was named Afghanistan. This story is not in the Bible, but has been handed down from generation to generation. I believe this story is true, like I said before God works in mysterious ways.

Alexander the Great had great respect for the Pashtun people; he said they were a lion like the one brave people confronting his soldiers with such great courage that he had not seen before. It is too bad he did not know they were related to him.

Many have tried and many have failed to subdue these people. Many Arabs have moved into Afghanistan and they are brothers to the Pashtun People.

### Matthew 2

*¹Now when Jesus was born in Bethlehem of Judaea in the days of Herod the king, behold, there came wise men from the east to Jerusalem,*

*²Saying, Where is he that is born King of the Jews? for we have seen his star in the east, and are come to worship him.*

The wise men I believe were Israelites from Iran, who traveled a long distance to see, and give gifts to the child that God would sacrifice for all humanity.

### The Tajik people

The Tajik people are also Indo- European, they speak mostly Persian, and a small percentage speak Pamiri in the high Pamirs. The Tajik people live in many countries, Afghanistan, Tajikistan, Uzbekistan, Kazakhstan, Kyrgyzstan, Turkmenistan, Pakistan, Russia, and China. There is no oral tradition stating they are related to the Israelites, but I most definitely believe they are. They are today the largest ethnic group in Balkh and the land of Bactria. Both the Pashtun and Tajik people are a mixture of Iranian, Israelite, and Mongolian people. Afghanistan is a very diverse Country, since Adam and Eve six thousand years ago, all three races, plus the eighth day race, and the sons of Cain have lived in this country.

The Tajik people are diverse genetically, mixing among different tribes for thousands of years. Ten percent of the Tajik people have blond hair and a big part of them live in the Pamir region. The Pamiri people, who live a hard life at elevations of thirteen thousand feet and above, could possibly be the indigenous people from Adam and Eve. If these people have lived here since Adam and Eve for six thousand years among these beautiful Mountains, and very harsh winters, it is truly remarkable, but it cannot be proven. Good people, living under extreme conditions, they are land locked by governments and have nowhere to go. I wish we could help them.

## The Kushans

The Kushans are an Indo-European people that lived in the Tarim Basin, where Noah and the Adamic people lived before the flood. Many European or Caucasian looking Mummies have been found in this region of China, going back before Noah. The Kushans migrated from the Tarim Basin to the land of Bactria, and settled in the region where Adam and Eve were created. The Eighth day man, cannot help it, they keep going back to where they had their beginning, the Garden of Eden.

The Asa, Saki, and Getae of the ten tribes of Israel all lived in the Syr Darya, Amu Darya, Indus river regions, and a big portion of these tribes moved west into Germany and became known as the Anglo Saxons. They then moved into Great Britain and became the English people. Three English-speaking nations today, Great Britain, United States of America, and Australia, are all fighting in Afghanistan for the freedom of our ancestors. The Adamic race cannot stay away from where they began. God works in mysterious ways.

This is the best I can do to convince you that the Garden of Eden is in Afghanistan.

Please go online: look up the Pastuns, Tajiks, and Kushans, from Wikipedia.

# Chapter 5

## Adam and Eve in the Garden of Eden

**Genesis 2:15-17 (King James Version)**

[15]And the LORD God took the **man**, and put him into the Garden of Eden to **dress it** and **to keep it.**

> Man = eth-ha-adham = the Adam

> Dress = to work, serve, and to labor

> Keep = to have charge over, to guard, to watch and protect

[16]And the LORD God commanded the man, saying, Of every tree of the garden thou mayest freely eat:

[17]But of the tree of the knowledge of good and evil, thou shalt not eat of it: for in the day that thou eatest thereof thou shalt surely die.

> The tree of the Knowledge of good and evil = Satan

God has prepared a special place for Adam to live in. A place about as close to being a utopia on Earth as you can get living in the flesh. The garden is near the city of Balkh, along the waters of the Balkh and Amu Darya. It cannot be a utopia because it clearly says he will dress it, and keep it. Yes, Adam had to work just as we do today. God gave us free will, and where there is free will utopia does not exist.

God placed Adam in the garden to till the soil, and to serve him. God gave him charge over the garden, to guard and protect his premium land. Adam is the boss man, he is responsible for himself, and if he does not produce, he does not eat.

*2 Thessalonians 3:10*

*[10]For even when we were with you, this we commanded you, that if any would not work, neither should he eat.*

# Why is God mentioning trees in the Garden of Eden?

# How can a tree be good or bad?

# How can a tree be evil and have Knowledge?

God teaches using symbolism, and here are some versus showing us what the trees are symbolic of, and mean.

*Judges 9:8-15 (King James Version)*

*[8]The trees went forth on a time to anoint a king over them; and they said unto the olive tree, Reign thou over us.*

*The trees = God's chosen people*

*The olive tree = the Anointed One (Christ)*

*[9]But the olive tree said unto them, Should I leave my fatness, wherewith by me they honour God and man, and go to be promoted over the trees?*

*[10]And the trees said to the fig tree, Come thou, and reign over us.*

*Fig tree = the fruit producer*

*[11]But the fig tree said unto them, Should I forsake my sweetness, and my good fruit, and go to be promoted over the trees?*

*[12]Then said the trees unto the vine, Come thou, and reign over us.*

*The vine = to bend*

*[13]And the vine said unto them, Should I leave my wine, which cheereth God and man, and go to be promoted over the trees?*

*[14]Then said all the trees unto the bramble, Come thou, and reign over us.*

*The Bramble (thorn tree) = Represents Satan the devil*

*The crown of thorns placed on Christ head was made from the bramble thorn tree*

*Bdellium comes from the thorn tree*

*[15]And the bramble said unto the trees, If in truth ye anoint me king over you, then come and put your trust in my shadow: and if not, let fire come out of the bramble, and devour the cedars of Lebanon.*

*The bramble = Satan*

*The fire = lies*

*The Cedars = Christians*

*Satan's lies will deceive the children of God*

*Matthew 3:10*

*[10]And now also the axe is laid unto the root of the trees: therefore every tree which bringeth not forth good fruit is hewn down, and cast into the fire.*

*The trees represent the people, good and bad.*

*The people that work against God will be judged and cast into the lake of fire*

**Mark 8:23-24**

*[23]And he took the blind man by the hand, and led him out of the town; and when he had spit on his eyes, and put his hands upon him, he asked him if he saw ought.*

*[24]And he looked up, and said, **I see men as trees, walking**.*

Being blind to the truth, then able to see the truth that the trees in the Garden of Eden are people.

### Ezekiel 31:16 (King James Version)

*[16]I made the nations to shake at the sound of his fall, when I cast him down to hell with them that descend into the pit: and all the **trees of Eden**, the choice and best of Lebanon, all that drink water, shall be comforted in the nether parts of the earth.*

*Trees of Eden = People of Eden*

*The many membered body of the tree of life will take in the living water of everlasting life*

### Revelation 2:7 (King James Version)

*[7]He that hath an ear, let him hear what the Spirit saith unto the churches; To him that overcometh will I give to eat of the **tree of life**, which is in the midst of the paradise of God.*

*Jesus was the tree of life in Eden, and now he sits in heaven on the right side of God*

## What does the bramble bush say he will do if he rules over the trees?

He says stand under my shadow, "a very small shadow" and if you do not, fire will come out of the bramble bush and devour the ciders of Lebanon that symbolizes the believers of Christ. More than anything in the world, Satan's desire is to deceive Gods Children, and to have them thrown in the lake of fire with him, and his angels.

God uses symbolism so we can reach a deeper meaning and understanding in His word. In addition, God uses symbolism so we will work for our understanding and truth. If you seek the truth, you will be blessed in the life to come.

### Genesis 2:16-17

*[16]And the LORD God commanded the man, saying, Of every tree of the garden thou mayest freely eat:*

*Every man and woman of all three races of people living in the Garden "the city of Balkh"*

*Eat = partake in friendship, business, and as neighbors*

<sup>17</sup>*But of the tree of the knowledge of good and evil, thou shalt not eat of it: for in the day that thou eatest thereof thou shalt surely die.*

*Satan is the tree of good and evil, if you hang out with him he will deceive you*

*If you are deceived by Satan you will die that very day*

*One day equals one thousand years*

<sup>18</sup>*And the LORD God said, it is not good that the man should be alone; I will make him an help meet for him.*

*There is no woman of Adam's race in the garden (all are sixth day humankind)*

*Woman in Hebrew is ishah*

<sup>19</sup>*And out of the ground the LORD God formed every beast of the field, and every fowl of the air; and brought them unto Adam to see what he would call them: and whatsoever Adam called every living creature, that was the name thereof.*

*Adam the first eighth day man (he is Ruddy in complexion to show blood in the face)*

*Adam is the first eighth day white man*

### 1 Samuel 16:12

<sup>12</sup>*And he sent, and brought him in. Now he was **ruddy**, and withal of a beautiful countenance, and goodly to look to. And the LORD said, Arise, anoint him: for this is he.*

*From Adam to David the bloodline is pure (David is ruddy complected like Adam)*

<sup>20</sup>*And Adam gave names to all cattle, and to the fowl of the air, and to every beast of the field; but for Adam there was not found an help meet for him.*

*Out of all the women in the city of Balkh not one was found to be a mate for Adam*

*Their DNA did not match Adams DNA*

Sixth day Mankind was in the Garden before Adam, but there were no eighth day women for Adam. For a pure distinct bloodline which Christ would come through, Adam would need an eighth day help meet.

### Genesis 2:21-25

*21And the LORD God caused a deep sleep to fall upon Adam, and he slept: and he took one of his ribs, and closed up the flesh instead thereof;*

*22And the **rib**, which the LORD God had taken from man, made he a woman, and brought her unto the man.*

*Rib = curve (a woman's curve or DNA curve)*

*Adam and Eve share the same DNA (God took the DNA from Adam to form Eve)*

*Men and Women have the same amount of ribs*

*23And Adam said, This is now bone of my bones, and flesh of my flesh: she shall be called Woman, because she was taken out of Man.*

*24Therefore shall a man leave his father and his mother, and shall cleave unto his wife: and they shall be one flesh.*

*25And they were both naked, the man and his wife, and were not ashamed.*

*Christ, and the Israelites will come through the DNA of Adam and Eve*

*There are still people in the Amazon that walk around naked without shame*

### Genesis 3

*1Now the serpent was more subtil than any beast of the field which the LORD God had made. And he said unto the woman, Yea, hath God said, Ye shall not eat of every tree of the garden?*

*Serpent = Satan*

*Subtle = Cunning, Crafty, Prudent, clever, shrewd, liar, and poison*

*Eat = Do not have an engagement with the tree of good and evil*

*²And the woman said unto the serpent, We may eat of the fruit of the trees of the garden:*

> *WE may socialize, and do business, with the sixth day humankind*

*³But of the fruit of the **tree which is in the midst of the garden**, God hath said, Ye shall not eat of it, neither shall ye touch it, lest ye die.*

> *Tree in the Midst of the Garden = Satan*
>
> *Have no relations with Satan, he will deceive you*
>
> *Touch = to lie with (to have sexual intercourse)*
>
> *The blood of Christ is 100% eighth day man*

**Genesis 3:4-7**

*⁴And the serpent said unto the woman, Ye shall not surely die:*

> *Satan lied to Eve, she will die before the day has finished*

*2 Peter 3:8 (King James Version)*

*⁸But, beloved, be not ignorant of this one thing, that **one day is with the Lord as a thousand years**, and a thousand years as one day.*

Satan Knows one day with the Lord equals a thousand years. Adam and eve do not know this; they believe one day is a 24-hour period. Adam will live to be 930 years old, probably believing Satan was right. Satan lied to them knowing they would die before Gods first day.

*⁵For God doth know that in the day ye eat thereof, then your eyes shall be opened, and ye shall be as gods, knowing good and evil.*

Satan is telling the truth; Cain will set them up as gods during his rein in Mesopotamia. Cain will make gods out of Satan, Adam, Eve, Abel, and himself thousands of miles away from Adam and Eve. Adam and Eve never knew they had become gods to other people in a far-off land. In their own land, they will become Patriarchs of their people, not gods. Satan lied to them about not dying in one day, knowing they would believe him. He also told them the truth about becoming gods, knowing they would not believe. Now we know why Satan is the great deceiver.

*⁶And when the woman saw that the tree was **good for food**, and that it was **pleasant to the eyes**, and a tree to be desired to makeone wise, she took of the fruit thereof, and did eat, and gave also unto her husband with her; and he did eat.*

*Good for food = desirable*

*Pleasant to the eyes = A very well built handsome man (Satan)*

*To make one wise = Knowledgeable*

*Fruit thereof = Satan's seed (Fruit of my loins)*

*Eat = Partake*

*Eve had sex with Satan, she touched him, and Adam also believed Satan's lies (he ate)*

Satan wholly seduced Eve and she had sex with him. Adam went along with it, being deceived by Satan also. Satan planted his seed in her, so his offspring could also claim Eve as their mother, (the mother of all living). Satan did not have sex with Adam there was no reason to do so, however he did have sex with Eve.

Eve ate an apple that is what I was taught. The woman on the Wendy's commercial asked, "where's the beef", I want to know "where's the apple". Not one apple is mentioned! Adams seed will produce good fruit (offspring) and Satan's seed will produce evil fruit (offspring). The offspring of the two brothers are still living and doing business together today. Can you do better than Adam and Eve and resist the temptations of Satan? You can if you truly have the desire to learn the truth that is hidden from us.

### Jeremiah 24:2 (King James Version)

*²One basket had **very good figs**, even like the figs that are first ripe: and the other basket had **very naughty figs**, which could not be eaten, they were so bad.*

*Adams seed will produce very good figs, and Satan's seed will produce very naughty figs.*

## Matthew 7:15-20 (King James Version)

¹⁵*Beware of false prophets, which come to you in sheep's clothing, but inwardly they are ravening wolves.*

*False prophets = False teachers (Pray that God will give you Discernment)*

*The wolf in sheep's clothing will lead you to the butcher block*

¹⁶*Ye shall know them by their fruits. Do men gather grapes of thorns, or figs of thistles?*

*Fruits = their good works or their evil works*

¹⁷*Even so every good tree bringeth forth good fruit; but a corrupt tree bringeth forth evil fruit.*

¹⁸*A good tree cannot bring forth evil fruit, neither can a corrupt tree bring forth good fruit.*

¹⁹*Every tree that bringeth not forth good fruit is hewn down, and cast into the fire.*

⁷*And the eyes of them both were opened, and they knew that they were naked; and they sewed fig leaves together, and made themselves aprons.*

Adam and Eve both knew the sin they had committed with Satan, and their nakedness was exposed. They placed fig leaves over their private parts where they had sinned. It was a shameful day for the both of them, and they both allowed this Evil man that thinks he can be god to seduce them.

Why God would not want Adam and Eve to eat an apple, it tastes delicious. People will always follow man's traditions above God's word! Why? I do not understand. To cover up what really happened in the Garden of Eden, the priest replaced the sexual act with an apple. There was no apple!!!

## Genesis 3:8-13 (King James Version)

[8] *And they heard the voice of the LORD God walking in the garden in the cool of the day: and Adam and his wife hid themselves from the presence of the LORD God amongst the trees of the garden.*

*Their sin opened their eyes and they knew they were naked*

[9] *And the LORD God called unto Adam, and said unto him, Where art thou?*

[10] *And he said, I heard thy voice in the garden, and I was afraid, because I was naked; and I hid myself.*

*Naked as a jaybird and very embarrassed of their sin that exposed their nakedness.*

*They now know good from evil.*

[11] *And he said, Who told thee that thou wast naked? Hast thou eaten of the tree, whereof I commanded thee that thou shouldest not eat?*

*God gave them one law, do not have anything to do with Satan, they are no longer pure and innocent*

*Today we are very near Satan's hour, and this time billions of people will have spiritual sex with Satan, and when Christ comes to marry his bride, and they have already married Satan, the shame will be world wide, and the people will be begging to die. (the wrath of GOD)*

[12] *And the man said, The woman whom thou gavest to be with me, she gave me of the tree, and I did eat.*

[13] *And the LORD God said unto the woman, What is this that thou hast done? And the woman said, The serpent beguiled me, and I did eat.*

*Beguiled = Wholly Seduced (had sex)*

*She touched him, (had sex) with Satan and from his loins the fruit will be evil.*

*2 Corinthians 11:3 (King James Version)*

*³But I fear, lest by any means, as **serpent beguiled Eve** through his subtilty, so your minds should be corrupted from the simplicity that is in Christ.*

*The Serpent seduced her and planted his seed in her*

*Subtle = Cunning, Crafty, Prudent, clever, shrewd, liar, and poison*

The shrewdest liar God has ever created deceived Adam and Eve; they succumbed to his lies, and committed a terrible sin. What about you, can you overcome his lies? Like Adam and Eve, the majority of God's children will crawl in bed with Satan. Learn Gods truth, and overcome Satan's lies. Most people today are in bed with Satan, and they do not know it. Leave Satan's bed and follow the truth.

### Genesis 3:14-15

*¹⁴And the LORD God said unto the serpent, Because thou hast done this, thou art cursed above all cattle, and above every beast of the field; upon thy belly shalt thou go, and dust shalt thou eat all the days of thy life:*

*The serpent is Satan*

*He deceived Eve, seduced her, and had intercourse with her*

*¹⁵And I will put enmity between thee and the woman, and between thy seed and her seed; it shall bruise thy head, and thou shalt bruise his heel.*

*Enmity = Hatred*

*There will be hatred between Satan's seed and Adams seed (Cain and Abel).*

*Bruise thy head = Satan will die in the lake of fire*

*(Hit a serpent over the head and he dies)*

*Bruise his heel = Jesus Christ is nailed to the cross*

*Satan's offspring, (the Kenites,) delivered Christ up for Sacrifice*

Genesis 3:16-24

*<sup>16</sup>Unto the woman he said, I will greatly multiply thy sorrow and thy conception; in sorrow thou shalt bring forth children; and thy desire shall be to thy husband, and he shall rule over thee.*

*<sup>17</sup>And unto Adam he said, Because thou hast hearkened unto the voice of thy wife, and hast eaten of the tree, of which I commanded thee, saying, Thou shalt not eat of it: cursed is the ground for thy sake; in sorrow shalt thou eat of it all the days of thy life;*

*<sup>18</sup>Thorns also and thistles shall it bring forth to thee; and thou shalt eat the herb of the field;*

*Adam ate of the tree, he agreed with Satan, he did not touch Satan (have sex)*

*Thorns and thistles = the thorn tree (Bramble bush) = Satan*

*Throughout life, we will have to deal with thorns and thistles*

*The thorns and thistles are greater today than ever before*

*The offspring of Cain will never leave us alone*

*<sup>19</sup>In the sweat of thy face shalt thou eat bread, till thou return unto the ground; for out of it wast thou taken: for dust thou art, and unto dust shalt thou return.*

*<sup>20</sup>And Adam called his wife's name **Eve;** because she was the **mother of all living**.*

*How can Eve be the mother of all living?*

*Sixth day man has been on the earth for six thousand years before Eve*

*From Eve to Mary (mother of Jesus) the umbilical cord is not broken*

*Through Eve, Jesus was born and sacrificed on the cross, and if you believe upon him, you will inherit everlasting life*

*If you believe in Christ, you are of the living, so Eve is "the mother of all living"*

*All peoples of the earth can have everlasting life even the sons of Satan/Cain*

Two thirds of the people on earth today do not believe in Christ. They will be taught during the millennium, and at the end of the thousand years, they will have an opportunity to follow Christ or Satan. Satan today deceives many Christians, and they are unaware of it. Wake up before it is too late. Unfortunately, many Christian's will follow the lies of Satan/Anti-Christ at the end of the sixth day.

*[21]Unto Adam also and to his wife did the LORD God make coats of skins, and clothed them.*

*[22]And the LORD God said, Behold, the man is become as one of **us**, **to know good and evil**: and now, lest he put forth his hand, and take also of the **tree of life**, and **eat**, and **live for ever**:*

*Us = Christ and the angels*

*To know good and evil (no longer innocent)*

*Graft yourself into the Tree of life*

*Believe in Jesus the Christ and live forever*

*[23]Therefore the LORD God sent him forth from the garden of Eden, to till the ground from whence he was taken.*

*The world's first farmer*

Sixth day humankind at this time for the most part did not cultivate the land they were mostly hunter-gatherers. Adam and his offspring will change all this, for they will invent the plow, and use beast of burden to till the soil.

*[24]So he drove out the man; and he placed at the east of the garden of Eden Cherubims, and a flaming sword which turned every way, to keep the way of the tree of life.*

*Adam and Eve along with their two sons are cast out from Eden*

*Driven out of the Garden, traveling east towards the Pamir Mountains*

*The Cherubims will not allow Adam and Eve to re-enter the Garden*

*The flaming sword protecting the way of truth*

*Adam and Eve no longer allowed to fellowship with Christ*

*The tree of life = Jesus Christ*

*During the millennium (the seventh day), the people that will follow Satan, will not see Christ Jesus for one thousand years, the same sentence was given to Adam and Eve in the garden*

Adam and Eve were innocent until they had sinned, and at that very moment, they knew they were naked. God gave them one law, they broke it, and their shame was grievous.

## Genesis 4

*¹And Adam knew Eve his wife; and she conceived, and bare Cain, and said, I have gotten a man from the LORD.*

*Knew = to mate*

*Eve knew Satan, and then knew Adam*

*Cain was born, his father is Satan, his mother is Eve*

God chose Cain to be Satan's son, (he was Satan's number one man "in the world that was" Cain's offspring will be a thorn in our side and even greater in the end times. The seed of Cain is beating down the United States of America, and 99% of the people are unaware of it. Most people are so caught up in their everyday lives; they never search for understanding of Gods truth.

*²And **she again bare** his brother Abel. And Abel was a keeper of sheep, but Cain was a tiller of the ground*

*Again = Yaw-saf (Hebrew) = Continued*

*After Cain was born she continued and gave birth to Abel*

*She gave birth to two sons with two different fathers*

Eve knew Satan, and then knew Adam. Satan planted his seed, and then Adam planted his. Both seeds are in her womb at the same time, and she conceived and had twins. The first-born was Cain, the son of Satan, the one she knew first. Then she gave birth to Abel, the son of Adam, the one she knew second. After giving birth to Cain, she said I have gotten a man from the Lord; this is true, all that is born of woman are from the Lord. Did she know that Cain the first-born was the son of Satan, Probably not? All she knew at the time is that she had received a son from the Lord. Her second son was Abel; did she know he was Adams son? She probably thought they were both Adams sons. She is a proud Mother; she received two sons from the Lord. How can Eve give birth to twins, and each twin having a different father? It has happened in modern times a woman giving birth to twins having two different fathers.

Does God say anywhere in the bible about Cain being the son of Satan the devil. The bible speaks of the children of Cain in the old and New Testament. Read two of these verses below.

### 1 John 3:12 (King James Version)

[12]*Not as Cain, who was of that **wicked one**, and slew his brother. And wherefore slew he him? Because his own works were evil, and his brother's righteous.*

*Wicked one = Satan*

*Cain's works were evil*

*Like father like son*

### John 8:44 (King James Version)

[44]*Ye are of your father the devil, and the lusts of your father ye will do. **He was a murderer from the beginning**, and abode not in the truth, because there is no truth in him. When he speaketh a lie, he speaketh of his own: for he is a liar, and the father of it.*

Jesus is speaking to the Scribes and Pharisees, and along with the Sadducees, they will have Jesus Crucified. Not all Scribes, Pharisees, and Sadducees are of the seed line of Cain, a small percent of the true tribe of Judah and Levi are Priest during the time of Christ.

Ye are of the seed line of Cain (Scribes, Pharisees, and Sadducees) and Cain is the son of the devil Satan. Who was the first murderer mentioned in the Bible? It was Cain of course! Jesus is not talking to the Israelites here, but the sons and daughters of Cain. Cain's progeny/offspring worked their way into the priest line beginning at the time of Solomon's rule (as scribes). From Scribes to Priest the sons of Cain moved right on in. By the time a remnant of Israelites moved back to Israel from the captivity of Babylon and Persia, nearly all the Priest were Kenites.

### 1 Chronicles 2:54-55

*55 And the **families of the scribes** which dwelt at Jabez; the Tirathites, the Shimeathites, and Suchathites. **These are the Kenites** that came of Hemath, the father of the house of Rechab.*

*The Kenites are the sons of Cain*

*The Kenites carry the DNA of Satan and Eve*

*Hemath and Rechab are Kenites*

### Revelation 2:8-9

*8And unto the angel of the church in Smyrna write; These things saith the first and the last, which was dead, and is alive;*

*9I know thy works, and tribulation, and poverty, (but thou art rich) and I know the blasphemy of them which say they are Jews, and are not, but are the synagogue of Satan.*

*They are not of the tribe of Judah, They are the offspring of Cain*

*The Kenite priest deceives the real Jews living in Jerusalem*

*Most of the Sadducees and Pharisees are the sons of Cain*

*The sons of Cain will have Jesus crucified, and they will have Rome do the dirty work*

*The Kenites will never get their hands dirty; they will always put the blame on others*

*Even the sons of Cain will bow down before Jesus on his second coming*

*They claim to be of the tribe of Judah and Levi, but they are not*

*The sons of Cain deceived the real Jews of Judah, Levi, and
Benjamin in Jerusalem, and turned them against Jesus*

*The Kenites are like one rotten apple in a barrel, it only takes one to ruin the whole barrel*

*The Kenites are a small population in Jerusalem, however
they have total power over the Jews*

### Genesis 4:3-24 (King James Version)

*³And in process of time it came to pass, that Cain brought of the fruit of the
ground an offering unto the LORD.*

*⁴And Abel, he also brought of the firstlings of his flock and of the fat thereof. And
the LORD had respect unto Abel and to his offering:*

*⁵But unto Cain and to his offering he had not respect. And Cain was very wroth,
and his countenance fell.*

*Abel was a Sheppard of sheep, for his offering he gave the very best that he
had in his flock. Abel was proud of his gift to God. Cain was a farmer, his yield
was probably abundant, but his offering was not the best of his yield. God is
disappointed in his offering.*

*⁶And the LORD said unto Cain, Why art thou wroth? and why is thy countenance
fallen?*

*God placed Cain in the womb of Eve, and he knows very well how evil he is. He was
probably Satan's number one man in the first earth age. Cain knows he has disappointed
God and he is in trouble. Cain has no remembrance of who he was in the first earth age*

*⁷If thou doest well, shalt thou not be accepted? And if thou doest not well, sin
lieth at the door. And unto thee shall be his desire, and thou shalt rule over him.*

*Did Cain love God? No, he did not; he loved himself, and disobeyed God*

*⁸And Cain talked with Abel his brother: and it came to pass, when they were in the field, that Cain rose up against Abel his brother, and slew him.*

*The first murderer mentioned in the Bible*

*Cain was jealous of his brother*

*⁹And the LORD said unto Cain, Where is Abel thy brother? And he said, I know not: Am I my brother's keeper?*

*Cain shows no respect to God*

*¹⁰And he said, What hast thou done? The voice of thy brother's blood crieth unto me from the ground.*

*¹¹And now art thou cursed from the earth, which hath opened her mouth to receive thy brother's blood from thy hand;*

*¹²When thou tillest the ground, it shall not henceforth yield unto thee her strength; a fugitive and a vagabond shalt thou be in the earth.*

*The sons of Cain will wander from one nation to another,
never having a home of their own*

From this day to present, Cain's descendants will not make good farmers. In fact, his offspring will never be farmers, even until this day. Hard dirty work is not in their vocabulary. Cain's people will seek occupations that will yield money not vegetables. Cain's offspring will become rich through ill-gotten gain, not by sweat.

*¹³And Cain said unto the LORD, My punishment is greater than I can bear.*

*¹⁴Behold, thou hast driven me out this day from the face of the earth; and from thy face shall I be hid; and I shall be a fugitive and a vagabond in the earth; and it shall come to pass, that every one that findeth me shall slay me.*

*Fugitive = on the run*

*Vagabond = to wander*

*As merchants and moneychangers, they rip off the citizens,*
*and provoke the people to anger*

*¹⁵And the LORD said unto him, Therefore whosoever slayeth Cain, vengeance shall be taken on him sevenfold. And the LORD set a mark upon Cain, lest any finding him should kill him.*

*His mark is his evil work toward humankind*

The mark of Cain was very distinguished in the beginning, but has worn smooth over a long period of time. Today Israelites and the sons of Cain live and work together, and even marry each other not knowing who they are. If a son or daughter of Cain believes in Christ, they will no longer be a child of Satan, but grafted in the tree of life. The Kenites (sons of Cain) have tried to keep their genealogy pure, but many Kenites have taken wives of other nations. Remember the Kenites are a race of their own, running back to Cain through the male line. No matter what wives they take the kenite line is pure on the male side.

*¹⁶And Cain went out from the presence of the LORD, and dwelt in the land of Nod, on the east of Eden.*

*Nod = wandering, fugitive, vagabond, and the land of nomads.*

*Mongolia is called the land of Nomads.*

*Cain is in a state of nod, a state of wondering.*

*Cain will travel from kingdom to kingdom, deceiving every*
*nation and race of people on the face of the earth.*

*His influence will be great around the world*

## Cain's Genealogy

*¹⁷And Cain knew his wife; and she conceived, and bare **Enoch**: and he builded a city, and called the name of the city, after the name of his son, Enoch.*

*This Enoch is not the Enoch of Adam*

*God wants us to be on our toes, some of the names are the same as Adams genealogy,*

*Cain wants you to believe he is of the genealogy of Adam, and he is not.*

*¹⁸And unto Enoch was born Irad: and Irad begat Mehujael: and Mehujael begat* **Methusael**: *and Methusael begat* **Lamech**.

*This Methusael is not the Methuselah of Adam*

*This Lemech is not the father of Noah*

*¹⁹And Lamech took unto him two wives: the name of the one was Adah, and the name of the other Zillah.*

*²⁰And Adah bare Jabal: he was the father of such as dwell in tents, and of such as have cattle.*

*Jabals occupation was husbandry, the domestication of animals.*

*Notice he is not a farmer.*

*Cain's people dwelled in tents, which means they were vagabonds.*

*²¹And his brother's name was Jubal: he was the father of all such as handle the harp and organ.*

*I believe Cain invented the musical instruments, and Jubal was a musician*

*²²And Zillah, she also bare Tubalcain, an instructer of every artificer in brass and iron: and the sister of Tubalcain was Naamah.*

*Sons of Cain = Kenite=Smith*

*Tubalcain is a smith*

*Tubalcain was a teacher of blacksmithing*

*Sons of Cain will become jewelers of precious stones and metals*

*Sons of Cain will become master stonemasons, passed down by Cain*

*²³And Lamech said unto his wives, Adah and Zillah, Hear my voice; ye wives of Lamech, hearken unto my speech: for I have slain a man to my wounding, and a young man to my hurt.*

*[24]If Cain shall be avenged sevenfold, truly Lamech seventy and sevenfold.*

*Lamech takes after his great grandfather Cain*
*The sons of Cain will kill the prophets of God, and Jesus Christ*

### Genesis 4:25-26

*[25]And Adam knew his wife again; and she bare a son, and called his name **Seth**: For God, said she, hath appointed me **another seed instead of Abel**, whom Cain slew.*

*Seth Adams second son (His first son Abel has no genealogy)*

*Another son to replace Abel, (Cain is not his brother, and Eve now knows this)*

*Through Seth will come Noah, Abraham, Isaac, Jacob, Judah, David, and Jesus*

*[26]And to Seth, to him also there was born a son; and he called his name Enos: then began men to call upon the name of the LORD*

According to Jewish Commentators, Enos showed great disrespect to God, by calling idols and stars "their gods." Enos is a frail sickly man yet he deceives his brothers and sisters with evil lies that will destroy the eighth day Adamic race, except for Noah's family. Enoch will prophesy against this evil, but the people will not listen to truth, people just have a tendency to follow evil. I am sorry to say it is going to happen again, Pastor Arnold Murray who I believe was Enoch, taught the truth on television, but most people chose not to hear the truth. The elect did and still listens to his son Denise, and they are ready to take on the anti-Christ/Satan.

### Matthew 24:37

But as the days of **Noah** were, so shall also the coming of the Son of man be.

### Hebrews 11:5

By faith **Enoch** was translated that he should not see death; and was not found, because God had translated him: for before his translation he had this testimony, that he pleased God.

# Chapter 6

## Cain's wonderings and evil works

God banished Adam and Eve out of the Garden of Eden, and they set out traveling east through rugged mountainous terrain, at very high altitudes. Their trip begins on the Balkh River, and runs into the Pison River, now called the Amu Darya River. They continue east up the River to the Pison/Amu Darya head, where the Vakhsh and Gihon/Panj Rivers connect. They travel east through the corridor of the Pamir and Hindu Kush mountains, a very beautiful view. Two Rivers come together at the Gihon head, the (Euphrates/Pamir River, and the Hiddekel/Wakhan River.)

Adam and Eve have a choice to make, the Euphrates, or the Hiddekel Rivers, and either one will get them to their destination. They may have sojourned here for a while, before choosing which River they would choose to follow. Cain will later name the two Rivers in Mesopotamia the Euphrates and Hiddekel/Tigris Rivers, after the two Rivers from which he played in as a young boy. They probably took the easiest route following the Wakhan Corridor to Lake Chakmaktin, traveling through the high Pamirs, and following the Kashgar River to the Tarim River head. The Euphrates riverhead ends at Lake Zorkul, which is a very beautiful lake, it is possible they may have taken this route, but no road exists for travel. Both lakes are over 13,000' in elevation, not an easy trip either way.

Adam and Eve with their two sons and belongings are on a 1200-mile trip through the rugged mountains of the Pamirs. Their destination is the Tarim basin in China. The passage through the high Pamirs has been in use for thousands of years before them. This route will later be called the ancient silk route, and mostly used by the Pamiri people, and tourist of today. Even today, this is a very difficult road to travel.

They must travel over the Kyzylart pass, which is 14,042 ft. above sea level. It was not easy back then, and it is not easy today. From here they will travel east down the Kashgar River. Two great rivers, the Kashgar and the Yarkand Rivers will come together, and form the Tarim River. Adam and Eve will homestead at the Tarim head, and the two boys' will grow up there. The land here is fertile, perfect for raising livestock and farming.

The Tarim River is the longest River in China, and no longer makes it to Lop Nor where it once ended. The great River no longer has a large flow of water due to pumping water for irrigation and drought. The Tarim River is home to the large and ancient Euphrates Poplar trees, and more will be said about these awesome trees, during the time of Noah.

Cain and Abel grew up on the Tarim River head, where Cain became a farmer, and Abel raised sheep. Adam was a very tall man at 8' tall, and his son Abel was 8' tall or near that. Eve would have been around 7'6" tall, a very tall woman compared to the sixth day man that averaged 5'6" tall. Cain, the son of (Satan and Eve) was 16' tall. I will explain later why he is so much taller. Adam was created around 4004 BC, and Eve soon after. My estimate of Adam's age is 110 years old, when Eve gave birth to Cain and Abel. How did I come up with that date?

The Mayan long count calendar began in 3114 BC. I believe this date was the date of Cain's death. By Jewish traditions, Cain is said to have lived to be 730 years old, add 730 years to 3114BC, and we get 3844 BC. This does not work, Seth was born in 3874BC, and this would make Seth older than Abel. No date is mentioned in Genesis of Cain and Abel's birth, so I am going to guess Cain and Abel were 20 years old When Cain slew his brother. This will make Cain and Abel born in 3894BC, and Cain died on 3114BC, making him 780 years old. The reason I believe Cain died on this date, is that the Mayan people were the offspring of Cain, and I will explain this later.

As we know Cain killed Abel, and God exiled Cain to a place called Nod, which means the land of Nomads. Mongolia and China is where Cain will rule over the

Mongolian race for about 70 years in the yellow River region. The yellow River is named after him, because of his yellow beard, and hair.

Most of the information about Cain comes from Mrs. Sidney Bristowe's book called (Sargon the Magnificent.) This book is necessary to read if you desire to learn more about Cain. This is one of my favorite books, and she was a very smart Lady. I learned a lot from this book, and I thank her for this unbelievable information.

Cain traveled east along the Tarim River, and then northeast into the Yellow River region, "the cradle of Chinese civilization." Cain will take a wife of the Mongolian race, and a new race will be known as the (Kenites) written in the bible. Cain will not stay in the land of Nod long, for Satan will lead him into Mesopotamia in 3800 BC.

Strong's concordance: 7014 Qayin (Kay-Yin) Kajin the first child (Cain) an oriental tribe from the East. Kenite = Sons of Cain, an Asian people from Mongolia/China.

The people in the land of Nomads are hunter-gatherers, not farmers, and Cain will teach them to farm and domesticate animals. Cain is a fugitive and his children will inherit the mark of Cain. They will wander from one Nation to another without having a land to call their own. The Kenites having the mark of Cain, is banished or killed everywhere they travel. The mark is set on Cain and his offspring, and all nations of the earth will seek to kill the sons of Cain, but they will survive and continue to deceive the children of God.

Cain has a great influence on the Mongolian race, and later will have a great influence on the Adamic race, and the twelve tribes of Israel. Cain will influence all races, tribes, and nations during and after his death.

Cain's special color is yellow, because of his yellow hair and beard. Even in ancient Greece, they called the color yellow, "Cain's yellow". The rulers of China were called the "rulers of the yellow people." The tiles of the Imperial temples and palaces are yellow, because yellow is the royal color. Their main River is called the yellow River named after Cain. The yellow River region is called "the cradle of Chinese civilization." I always wondered why the Chinese are called the yellow people. They are not yellow in skin color; they are called the yellow people because of Cain, who taught them many things to improve their lively hood.

Cain is the first giant on the earth, and he is smarter than anyone on earth except for Adam. His father is Satan who knows the plan of God and will guide Cain throughout his life. Cain has white skin like Adam and Eve, and has yellow hair and a beard, which the Mongolians are not used to seeing. Mongolians have black hair, and they usually do not grow beards. Cain will teach the Mongolians many things during his short stay in the yellow River area.

Cain is in a state of wondering; he leaves the Tarim River region, and travels into present day China. He taught the Mongolian people in this land, of his Father the Dragon, "the old serpent the devil." He calls the people of the land of Nod, the children of Bel. Bel is the Dragon, and the Dragon is Satan. Cain's desire is to change all of God's children, and make them the children of Bel.

The influence of Cain is still in China today and the hills that nearly encircle Peking are still called the protecting Dragon. The Chinese have a Dragon festival ever year on the fifth day of the fifth month not knowing that the Dragon represents Satan the Devil. Cain taught the people agriculture, and he is known as the Devine Agriculturist. Remember Cain was a farmer taught by Adam.

Shakespeare wrote, "A little beard, a Cain colored beard"

Cain the first Emperor of the region we call China

Cain was the first Yellow Emperor, and when he came into the land of the yellow River, he taught the people many things that would improve their lives. Little did they know, Cain with the yellow hair and beard, was the son of Bel the old dragon, (Satan the devil.) He taught the people farming, husbandry (breeding of livestock), weaving, writing, music, astrology. He taught them how to farm for a more sustainable life style. He taught them how to read the stars, so they would know the seasons, giving them important knowledge on when to plant and when to harvest. Cain has taught the people of the yellow River many things that will improve their way of life, they will become a great nation, and the country today is China.

The sixth day races are taught a new way of living not known to them for six thousand years or more. The six-day man have learned or invented very little since God put them on the earth. Now we have two new races of people, the Adamic people, and the Kenite people (sons of Cain). The quality of life will be greatly improved by both races. In the early 1900s, we put on film, people living in the Amazon River areas that have not progressed for twelve thousand years. Why have they not progressed?

The reason is, neither the Adamic, or Kenite races have ever reached them. They live in remote areas where the great sea king Cain or the sons of Adam had not discovered them. If it were not for Adam and Cain, we would still be living like the Amazon tribes, and other remote peoples around the world. Now we know why these people walk around naked like Adam and Eve did in the beginning. They have not received laws, they do not know good from evil. Without law's, they have no sin, so they remain naked like Adam and Eve before they sinned.

God created mankind on the sixth day, and for six thousand years they learned nearly nothing, on the seventh day God rested, and on the eighth day God created a man to till the ground. If God had not created Adam, humankind would not have progressed any further. Humankind cannot progress on their own; God has given us direction through Adam on how to live a better life. In addition, remember Adam taught Cain, who was formed and molded by God. Cain flees to the land of Nod, and is now under the direction and guidance of Satan.

In the first earth age before you were born in flesh, all people were male; there was no need of a female at that time. We did not live in flesh like the animals that needed two sexes to procreate. Once God placed us in flesh bodies, half of the people would be female. All angels in the Bible are male. Does this mean when we go back to heaven we will all be male once again? I do not know, and we will have to wait and see. Read Matthew 22:29-30 Below.

### *Matthew 22:29-30*

*[29]Jesus answered and said unto them, Ye do err, not knowing the scriptures, nor the power of God.*

*[30]For in the resurrection they neither marry, nor are given in marriage, but are as the angels of God in heaven.*

When Cain moved into the yellow River region, the people were nomadic, and hunter gathers like all the people of the world at that time. In the land of Nod, Cain will take a wife, and will have many sons and daughters. Genghis Khan or "Khagan of the Mongol empire" was a direct descendant of Cain. Khan and Khagan both are names meaning King Cain. King Cain or Koenig means King Cain (the great Khan,) (the first yellow Emperor.)

King Cain in what we call China today did not stay there long, however, his seed line possibly from other wives continued to invent, and to improve the lifestyle of the Mongolian race. Many inventions came from Cain and his offspring, the making of clothing, silk, homes, farming, husbandry, dyes for clothing, building carts with wheels, and all the things the Adamic race was doing at the same time. The world changed very quickly after Adam and Cain entered the flesh world.

*There is a big difference between Adams race and Cain's Race. Adam taught his children morals and to love only God. Cain taught the opposite, he hated God; he invented thousands of creatures that were not natural, men with bodies of animals, and lions with wings, creatures that God had not created. He taught men to sacrifice men, women, and children, and the eating of human flesh. He taught cannibalism first to the Mongolians, and then the black and white races. Cain was the first to take men for bedmates in the yellow river region. Cain is the evilest flesh man to live on the earth, he despised God, and his evil influence has remained and increased today.*

*Cain taught unnatural behavior contrary to God*

*Cain taught human sacrifice*

*The ancient Chinese practiced cannibalism according to old historians*

*The Incas, Mayan, and Aztec people sacrificed their people over agriculture (sons of Cain)*

*Abel was the first to be sacrificed related to agriculture*

*Cain continued his Sacrifice and eating of human flesh*

*In the land of Canaan people sacrificed their children to Baal worship*

*The Dragon was the serpent in the Garden; he had many names,
Lucifer, Satan, Bel, and the Devil. These are just a few of them.*

Still wandering in a state of nod, Cain is moving on. Cain travels into Tibet, then into India. From India, he will travel through Pakistan, and then into Iran. From Iran, he will travel west into Mesopotamia, along with many people from the land of Nod, which is Mongolia and China. Two new races (the Kenite and Mongolian races) will enter into Mesopotamia, and will be known as the Sumerians. The peculiar race with oblique eyes, known as the black heads, are the Mongolian race that came from the yellow river region and Tibet. The Akkadians were the sixth day black and white races that were the indigenous people already there in Mesopotamia, modern day Iraq.

Cain has reached Babylon in 3800BC, 1400 years before the grandsons of Noah will enter into this land. In Mesopotamia Cain will set up a kingdom more advanced than the Greek and Roman era. However, evil will not stand, and the empire will fall.

Satan knows God's plan, he leads Cain to Babylon before the Adamic race will arrive there. He plants his lies before his own children so they will deceive the children of Noah when they arrive in Babylon. He does a good job; from the offspring of Abraham to the time of Christ, the people will be deceived by the great lies of Cain with the help of Satan. Today humankind is still influenced by Cain's lies, and Satan's evil demon spirits.

Cain with his family, and the Mongolia people who followed him to this land, will make a permanent homestead. Four different races of people are now living together in Mesopotamia soon to be named Babylon. Cain will encourage the races to mix with exception to his race; he will try to keep his offspring pure. Cain's offspring will have Jesus crucified on the cross. Today Cain's offspring is trying to overthrow the world, with "the new world order," or "the one world system." The sons of Cain use money to take power, to control the US, and European States. They will fail, but Satan will not.

<u>Strong's Concordance:</u>

Babel or Babylon = "confusion (by mixing)"

The Assyriologists today are very confused with the Babylonian writings, by the Priest and Scribes; they mixed the languages and created babble to deceive Gods children. Notice Babylon is situated on the Euphrates River where Cain named the River where he once grew up on, at Lake Zorkul, or Lake Chakmakin in the Pamir plateau.

The first thing Cain did was to name the Rivers. The east River he named the Hiddekel, which is known as the Tigris River today. The Jews and ancient Hebrews have always called the Tigris River the Hiddekel. The west river he named the Euphrates, and it is still called that today. Two Great Rivers in the Pamirs that he knew well, he renamed in Mesopotamia. One other River he grew up with as a young child was the Balkh River in the Garden of Eden. The Balkh River was a tributary to the Pison River, the first River mentioned in Genesis. Once Cain surveyed the land, he named the largest tributary River flowing into the Euphrates the Balikh River. The Balkh River of Bactria Afghanistan became the Balikh River in Mesopotamia/Babylon. He also probably named other tributaries flowing into the Tigris and Euphrates Rivers.

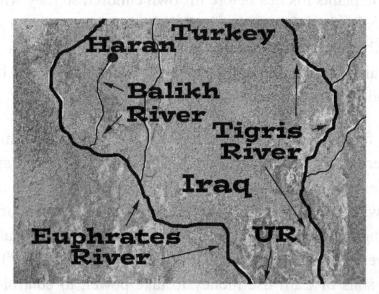

Cain is around 94 years old when he arrives into the land of Mesopotamia. I do not believe he conquered this land; he just walked in with his people and made himself at home. He immediately became King over all the people in this fertile land. His stature at 16 feet, along with his physical strength, superior intelligence, and with a large group of Mongolians, had very little or no resistance from the indigenous people of this fertile region. Cain has the spirit of Satan in him, and his goal is to destroy the bloodline of the Adamic race, so Jesus cannot be born of woman. Cain, the king of the Mongolian race, now makes himself king over the black and white race, and appoints himself as high priest.

## Cain's evil works in Babylon

Cain and his sons and their sons will build cities in Babylon, ruling over the Black Heads/Mongolians, the Africans, and the sixth day Whites. Cain will live 684 more years as king living as a god in Babylon. Babylon will be his home base; from here, he will travel throughout the world planting seeds of deceit into the minds of Gods innocent children. The Mongolians, the Blacks, the whites, and the eighth day man will receive his lies, and all of humanity will be deceived, as Satan deceived Adam and Eve.

During the time of Sargon the Magnificent (who is Cain), the people lived at a higher level. Their culture and order were more advanced, than the Greeks, Romans, and the Egyptians at the peak of their time. The art in Babylon has never been equaled since the time of Cain, and after his death. Degradation began under Cain, and most of the high living standards was lost. Cain's intelligence and tall stature makes him look supernatural, and there is no human on the face of the Earth like him. However, he is flesh and not supernatural.

Some Scholars Believe black heads were African, and others believed they were a peculiar white race. I believe they were the Mongolian race of people probably from the Yellow River region, and Tibet in present day China. He called them "the children of bel," which means the children of the devil. He also called them the "children of the sun", which Cain was and is worshipped as the great sun god. Chinese still today call themselves "the children of the dragon."

Cain of Akkad is said to have ruled over the blackheads, and in Chinese tradition, the first ruler (Cain) changed the black-haired people from hunter-gatherers to farmers, and a pastoral people. Their Culture and standard of living greatly improved and transformed the people into a higher standard of living. Cain founded the Chinese empire, giving them a better and more productive lifestyle. Cain introduced the Chinese to Art, architecture, science, and philosophy. Cain gave them the twelve constellations, and Enoch from Adam gave the Adamites their twelve constellations.

Unfortunately, Cain introduced to them very negative beliefs that totally went against God. Human sacrifice, Cannibalism, belief in many gods, and many other sins were taught to the Chinese.

A Sumerian on left with three Semites
Semites are sons of Shem

Sumerian with oblique eyes
Sumerians are Mongolians

http://www.v-stetsyuk.
name/en/China.html

As you can see, the Sumerian does not look like the white or black race. In addition, the Sumerian is much shorter than the three Caucasian men are, just as they are today. I am aware that the Chinese are getting taller today.

Pray for the Chinese Christians, they are being persecuted, and their churches are being destroyed. They have been forced to go underground for their belief, and why does the communist government see them as a threat. Christians do not blow up people, and they do not overthrow governments. Communism has always been anti-Christian, why; it was founded by the Kenites.

Cain was a very busy man, he had a very big job to fulfill, and that is to deceive all of God's children equally. I believe Cain ruled over the entire world, all nations, and all races. Except for the eighth day man at present and future, they will endure greater sin through Satan's fallen angels. Have you ever wondered why all nations around the world believe in dragons? Even the north and South American Indians believe in dragons. The dragon represents the devil, and Cain introduced it to the world.

You are probably wondering how Cain could have traveled such long distances. First, he had 760 years to do it in, second, he had no enemies, he could travel freely, not like Alexander, who had to fight and shed blood everywhere he traveled. Cain was called the Sea King; he traveled by boat, and by land. He traveled through Europe, Africa, Asia, and maybe the Americas. Remember Satan guides Cain, he learns to build boats that are capable of crossing the oceans. The weather during this time was stable, and ocean voyages were much easier. Therefore I believe the Polynesians were able to travel from Asia to the Americas.

The three races, Mongolian, Black, and white have been living in the Americas 6000 years or more before Cain's children of the sun migrated into Mexico and South America. With them, they bring the evil ways of Cain, the sacrifice of humans, and eating of human flesh.

The Hawaiians and Tahitians worshipped the god of Kane/Cain not knowing Cain was the son of Satan. The Iku-pau claim to be direct descendants of Kane. They were "the children of the sun" and they worshipped the sun god (Cain.) The worship of Cain was common throughout Polynesia, and the Iku-Pau people taught them this belief. The Iku-Pau are the sons of Cain, they will migrate to South America. To learn more read the book by W.J. Perry (The children of the sun) also look up Iku-Pau people on-line or (The Kane worship.)

Cain claimed to be the creator of heaven, the earth, the animals and humankind; he was (the great sun god, and the great sea god.) He spread this belief around the world. In Polynesian belief, he had two other gods that assisted him, and their names were Ku and Lono. These two gods may have represented Adam and eve.

*The children of the sun are descendants of Cain, and they rule over the Polynesians*

*Iku-Pau = Descendants of Cain (Kenites)*

*Kumuhenua = Cain*

*Kane or Cain is the sun god that rules over the children of the sun*

From Babylon to China, then down to Australia, and out to Polynesia, "the children of the sun," worshipped Cain. His kingdom does not stop here the Americas are next. The Polynesians today are not the descendants of Cain they are a good people, remember the kenites are always a small population, wherever they go they take control.

The Iku-Pau were direct descendants of Cain, from a Mongolian wife. Some of these people may have traveled farther east and landed in the Americas later after the rule of Cain. I believe these people were the Olmec people who settled in south central Mexico. The Olmec culture began around 1600 BC, and ended around 300 to 400 BC. Cain was no longer around but he gave them something no other culture had, and that is the long count Calendar. Cain revealed his secretes to the Iku-Pau people and they migrated to the Americas.

## How could anyone know about the 26,000-year cycle?

There is only one man that could possibly know of this cycle and it is Cain. How did Cain know this? He was taught by his "all father" Satan the devil. For man to know this at that time they would have had to kept records for 26,000 years, something I do not believe possible. Before Cain, people were hunter- gatherers, and they had no written language.

The Mayan People are the same people, "the offspring of Cain", but a more advanced people. I believe the Olmec people relocated, and became more advanced, and are now the Mayan people. I would like to mention one thing; I do not believe the people today who claim to be Mayans are of the seed line of Cain, I believe they died out many years ago. The good people of the Mayan's today are not of Cain.

During the time of Cain, the temperatures were mild, the days were not hot, and the nights not cold. There was no jet stream to cause great storms, and it did not rain. You could look at the Sun during anytime of the day. The ozone was thicker, which allowed less radiation to enter the earth. The oxygen was twice what it is today. Men lived to be 900 years old, but after the flood, the radiation increased, and the oxygen percentage decreased. The generation decreased down to 120 years, and then to a 70 years generation.

The sons of Cain, left the Yellow River region/China, traveled to Hawaii, and other Polynesian Islands. One group traveled to Mexico, and the Yucatan Peninsula, now known as the Olmec people. They landed in Mexico 253 years before Noah's flood, and 514 years after Cain's death. The Olmec's became the Mayans, and they built large pyramid structures to sacrifice people for agriculture, as Cain did to Abel. Many years later, it was getting hot in the Yucatan Peninsula, and so the Mayans moved north to the high mountains of Mexico. The Mayan's become the Aztec people, and founded an Aztec state on Lake Texcoco in the 1300s, and was destroyed by Cortez in 1521. The Aztec people continued human sacrifice, and eating of flesh, which Cain had taught them. Cortez was disgusted with what he had witnessed, and "the sons of Cain" were wiped out.

The Sumerians, Egyptians, Tibetans, Mayans, and Hopi, all believed in the 26,000-year cycle, and they based their calendars on this great cycle. Cain's influence was worldwide.

Some of you may not know of, or understand the 26,000-year cycle called the great cycle. The Earth has a slight wobble like a spinning top we played with as children. The top has a very fast wobble, but our earth has a very slow wobble. The earth completes one wobble cycle every 25,625 years, just short of 26,000 years, but we like to round off, it is easier to remember. This is why we do not always have the same North Star; in fact, we are losing Polaris as our north star at this very moment.

The Mayas divided the great circle of 25,625 years into five periods equaling 5125 years per lesser cycle. Their year begins August 11, 3114 BC the day Cain died. I do not believe this is a stretch, I believe the Mayan calendar is based on Cain's death. The Mayan calendar ends on December 21, 2012 the winter solstice.

If we use the astronomical calendar, which is 3113, and subtract 5125 years, we have the year of 2012.

Since the beginning, there have been six Aquarius cycles with both the smaller and larger wheels of the calendar. The seventh is said to be on December 21, 2012 and the Higgs boson was discovered that year. The Higgs Boson is called the "god particle," it is said to give mass to matter. The seventh Aquarius, and seventh day, are coming very soon. Satan's hour will happen at the end of the sixth day. Christ Jesus will come down from heaven to start the seventh day, the millennium.

### Matthew 24:20

*20But pray ye that your flight be not in the winter, neither on the sabbath day:*

> *The end of the sixth Aquarius cycle is when Satan will come down,*
> *he will gather his Kenites, and they will deceive the world.*

> *Satan's flight will be out of season, don't get on that flight*

The Mayan calendar says nothing about the world coming to an end, but it will be a time of change, and he will certainly change our times. The calendar will mark Satan's end, and Christ second coming, and the Millennium will begin.

Did Cain create a calendar that predicts Satan's reign on this Earth? It is a possibility!

The raiser of taxes written in Daniel 11:20 will precede or usher in Satan. Can it be President Obama; well yes, it is possible because the Supreme Court declared Obama Care as a tax. However, that is speculation; it could be someone unknown in the near future. Then Satan will soon arrive in Jerusalem standing on mount Zion claiming to be God. He will kill the two witnesses, and they will rise in three days. Christ will come down from heaven, and the seventh day will begin. All we can do is sit back and watch, whatever happens remember it is God's plan.

### Mark 13:14

*14But when ye shall see the **abomination of desolation**, spoken of by Daniel the prophet, standing where **it** ought not, (let him that readeth understand,) then let them that be in Judaea flee to the mountains:*

*Abomination of desolation= desolator = Satan*

*It = He*

*Satan will stand on mount Zion proclaiming to be god*

Cain not only traveled to Asia he also traveled the Mediterranean into Europe and Africa, and possibly the Americas. Crete was an ancient colony of Babylon ruled by King Minos. Sir Arthur Evans wrote, "That there once lived in Crete a priest king of gigantic size who is suspected of sacrificing human beings, and perhaps, of cannibalism". King Minos was King Cain, the first giant and first priest to rule on the earth. Many priests, scribes, and many rulers came from his loins.

The French uncovered many interesting discoveries on Crete. The women's attire was like the Victorian era, and the water and sewer system was thousands of years ahead of their time. In fact, it took over 3000 years before the Romans would accomplish this sanitary system. The French found a bronze sword in-laid with gold, crystal, and amethystine, and the sword was longer than any ever seen in Europe. Why was it so long? It was made for a giant, and the giant was Cain.

King Cain also ruled over Egypt, and set up a priest to rule over the people and to influence the Pharaohs. Many of the priests that ruled over Egypt were the sons of Cain. Cain established a priest line that ruled over many nations, and are still to this day. Ramses II was of the offspring of Cain, and some scholars say ruled during the time of Moses. Ramses II did not rule during the time of Moses, he ruled during a later period.

The 19th dynasty, which includes Ramesses I-II and Seti I ruled after the exodus of Moses. The Exodus was around 1491BC, and Ramesses ruled around 1280 BC to 1212 BC, if these dates are accurate. The 18th dynasty probably ruled during the time of Moses, during Thutmose I in 1493 BC to 1479 BC. Thutmose is pronounced Thut-mosa, or Thutmoses, and Moses bears the name, from whom he was adopted by king Ahmose I sister.

I have read many books on the Pharaohs of Egypt and the dates do vary. The three pharaohs Seti I, Rameses I, and Ramses II were of the priest line of Egypt. Rameses, I was not of the royal lineage, he was a son of the troop commander named Seti. Rameses was a priest of the Amun, his family had high status and somehow, he became Pharaoh of Egypt. The high priests were always trying to take power from the Pharaohs. In this case they did! The Rameses families were Priests of the "children of the sun", Cain's offspring.

Cain's offspring were called the "children of the sun" (the children of Ra), and the Amun were priests that worshipped Amun-Ra. In other words, they worshipped (Cain the sun god.) The sons of Cain have ruled over the Egyptians, Babylonians, the Jews, the Israelites, the Persians, the Greeks, the Romans, and many other kingdoms, states, and nations.

The same priests took over as high priests in the land of Judah. They became the Pharisees, Sadducees, lawyers, moneychangers, and scribes. During the time of Jesus, they had full religious control over those living in Judea including the Jews and Israelites. Unbelievably the Scribes of Judea have copied down the word of God from the time of Solomon, to Christ, and to present, and most of the scribes are the sons of Cain. They deceived the people of the tribe of Judah, and Israel. Many of the tribe of Judah and Israel are still deceived today by the sons of Cain. The sons of Cain were few in the days of Jesus and few today, yet they have deceived many people by playing the role of Levite priests. Cain knows the best way to control people is through religion, education, money, and government and the sons of Cain are masters of all four.

Satan is coming soon; he will stand on mount Zion in Jerusalem "where he ought not," and claiming to be God. King Cain was the king of the world during his time, and Satan will make himself god of the world in the very near future. He will deceive a high percentage of the people on this earth today. Adam and Eve did not have a chance against Satan in the Garden of Eden, and it is no different today.

## Bible verses of Cain's offspring the Kenites

### 1 Chronicles 2:55

*55And the families of the scribes which dwelt at Jabez; the Tirathites, the Shimeathites, and Suchathites. These are the Kenites that came of Hemath, the father of the house of Rechab.*

*The children of Cain are very smart; they are the scribes, (the bookmakers)*

*Jabez = Sorrow (near Bethlehem) 990BC to 500BC*

*Kenites = Sons of Cain*

*Hemath and Rechab are the sons of Cain*

### Jeremiah 35:6-19

*⁶But they said, We will drink no wine: for Jonadab the son of Rechab our father commanded us, saying, Ye shall drink no wine, neither ye, nor your sons for ever:*

*Wine represents the blood of Christ (His sacrifice)*

*The sons of Cain will not believe in the Sacrifice of God's Son (Christ our savior)*

*⁷Neither shall ye build house, nor sow seed, nor plant vineyard, nor have any: but all your days ye shall dwell in tents; that ye may live many days in the land where ye be strangers.*

*Remember what God said to Cain in Genesis 4:12*

*When you till the ground, it will not produce.*

*You will be vagabonds on the earth*

*Wanderers going from one place to another not having a permanent home*

*Cain's children will have no country to call their own*

*⁸Thus have we obeyed the voice of Jonadab the son of Rechab our father in all that he hath charged us, to drink no wine all our days, we, our wives, our sons, nor our daughters;*

*⁹Nor to build houses for us to dwell in: neither have we vineyard, nor field, nor seed:*

*¹⁰But we have dwelt in tents, and have obeyed, and done according to all that Jonadab our father commanded us.*

*[11]But it came to pass, when Nebuchadrezzar king of Babylon came up into the land, that we said, Come, and let us go to Jerusalem for fear of the army of the Chaldeans, and for fear of the army of the Syrians: so we dwell at Jerusalem.*

**The sons of Cain moved in Jerusalem, and became scribes,
priests, lawyers, merchants, and moneychangers.**

**You will not see farmer listed as an occupation on their resume**

**They moved back into Jerusalem around 496BC, nearly 500 years before Jesus was born**

**They will have 500 years to take over as high priest, most of this will happen in Babylon**

**They will begin as scribes "the smart ones"**

*[12]Then came the word of the LORD unto Jeremiah, saying,*

*[13]Thus saith the LORD of hosts, the God of Israel; Go and tell the men of Judah and the inhabitants of Jerusalem, Will ye not receive instruction to hearken to my words? saith the LORD.*

**The Israelites do not listen to their Father the God of Abraham**

**They do not listen to the true prophets of God**

*[14]The words of Jonadab the son of Rechab, that he commanded his sons not to drink wine, are performed; for unto this day they drink none, but obey their father's commandment: notwithstanding I have spoken unto you, rising early and speaking; but ye hearkened not unto me.*

**The Kenites listen to their Father the devil, and they obey
Nevertheless, they do not obey the God of Abraham**

*[15]I have sent also unto you all my servants the prophets, rising up early and sending them, saying, Return ye now every man from his evil way, and amend your doings, and go not after other gods to serve them, and ye shall dwell in the land which I have given to you and to your fathers: but ye have not inclined your ear, nor hearkened unto me.*

**Kenites will not listen to the true prophets of God**

¹⁶*Because the sons of Jonadab the son of Rechab have performed the commandment of their father, which he commanded them; but this people hath not hearkened unto me:*

¹⁷*Therefore thus saith the LORD God of hosts, the God of Israel; Behold, I will bring upon Judah and upon all the inhabitants of Jerusalem all the evil that I have pronounced against them: because I have spoken unto them, but they have not heard; and I have called unto them, but they have not answered.*

¹⁸*And Jeremiah said unto the house of the Rechabites, Thus saith the LORD of hosts, the God of Israel; Because ye have obeyed the commandment of Jonadab your father, and kept all his precepts, and done according unto all that he hath commanded you:*

*The Kenites obeyed their father Jonadab, the Israelites did not obey their father*

¹⁹*Therefore thus saith the LORD of hosts, the God of Israel; Jonadab the son of Rechab shall not want a man to stand before me for ever.*

*Because they obeyed their father, God gives them a blessing with a higher intelligence*

*They are not blessed with children, usually only having one child*

## Cain makes good on Satan's promise

### Genesis 3:5

⁵*For God doth know that in the day ye eat thereof, then your eyes shall be opened, and ye shall be as gods, knowing good and evil.*

Cain invented the concept of more than one god through his personal hatred and revenge of God, and with the help of Satan. We have one true God, the creator of the universe, but Cain deceives the multitudes by his evil lies. He made gods out of Satan, Adam, Eve, Abel, and himself. People today still believe in many gods. If you do not believe it, watch the history channel. Watch the shows about aliens; the aliens are the gods that traveled from a distant planet from our galaxy or a distant galaxy. They do not understand, that these Aliens are from the great city that sits over Jerusalem. The spaceship that Ezekiel described in the bible came from the great city, not from another solar system. Many people still believe in the Greek, Roman, and Egyptian gods, all having their beginning from Cain.

## The god's Cain created

*Satan = Mul-lil or Enlil, Bel, and Akki, "god of the lower world" "lord of the surface of the earth" "god of the earth" "god of flesh man" "Akki the drawer of water" "prince of the world"*

*Adam = Anu =Amu "ruler and god of heaven" "the king of angels" "lord of the city Erech" "father of the gods"*

*Eve = Ea, Isthar, Nintu, Davkina, Ashtoreth of the Canaanites, Astarte of the Phoenicians, Isis, Osiris, Diana, Venus, Artemis, and Aphrodite. "The god of water" "water nymph" "great mother" "mother of mankind" "lady of Eden" "goddess of birth" "the god of culture" "the Author of intelligence" "daughter of the moon god" "wife of bel (Satan)" "Queen of heaven"*

*Abel = Tammuz, Adonis, Attis "son of Ea" "a shepherd" "Adonis and Attis both are names of a pig or boar" Cain had no respect for Abel his brother, he was considered the god of pigs. Tammuz translates to Domuz in Turkish, and domuzi in Chinese and they both mean pig. Demeter whom represents Eve in Grecian mythology relates to the little pig. Demeter represents Eve and the little pig represents Abel. Cain deified Adam as god of heaven, Eve as Queen of heaven and insulted Abel as god of the pigs. Cain the evil one will have his day*

*Cain = Merodach, Marduk, Sargon, Adar, Kian, Ares, Sun god, Sargon of Akkad, All – father, Insullanu, Kuon (dog), "The first high priest", "The son of Bel", "the deviser of constituted laws" "lord of the date" "The first sea king (Minos)", "Devine agriculturist" "The first free thinker" "The first born of Eve" "Adar said to be a giant" "Cain the sun god" "of that wicked one (Satan)" "The protégé of the devil" "Isullanu the gardener of Adam" "The great irrigator" "Ruler of the children of the sun"*

As you can see there are many names addressed to Satan, Adam, Eve, Cain, and Abel. Cain fabricated Satan as a god, and then made gods of the living, Adam the god of heaven, Eve the god of water, Abel the god of pigs, and Cain the sun god. The gods that Cain manufactured while in Babylon were adopted by Greece, Rome, and Egypt. The names were changed, more gods were invented, and the fictitious stories increased.

During the time of Cain that lasted 780 years, he governed, created laws, and ruled with total authority. He became Sargon the Magnificent, the king of the world. He influenced every race, nation, tribe on the face of the earth. Cain did not have supernatural abilities; he had 100 % use of his brain, which made him seem supernatural. He was a giant; his intelligence was far superior to anyone on earth except Adam. His mentor was Satan the archangel, and he was taught well. His sway with humankind today is greater than it has ever been. Even the chosen children of God are deceived, and many have become proselytes being misguided by Cain's progeny.

Cain was the king of the earth in a flesh body, in the very near future Satan will stand in Jerusalem in a transfigured body. He will claim to be god, the Messiah, Allah, Buddha and others, and he will be everyone's god. He will perform miracles that flesh man has never seen before, snapping his fingers, and lightning coming down from the sky, and many others. All these miracles we will see on television. Can we overcome this liar? Yes, learning the truth, having enough oil in your lamp, and you will overcome.

*Bel the name of the dragon or devil, was written in stone, in Babylon*

*In addition, Bel is written in the Bible. Here are three verses*

### Isaiah 46:1

*¹Bel boweth down, Nebo stoopeth, their idols were upon the beasts, and upon the cattle: your carriages were heavy loaden; they are a burden to the weary beast.*

*Bel = Devil, Dragon, Satan*

*Nebo = Prophet (the devils prophet)*

Strong's concordance: Nebo: A Babylonian deity who presided over learning and letters; corresponds to Greek herms, Latin mercury, and Egyptian Thoth.

### Jeremiah 50:2

²*Declare ye among the nations, and publish, and set up a standard; publish, and conceal not: say, Babylon is taken, **Bel** is confounded, **Merodach** is broken in pieces; her idols are confounded, her images are broken in pieces.*

*Bel is Satan and Merodach is Cain*

*Bel and Merodach are written in the Babylonian tablets and the Bible*

*Confounded = all dried up*

*The truth has come out; God's prophet has revealed Cain's gods*

*The Idols are dried up*

### Jeremiah 51:44

⁴⁴*And I will punish **Bel in Babylon**, and I will bring forth out of his mouth that which he hath swallowed up: and the nations shall not flow together any more unto him: yea, the wall of **Babylon shall fall**.*

*Babylon = Confusion "by mixing people, creating mongrels, mixing language, creating idols, and using lies to deceive people into unnatural thought and behavior"*

*The wall of Babylon will not stand*

## Ashtaroth another name for Eve is it written in the Bible

## Ashtaroth is written eleven times

### Joshua 12:4

⁴*And the coast of Og king of Bashan, which was of the remnant of the giants, that dwelt at Ashtaroth and at Edrei,*

*Og = (long-necked) a giant of Rephaim*

*Rephaim = tribe of giants*

*Ashtaroth = Star, Eve, false goddesses*

*Edrei = "goodly pasture" "like the garden of Eden", city of Bashan, north of Jabbok river*

## Joshua 13:12

¹²*All the kingdom of Og in Bashan, which reigned in Ashtaroth and in Edrei, who remained of the remnant of the giants: for these did Moses smite, and cast them out.*

> *Bashan = "fruitful" east of Jordan known for its fertility of giants*
> *(This land acquired by the half tribe of Manasseh)*

> *Remember Cain was a giant from the seed of the archangel Satan*

> *Coming up the giants during the time of Noah*

## Judges 2:13

¹³*And they forsook the LORD, and served Baal and Ashtaroth.*

> *Baal = "Baal worship" worship of the many gods created by Cain*

> *The Israelites worshipped Baal and Eve*

## 1 Samuel 12:10

¹⁰*And they cried unto the LORD, and said, We have sinned, because we have forsaken the LORD, and have served Baalim and Ashtaroth: but now deliver us out of the hand of our enemies, and we will serve thee.*

> *Eventually the Israelites will leave this land of Baalim and*
> *Ashtaroth and will be true to their one and only God*

## Judges 10:6

⁶*And the children of Israel did evil again in the sight of the LORD, and served Baalim, and Ashtaroth, and the gods of Syria, and the gods of Zidon, and the gods of Moab, and the gods of the children of Ammon, and the gods of the Philistines, and forsook the LORD, and served not him.*

*Cain is the originator of these gods*

*Molech sacrifice: the most evil ever*

*Molech = king, (king Cain)*

In Molech /Moloch sacrifice was an abomination to God. Young children were sacrificed in the most horrible way imaginable. A hollow figure of a head of an ox made of bronze was heated up by fire, and young little ones were place into it, and slowly burned alive. The sacrificing evil priest beat on their drums to keep the parents from hearing the screams. This evil all started with Cain. When Cortez saw the evil that was being done by the Aztec priest, (the sons of Cain) he destroyed them and saved the people that were being sacrificed.

It is hard to believe that some of God's chosen people, Judah and Israel, performed this evil and cruel act. God never intended for any of his children to do such atrocious acts and behavior. None of these evil beliefs and sacrifices would have happened if it were not for the evil one (Satan) and the one that taught God's children these cruel deeds, (Cain.)

The great and magnificent king he called himself was the instigator and presenter of evil to all races and nations of the earth. Today we all of humankind have an opportunity to overcome Cain's evil. Learn and understand the truth, and the truth will give you freedom.

During the time of Cain, the people of the earth lived under a one-world system ruled by King Cain. The elitist today is trying their best to create a one-world system, and we are very close today. The one world system will fail, (the deadly wound), and Satan will stand in Jerusalem claiming to be god. Satan will heal the wound, and the one world system will be in place. The world will whore after anti-Christ, thinking he is God, Jesus, Buddha, the Messiah, and the prince of peace. He was the archangel that protected the mercy seat of Christ, and he wanted that seat because of his pride. His seat will be in the lake of fire, and his soul will be burned to ashes forever and ever.

### *Revelation 13:12*

*[12] And he exerciseth all the power of the first beast before him, and causeth the earth and them which dwell therein to worship the first beast, whose deadly wound was healed.*

*The sons of Cain have done a good job preparing the world for Satan's hour*

The Jews, Israelites, Christians, Muslims, Buddhist, Atheist, Hindu's, and many others will worship the Dragon. The Kenites will gather to him, for they are his offspring. Learn God's word, through Shepherds Chapel, and you will have your armor in place to do battle with Satan.

# Chapter 7

## The generations of Adam

**Genesis 5**

[1]This is the book of the generations of Adam. In the day that God created man, in the likeness of God made he him;

[2]Male and female created he them; and blessed them, and called their name Adam, in the day when they were created.

[3]And Adam lived an hundred and thirty years, and begat a son in his own likeness, and after his image; and called his name Seth:

[4]And the days of Adam after he had begotten Seth were eight hundred years: and he begat sons and daughters:

[5]And all the days that Adam lived were nine hundred and thirty years: and he died.

> Adam was born in 4004BC and died in 3074BC living 930 years
>
> Eve's age is not mentioned, but probably lived into the 900s
>
> Cain was born in 3894BC and died in 3114BC (approximately)
>
> Adam lived 71 years after Cain's death

[6]And Seth lived an hundred and five years, and begat Enos:

*⁷And Seth lived after he begat Enos eight hundred and seven years, and begat sons and daughters:*

*Seth married one of his many sisters*

*⁸And all the days of Seth were nine hundred and twelve years: and he died.*

*⁹And Enos lived ninety years, and begat Cainan:*

*¹⁰And Enos lived after he begat Cainan eight hundred and fifteen years, and begat sons and daughters:*

*¹¹And all the days of Enos were nine hundred and five years: and he died.*

*¹²And Cainan lived seventy years and begat Mahalaleel:*

*¹³And Cainan lived after he begat Mahalaleel eight hundred and forty years, and begat sons and daughters:*

*¹⁴And all the days of Cainan were nine hundred and ten years: and he died.*

*¹⁵And Mahalaleel lived sixty and five years, and begat Jared:*

*¹⁶And Mahalaleel lived after he begat Jared eight hundred and thirty years, and begat sons and daughters:*

*¹⁷And all the days of Mahalaleel were eight hundred ninety and five years: and he died.*

*¹⁸And Jared lived an hundred sixty and two years, and he begat Enoch:*

*¹⁹And Jared lived after he begat Enoch eight hundred years, and begat sons and daughters:*

*²⁰And all the days of Jared were nine hundred sixty and two years: and he died.*

*²¹And Enoch lived sixty and five years, and begat Methuselah:*

*²²And Enoch walked with God after he begat Methuselah three hundred years, and begat sons and daughters:*

*[23]And all the days of Enoch were three hundred sixty and five years:*

*Enoch lived 365 years and maybe three months = 365.25 years*

*Enoch lived one year for every day in a solar year*

*[24]And **Enoch walked with God**: and he was not; for God took him.*

*Enoch was transfigured like Elijah and probably Moses*

*Two of these three men could be the two witnesses at the end times*

*[25]And Methuselah lived an hundred eighty and seven years, and begat Lamech.*

*[26]And Methuselah lived after he begat Lamech seven hundred eighty and two years, and begat sons and daughters:*

*[27]And all the days of Methuselah were nine hundred sixty and nine years: and he died.*

*Old as Methuselah 969 years old*

*The Adamic race has grown, the population is possibly in the millions*

*[28]And Lamech lived an hundred eighty and two years, and begat a son:*

*[29]And he called his name **Noah**, saying, This same shall comfort us concerning our work and toil of our hands, because of the ground which the LORD hath cursed.*

*Noah = Rest, comfort*

*Noah was born in 2948BC*

*[30]And Lamech lived after he begat Noah five hundred ninety and five years, and begat sons and daughters:*

*[31]And all the days of Lamech were seven hundred seventy and seven years: and he died.*

*777 years old*

*7 means completeness, spiritual, and perfection*

*The most sacred number of the Israelites*

*Second most used number in the bible, and the number 1 is first*

³²*And Noah was five hundred years old: and Noah begat Shem, Ham, and Japheth.*

*Through Shem Jesus would be born*

*The three sons were his first children, and they were born
at a perfect time according to God's plan*

Adams offspring are nearly destroyed, only eight are left after the flood. The bloodline must remain pure, so Jesus can be born from a virgin. Through Shem, the bloodline to Jesus will continue without blemish. God will bless Ham and Japheth with many children, and the eighth day man continues.

# Chapter 8

## The Giants, biblical and history

The question is, did giants really walk the earth in ancient times, or is all this giant stuff just made up. Well the bible says so if you believe in the word of God. Does history or archaeology say or show any evidence that giants once walked the earth? Have we found any bones to prove there were giants in the past? The answer is yes. Why do the scientist, archaeologist, historians, scholars, and museums refuse to acknowledge the giant's existence on the earth? For them supporting the idea that giants did walk the earth, this would back the bible, and they cannot have that. If giants were not in the bible, they would be all over it.

*Genesis 6:1*

*[1]And it came to pass, when men began to multiply on the face of the earth, and daughters were born unto them,*

*Since Adam 1500 years have gone by, and eighth day humankind has increased abundantly*

*From Joseph to Moses the population increased from 70 souls to 2 million souls*

*The Adamic race may have been in the millions during the flood*

*[2]That **the sons of God** saw the daughters of men that they were fair; and **they took them wives of all**, which they chose.*

*Fair = beautiful, goodly, pleasant, agreeable*

*All the daughters of Adams progeny were taken (had sex with the fallen angels) except for Noah's family*

*[3]And the LORD said, My spirit shall not always strive with man, for that he also is flesh: yet his days shall be an hundred and twenty years.*

*120-year generation*

*Adam lived 930 years, Noah 950, Abraham 175, Isaac 180, and Jacob 147*

*After Jacob, no one lived beyond a 120 years*

*[4]There were **giants** in the earth in those days; and also after that, when the sons of God came in unto the daughters of men, and they bare children to them, the same became mighty men which were of old, **men of renown**.*

*Giants = Progeny of Nephilim*

*Sons of god = fallen angels (Nephilim)*

*Daughters of men = progeny of Adam*

*Nephilim = naphal "to fall" "the fallen ones"*

*Old men of renown" = Gibbor = the Giants*

## Jude 1:6

*[6]And the angels which kept not their first estate, but left their own habitation, he hath reserved in everlasting chains under darkness unto the judgment of the great day.*

*The angels disobeyed God, and left heaven, not being born of flesh*

*Because of their great sin, they have been sentenced to the lake of fire*

The fallen angels (angels of Satan) left their habitation in heaven "that great city" not being born of flesh, having sex with the daughters of Adam. The angels had come down from heaven, possibly before Noah was born, and during that time, Enoch was prophesying against the fallen ones of Satan. The angels were not touching the sixth day man, only the eighth day man. The offspring from the seed of Satan's angels were giants that ranged from 12' to 22' in height and they continued to do evil upon the earth. All children of God are to go through the flesh except the arc archangel, like Michael, Gabriel, and Satan. Yes, Satan is an

141

archangel, and he will not be born of women, while preachers today teach the opposite that Satan will be born of women. By the time Noah is six hundred years old, the entire Adamic race has mixed with the seed of the fallen ones. Noah's family is the only people left with a 100% DNA from Adam's seed. Christ can only be born from a pure generation from Adam.

## How do we know there were giants on the earth? Where is it in the bible, where is it in Archaeology, and where is it in history, or legend?

Let us start with the most famous giant of them all Goliath. Most of us have read or listened to the story of how David slew the giant. Scholars have also told us that Goliath was 9'9" tall, and in my book, that does not qualify Goliath to be a giant. The bible says he is a giant, and I am definitely not going to argue with the bible. However, I will argue with the scholars.

## Who is Goliath, and how tall is he?

Before we were born in flesh, we were sons of God (angels). Our first estate is the holding area in the great city, that 1500-mile high building. The angels disobeyed God; they left the great city, and wholly seduced the seed-line of the Adamic race. The angels that had fallen were Satan's very best. Their purpose was to destroy Adams pedigree to prevent Jesus from being born.

The fallen angels have received their death sentence, they chose not to go through the flesh, and their destiny is the lake of fire.

### John 3:3

³*Jesus answered and said unto him, Verily, verily, I say unto thee, except a man be born again; he cannot see the kingdom of God.*

*Again = from above "a higher place" (The great city)*

*All of God's children living in the great city must be born of woman*

*If an angel refuses to be born in the flesh, the angel will not enter in the kingdom of God (everlasting life)*

*Satan and his angels is sentenced to death in the lake of fire*

# Are there evil angels?

### Psalm 78:49

*⁴⁹He cast upon them the fierceness of his anger, wrath, and indignation, and trouble, by sending evil angels among them.*

*Angels are the people who are in heaven, some followed God, and others chose Satan*

*Anyone in flesh or spirit that loves and worships Satan is evil whether on the earth or in heaven*

### Joshua 11:22

*²²There was none of the Anakims left in the land of the children of Israel: only in Gaza, in Gath, and in Ashdod, there remained.*

*Anakims = A tribe of giants "offspring of the fallen angels"*

*Gaza = the strong, Gath = winepress, Ashdod = the powerful, all in the land of the philistines*

### 1 Samuel 17:4-7

*⁴And there went out a champion out of the camp of the Philistines, named Goliath, of Gath, whose height was six cubits and a span.*

Goliath = Splendor

Gath = his home town

Goliath is the last of the giants "the Anakims"

The bible tells us, Goliath is six cubits and a span. The question is what does the cubit measures out in length. The span is half a cubit, so if we knew the length of a cubit we would have Goliaths height. However, it is not that simple, the cubit varies from nation to nation, and also the date and location. The cubit length is determined by measuring from the elbow to the middle finger. A man standing 5'6" tall would range from 17 inches to 18 inches, and 18 inches is the standard for a cubit today. A man that stands 6-foot-tall would vary from 18 inches to 22 inches a significant difference. In ancient times, the cubit deviated slightly, and I will determine Goliaths height by one of these cubits.

Royal Babylonian cubit = 21.81"

Ancient Egyptian cubit = 20.6"

Biblical Cubic = 21.8"

Assyrian cubic = 21.6"

Ezekiel cubic= 20.5"

Hebrew long cubic = 20.67"

As you can see the cubic does not vary that much. I have a choice, I can average them out and that comes to 21.16 feet, which would be close to the Assyrian cubit. The Ezekiel cubic is the shortest and I will go with that.

Six cubits times 20.5 inches = 123 inches

One span = half a cubic = 10.25 inches

123 inches + 10.25 inches = 133.25 inches divided by 12 inches = 11.1 feet tall

Using the Assyrian cubit his height would have been 11.7 feet tall

Goliath barely made giant status; he was probably a third or fourth generation giant. The offspring of fallen angels are only male, therefore when giants mate with flesh women, their children no longer have supernatural abilities and their size diminish quickly. Goliath was the last of the giants of the Anakims, and the last in Philistine/Canaan. The giants during the time of David were not the first, and not the last, Satan's angels will continue planting giants in strategic locations, until Christ puts a stop to it.

[5]*And he had an helmet of brass upon his head, and he was armed with a coat of mail; and the weight of the coat was five thousand shekels of brass.*

*One shekel = .35 troy ounces*

*One troy ounce is ten percent heavier than the ounce*

.35 troy ounce = .385 ounces

5000 shekels x .385 = 1925 ounces

1925 ounces divided by 16 ounces = 120 pounds

*[6]And he had greaves of brass upon his legs, and a target of brass between his shoulders.*

*[7]And the staff of his spear was like a weaver's beam; and his spear's head weighed six hundred shekels of iron: and one bearing a shield went before him.*

*600 shekels x .385 = 231 ounces*

*231 ounces divided by 16 ounces = 14.43 pounds*

Goliaths Coat of mail weighed 120 pounds, and his spearhead weighed 14 pounds. This is a lot of weight for a 180lb man, but for an eleven-foot man that probably weighed around 800 to 1200 pounds, "hardly noticeable".

# Is there a larger giant mentioned in the bible?

### Deuteronomy 3:11

*[11]For only **Og king of Bashan** remained of the **remnant of giants**; behold his bedstead was a bedstead of iron; is it not in Rabbath of the children of Ammon? **nine cubits** was the length thereof, and four cubits the breadth of it, after the cubit of a man.*

*Og = long-necked*

*Remnant of giants known as the Anakims*

Og is a very tall giant, his bed is nine cubits in length, so how tall is he? The nine cubits by 4 cubits is the same measurements as Marduk's tomb in Babylon. Remember Marduk is Cain, and I estimated Cain to be sixteen feet tall before I knew of his tombs dimension. Since the tomb of Cain is in Babylon during ancient times, and Og lived during this era, I have decided to use the Royal Babylonian cubit at 21.81 inches.

*9 cubits at 21.81 inches = 196 inches = 16.33 feet or 16' 4"*

*The length of his bed or tomb is 16'4"*

*Og was 16 feet tall "now that's a giant"*

Can you imagine a 16' tall man; a man that tall would have to bend over to walk under an interstate overpass. Og would be one to two feet shorter than a male Giraffe, which is the tallest mammal on earth. He probably weighed well over 1500 pounds, and could probably lift more than a ton. Some people believe the giants were used to help build the Pyramids, Stonehenge, and other large stone structures. It is possible, some may have worked on these great structures, but I believe expert masons, and a multitude of laborers did most of the work. I personally do not believe there were enough giants to build the pyramids, but they certainly could have helped with the heavy lifting and dragging of large stones. However, these large stone structures all around the world may have been built in the first earth age. We really do not know the age of these structures.

### Numbers 13:32

*32 And they brought up an evil report of the land which they had searched unto the children of Israel, saying, The land, through which we have gone to search it, is a land that eateth up the inhabitants thereof; and all the people that we saw in it are **men of a great stature**.*

*Stature = great in size, superhuman, abnormal, and very wicked*

*33 And there we saw the giants, the sons of Anak, which come of the giants: **and we were in our own sight as grasshoppers**, and so we were in their sight.*

*Anuk = neck*

*The giants were 12 to 22 feet tall making the Israelites seem like grasshoppers*

The first angel to have sex with a flesh woman was Satan, the result was a male giant, and his name was Cain. The first influx of fallen angels came before, and during the time of Noah. The second influx of fallen angels (Nephilim) was during the time of Moses. The evil angels, (the followers of Satan) were trying to prevent the Israelites from entering the promise land. They know Gods Son will be born, and sacrificed in this land. Satan will never allow the Israelites to have rest and peace, in their new land.

### Deuteronomy 2:21

*21A people great, and many, and tall, as the Anakims; but the LORD destroyed them before them; and they succeeded them, and dwelt in their stead:*

*Many giants in the land of Moab and Canaan*

*The Anakims were destroyed and the land was given to the tribe of Manasseh*

### Joshua 13:12

*12All the kingdom of Og in Bashan, which reigned in Ashtaroth and in Edrei, who remained of the remnant of the giants: for these did Moses smite, and cast them out.*

*Bashan east of the Jordan River*

*Ashtaroth = star*

*The Anakims were killed off by the Israelites in the land of Moab (Jordan)*

The bible says there were men of great stature that were the progeny of fallen angels. I do not need history or archaeology to prove the existence of giants, the bible says so, and I believe it. Nevertheless, there just happens to be a little of both.

## Archaeology proof of giants

If you go online, you will find plenty of proof that giants did exist, and many of these giants having red hair, six toes, six fingers and double rows of teeth. If there were giants back then, why do we not see them today? The reason is God sentenced Satan along with his angels to death. They will no longer be allowed to leave heaven; they are in a holding area until Michael the archangel releases them onto the earth. When the deadly wound occurs, which will soon come to past. Satan will be cast out of heaven along with his angels, and he will stand on Mount Zion claiming to be God.

### 2 Peter 2:4

*⁴For if God spared not the angels that sinned, but cast them down to hell, and delivered them into chains of darkness, to be reserved unto judgment;*

Satan's angels have visited the earth many times, and each time producing offspring of an unnatural gigantic size. The angels only produce males of giant stature, and some with large coned heads with very large brains. The progeny of the angels can breed male and female giants by mating with flesh women. The giants will reduce over many generations, but the gene pool is still with us today. Some Giants may have six Fingers and toes, a double row of teeth, and red or yellow hair.

Giant Sumerian

Sumerian Giant 16 feet tall or better     Giant Egyptian 8 feet tall or better

### 2 Samuel 21:20

*²⁰And there was yet a battle **in Gath**, where was **a man of great stature**, that had on every **hand six fingers**, and on every **foot six toes**, four and twenty in number; and he also was born to the giant.*

Many giants discovered had six fingers and six toes. People today are born with six fingers, toes and double rows of teeth, passed down by the genes of ancient giants. I believe the last influx of the fallen angels (Nephilim) was in South America, where many records and sightings occurred during the explorations of the Spaniards. Cain and his sons may have had six toes and six fingers, and as we know, six represents Satan.

Naram-Sin the grandson of Cain wearing a horned helmet depicts him as the moon god. Sin or Suen translates into moon god, and, the moon represents Satan. (The moon can only reflect light not produce it.) Notice Naram-Sin is twice as tall as the others shown on the Stele. Naram-Sin the third generation of Cain is still very tall at around eleven feet, if the average person depicted on the stele is 5'6" tall.

Go online and type in (Naram-sin Stele) His victory stele is shown at the Louvre in Paris.

Unfortunately, a lot of evidence has been put away in museums never to be seen by the public again. God forbid this evidence would prove the bible correct that giants once walked the earth. If you desire to learn more, search (Giants and mummies) (red hair giants) or (New giant skulls found) a video on you tube a must see. It is up to you to discern the content, not everything is true.

## History and legend of Giants walking the earth

Why is it important to know the history of the giants? Many people with faith believe the word of God, and need no more. Some people are like Thomas the apostle who needs proof that the man standing before him was Jesus. Whether you have much faith or little faith, history can expand your belief. Let me qualify these giants; they are not the giants of today that usually have a pituitary gland disease. The fallen angels impregnated the Adamite women, and giants (Gibbor) are the result. Giants are no longer among us today because the fallen angels are locked away, and no longer able to impregnate woman.

The fallen angels during the time of Noah tried to destroy the unbroken seed line that Jesus would be born from, and Noah's family prevailed. Again, the fallen angels will come to the earth during the hour of Satan, and they will try to steal as many souls as possible before Christ second coming. The reason for the giants was to prevent Jesus from being born and to scare the Israelites from entering into the land of Canaan.

Scholars passed down my favorite legend, "Brutus founder of London", from Gildas Albanius of the 5th century AD, Nennius of the 9th century AD, Geoffrey of Monmouth 1150AD, and Professor Waddells book written in the 20th century. The story was told, by word of mouth, by the Welsh monks, or Druids, and was first written down by Gildas Albanius, a British cleric around 550AD.

Aeneas, a Trojan prince, escaped by boat to Latium. Latium is where Rome was founded by Ascanius offspring, who was Aeneas' son. Ascanius' wife died giving birth to their son Brutus, and it was foretold that Brutus would kill his mother and father.

Young Brutus accidentally shot his father during a hunting trip with an arrow killing him thus; he killed his mother and father. For this heinous crime, Brutus was banished from Italy by his relatives. He traveled to Greece where many of his countrymen from Troy were being held. He obtained ships and supplies, and sailed off to an unknown land. His destiny, all planned by God, was the Island called Albion, or White Island. Giants were said to live on this Island, the fallen angels had impregnated the daughters of this land a generation or two before Brutus made his landing in 1103BC.

One thing I have not mentioned is Brutus is a direct descendent of Judah, one of the twelve patriarchs of Israel. Judah had two sons by Tamar, the first was Pharez and the second was Zarah. Through the royal king line of Pharez, King David would be the first king of the tribe of Judah. The last king would be Jesus the Christ. Through Zarah's royal line, many of Europe's kings are descended. After the crucifixion of Jesus, the Pharez line joined with the Zarah line through the line of Mary and Joseph, the Desposyni line.

Jesus would visit Glastonbury England many times with his uncle Joseph of Arimathea during the years when he is not mentioned in the bible. At age 12-29. Jesus built the first church out of wattle, in Glastonbury England. All twelve tribes of Israel will come and settle on this island. A few hundred years after Jesus built the church the Engle/Anglo will enter England with a sword to conquer. Later Christianity will conquer the Anglo Saxons, and they are the last of the twelve tribes of Israel to enter Great Britain.

Now we know why Satan sent the fallen angels down to the Island of Albion to prevent the coming of Brutus. After the landing of Brutus, the Island was renamed Brutus land, and then altered into Britain, and Great Britain. Eventually all twelve tribes of Israel will settle and conquer this land. Brutus became the first king of Britain, the first lawgiver, and founder of new Troy, later renamed London, after his son.

*Britain = Covenant Land (God's promise to the twelve tribes of Israel)*

Before Brutus landed in Albion, he was warned of the Giants in this land by a dream he had in the temple of Diana.

*Brutus! There lies beyond the Gallic bounds an island which the western sea surrounds, by giants once possessed, now few remain to bar thy entrance, or obstruct thy reign, to reach that happy shore thy sail employ, their fate decree to raise a second Troy, and found an empire in thy royal line which time shall never destroy nor bounds confine.*

**From Waddell's Book pg. 152-153**

Brutus and company landed in Totnes in Devon England 1100 years before Christ, an area that had few giants. On his arrival, the giants fled to the caves in the mountains never to be seen again. Corineus a man of great courage was given the land, (now called Cornwall,) in south England to rule over, which had many giants. Corineus and his people later called the Cornish people fought and destroyed all the giants but one, his name was Gogmagog. He was a mean, vile, and wretched giant, taller than all the other giants, who according to Geoffrey of Monmouth stood twelve cubits and had incredible strength. Using the ancient Egyptian cubit at 20.6 inches in length, Gogmagog would have stood 20 feet tall, and using the modern 18-inch cubit, he would have stood 18 feet tall. Either way, he was taller than OG or Cain, which makes him the tallest man written of in history.

Corineus wrestled the giant and somehow threw him off the cliff onto the rocks below, near the sea, which is called Lam Goemagot today. How can a six-foot man defeat a twenty-foot man? The same way David destroyed Goliath, with the help of God. The giants were not successful in keeping the royal line of Judah from establishing a king line of the tribe of Judah, which has continued until this day in Great Britain. Our Queen in Great Britain, Queen Elizabeth, has both the royal seed lines of Zarah and Pharez, the two sons of Judah.

## Captain Magellan and the Patagonian giants
## The Spanish world explorers

Captain Magellan and his crew on a long voyage around the world encountered very tall humans estimated to be 12' to 15' in stature, while wintering in a harbor in present day Argentina. He named these people, the Patagonian giants, and possibly meaning big feet. Pata means foot, but the suffix gon is unknown, so the meaning is uncertain.

Antonio Pigafetta one of the 17 survivors that circumnavigated the earth on Magellan's expedition chronicled the whole exploration, including the encounter with the giants on the southeast portion of South America. He arrived back in Spain on the ship (The Victoria) on September 8, 1522.

Antonio Pigafetta written account

*"One day we suddenly saw a naked man of giant stature on the shore of the port, dancing, singing, and throwing dust on his head. The captain-general* (Magellan) *sent one of our men to the giant so that he might perform the same actions as a sign of peace. Having done that, the man led the giant to an islet where the captain-general was waiting. When the giant was in the captain-general's presence he marveled greatly, and made signs with one finger raised upward, believing that we had come from the sky. He was so tall that we reached only to his waist, and he was well proportioned..."*

Captain Cooke actually captured a giant and tied him to the mast of the ship. The giant untied himself, and jumped overboard never to be seen again. The giant was referenced to be over nine feet tall.

Captain Magellan and Captain Cooke both wrote of these giants in their log books, but by the end of the 1800s these interesting records were debunked. I suppose the higher critics considered it a bunch of exaggerated nonsense. If these writings would have supported evolution it would be in our history books today, and taught in our schools. Captain Magellan wrote in his logbook that the giants were so tall they only came up to the giants' waist. If Magellan was exaggerating the giant's size, why did none of the 17 survivors refute his writings?

Sir Francis Drake in 1579 wrote down a meeting with very tall natives in Pantagonia. Anthonie Knivet wrote down claiming to have seen dead bodies 12 feet long. William Adams claimed a fearful encounter with very tall natives in 1590 while onboard a Dutch ship. Commodore John Byron 1766 had seen natives in Patagonia estimated to be 9 feet tall. The accounts were revised in 1773, saying the natives were around 6'6" tall. In 1773, 6'6" would be considered very tall for any race of people. President Abraham Lincoln was 6'4" tall when the average man in the USA was around 5'8" tall. When Charles Darwin encountered the Patagonian's in the 1830s, he said they were 6' tall. Some were taller, but most were 6'. Of course, Charles Darwin debunks the stories as an exaggerated made up myth. He described the natives as being sub-human, and a missing link from the ape family. He denied giants ever existing on the earth, and of course, he had to, it would prove the Bible correct.

If you noticed from the 1500s to the 1800s, the average height decreased quite a bit. From 12' to 6' how did that happen? It is easy! Each generation of giants, reduce in size, because the DNA dilutes down from the original giants, fathered by the fallen angels of Satan. The giants are only male, and they must mate with the native women of the area where they were born. Therefore, by the 1800s, they were very close to being of average height. Now remember the offspring of the fallen angels are only male, when they mate flesh women, the offspring can be male or female. They reduce down every generation.

Humankind has always been fascinated with the giants. Ancient mythology, folklore, and the bible have given us many stories about them. Many stories are myths, like Jack and the bean stock, Paul Bunyan, and many more around the world. Saxo Grammaticus believed they had to exist, because how can you explain the large stone walls, and monuments like Stonehenge, and the Pyramids of Egypt. He said only the giants could have built these amazing structures. Well I am not so sure about that, but I do know the Bible does declare the giants once walked this earth, and I do believe the bible.

Today there are no giants among us descended from the seed of the falling angels. Giants today have no DNA connection with them; in fact, they do not qualify as giants in my book. The sons of Cain called Kenites in the bible are the only offspring that have kept their DNA above one percent. The Kenites will always live among the ten tribes of Israel, and the tribe of Judah and Benjamin. Kenites have always been in the religious business, and some are Protestant Preachers, Catholic Priest, and Jewish Rabbis, that are of the sons of Cain. Do not let it alarm you, the Kenites have been writing down God's word as scribes, since the time of Solomon.

In Gods book and in my book the giants did exist. If you choose not to believe in giants, it is perfectly ok. God created us and gave us all free will he loves our different traits, personalities, and our opinions however he always requires love.

# Chapter 9

## Noah's flood

## Was the whole earth flooded?

## Where did Noah and his people live, at the time of the flood?

Cain killed Abel, and Cain fled to the land of Nod, which is Mongolia and China. Seth, the only child left, is living with Adam and Eve on the Tarim River. Eve continues to have more children, Seth marries his sister, and Enos is born. At this time, there is no law against marrying your sister, and there is no other way to keep the bloodline pure. By the time Noah is born, thousands of Adamites are living in the Tarim Basin in China. The offspring of Adam are living with few laws, and without laws, they go astray.

### Genesis 6:5-8

[5] *And God saw that the wickedness of man was great in the earth, and that every imagination of the thoughts of his heart was only evil continually.*

*The earth is the (Tarim Basin) where Adams offspring are living*

The fallen angels seduced the daughters of Adam, and they gave birth to giants. The giants were 12' to over 22' tall, and they were very evil. The earth (Tarim Basin) was consumed by evil, and every kind of sin committed. The people were more evil than the time of Sodom and Gomorrah.

*⁶ And it repented the LORD that he had made man on the earth, and it grieved him at his heart.*

*⁷ And the LORD said, I will destroy man whom I have created from the face of the earth; both man, and beast, and the creeping thing, and the fowls of the air; for it repenteth me that I have made them.*

*⁸ But Noah found grace in the eyes of the LORD.*

*Noah's family was not Wholly seduced by the fallen angels*

*Noah to Shem to David to Jesus, and the bloodline is unbroken*

### Genesis 6:9-22

*⁹ These are the generations of Noah: Noah was a just man and perfect in his generations, and Noah walked with God.*

*¹⁰ And Noah begat three sons, Shem, Ham, and Japheth.*

*¹¹ The earth also was corrupt before God, and the earth was filled with violence.*

*¹² And God looked upon the earth, and, behold, it was corrupt; for all flesh had corrupted his way upon the earth.*

*¹³ And God said unto Noah, The end of all flesh is come before me; for the earth is filled with violence through them; and, behold, I will destroy them with the earth.*

*Noah's family is the only pure Adamic seed line left*

*The others have mixed with the fallen angels*

*The eighth day mankind living in the high Pamirs were not touched by the fallen angels*

*After the flood some of these people, migrated back to the Tarim basin and mined salt.*

*Their mummies have been found*

*Read the book, (The Mummies of Urumchi) by Elizabeth Wayland Barber*

*Genesis 6:14*

*¹⁴ Make thee an ark of gopher wood; rooms shalt thou make in the ark, and shalt pitch it within and without with pitch.*

*What is Gopher Wood?*

*Pitch = Asphalt*

*¹⁵ And this is the fashion which thou shalt make it of: The length of the ark shall be three hundred cubits, the breadth of it fifty cubits, and the height of it thirty cubits.*

*Based on Biblical Cubit = 21.8"*

*Length = 300 cubits x 21.8" = 545'*

*Breadth = 50 cubits x 21.8" = 91'*

*Height = 30 cubits x 21.8" = 55'*

*Three stories divided by 55' = 18'*

*The tallest mammal the Giraffe is 18'*

*148,785sf of living and storage area*

*Plenty of room for all the animals*

Only the animals that lived in the Tarim basin area were gathered, there is no way Noah could have gathered two of all the animals around the world. Unless God had provided them to Noah.

*Genesis 6:16-22*

*¹⁶ A window shalt thou make to the ark, and in a cubit shalt thou finish it above; and the door of the ark shalt thou set in the side thereof; with lower, second, and third stories shalt thou make it.*

*¹⁷ And, behold, I, even I, do bring a flood of waters upon the earth, to destroy all flesh, wherein is the breath of life, from under heaven; and every thing that is in the earth shall die.*

*In the first Earth age, the whole Earth was destroyed by water*

*The second flood (Noah's flood) was not world wide*

*Earth = eh'rets = country, territory, land, and ground "not the whole world"*

*Breath of Life = Living Spirit*

*Every human and creature shall die that lives in the Tarim Basin (Noah's Earth)*

*¹⁸ But with thee will I establish my **covenant**; and thou shalt come into the ark, thou, and thy sons, and thy wife, and thy sons' wives with thee.*

*Covenant= Alliance, Pledge, agreement, promise*

*Eight Adamic souls will go on the boat*

*Eight means new beginning "Noah's family will start a new beginning"*

*¹⁹ And of every living thing of all flesh, two of every sort shalt thou bring into the ark, to keep them alive with thee; they shall be male and female.*

*The Mongolian, Black, and White races may have entered the boat with one couple each representing their race*

*By the time of Noah, the Sixth day man had populated the whole Earth*

*²⁰ Of fowls after their kind, and of cattle after their kind, of every creeping thing of the earth after his kind, two of every sort shall come unto thee, to keep them alive.*

*²¹ And take thou unto thee of all food that is eaten, and thou shalt gather it to thee; and it shall be for food for thee, and for them.*

*²² Thus did Noah; according to all that God commanded him, so did he.*

From Adam to the beginning of the flood 1,656 years have passed. Noah is 600 years old and Adam has been dead for 726 years. Methuselah lives longer than anyone ever recorded at 969 years old. When he died, the flood began in 2348 BC, that is 4364 years ago (based on 2016). There is no way to know how many Adamic souls were on the earth at the time of the flood. There could have been millions, therefore I believe some people left the Tarim Basin and survived the flood. Some going east into China, others south into India, and others west into Persia, Mesopotamia, Egypt, and others elsewhere. Most probable the people of Adams pedigree mixed with the Indigenous people wherever they settled.

Enoch walked with God 365.25 years, one year for every day of the solar year. Some people believe he built the Great Pyramid in Egypt, and maybe he did, but we have no proof. He did preach against the mixing of the fallen angels while living in the Tarim basin, and tried to keep the eighth day race pure. Enoch named the twelve constellations, and I believe invented the first writings. He was so good, and so pure; God took him flesh and all. Yes Enoch, Elijah, and Moses are still in their flesh bodies today waiting for the time Satan will stand in Jerusalem. Michael will cast out Satan and his seven thousand angles to the earth, and Enoch, Moses, and Elijah will have a big part in the last days. I believe two of these three men will be the two witnesses written of in Revelation.

Noah was also a man of God, and he walked with God and stayed pure to the end of his days. When I say pure, it does not mean he did not sin, but he loved and obeyed God all his days. I believe Noah was born in the Tarim Basin at the head of the Tarim River. He grew up in very troubling times, when Satan was trying his best to destroy Adams offspring. He knew that Yeshua the Christ would come through this seed line. Over his six hundred years, he saw the invasion of the fallen angels corrupting the children of Adam, and slowly taking away the pure pedigree of Adam and Eve.

Year after year women were wholly seduced, and the pure seed line was reduced to eight souls. God has always had at least one good man on the earth, like Pastor Arnold Murray today teaching God's elect.

## What is Gopher Wood?

God told Noah to build an ark of gopher wood. What tree is that? There is one amazing tree, which lives under extreme conditions in the Tarim basin, which is the Euphrates Poplar. The tree has been living in this region for thousands of years, and ancient stumps refuse to rot in the dry desert sand. The tree today is not strait, it twists and turns like Elvis Presley and would not make good lumber for a large vessel. However, in the days of Noah it was a completely different ballgame. Today the wind blows very hard in this region and the trees twist, but in Noah's time, the weather was stable and the trees grew tall and strait.

The Euphrates Poplar is a beautiful tree; it refuses to die under the extreme conditions of the Tarim Basin. No wonder it was named Euphrates, which means fruitful. Adam and Eve reared their young boy Seth on the Euphrates River and his seed became fruitful. Noah built his boat out of Euphrates Poplar and his seed became very fruitful. From the River and from the boat, which saved the offspring of Adam, his offspring will be fruitful. On the other hand, should we say his seed would be Euphrates? Do I believe the Gopher tree could be the Euphrates Poplar, yes I do?

Euphrates Poplar in Tarim Basin: The trees are very beautiful and are yellow, red, and green in color, please go on-line and look at these beautiful trees in the Tarim basis.

The Tarim basin has the largest population of Euphrates Poplar trees, and the largest poplar trees in the world. Some trees can live over three thousand years, and can live in extreme conditions and have lived in this region for over 60 million years. Amazing today it is called the Euphrates poplar, which would be the gopher tree during the time of Noah.

In 2008 (Euphrates poplar Coffins) were found at the Hotan River where it joins the Tarim River. The coffins were 9'2" long, and the bodies were 7'2" tall. An ancient tribe of tall Caucasoid Mummies with light hair, round eyes, long nose, and light beards were in these coffins. These people very well could be the Adamic people I believe lived here in the Tarim basin. I estimated the height of Adam to be 8' tall, and their height at this date has diminished a small amount.

Since the coffins were 9 feet long, this gives us the height range of these people from 7 feet to 9 feet in stature.

Queen's University in Belfast estimated the date of the tombs to be 4600 years old, and the year of the flood was 4348 years ago. These tombs were here 252 years before the flood. The Adamic race of people were living on the Tarim River among the giant beautiful Euphrates Poplar trees during the time of Noah.

Now we have a very good idea of where Noah's people were when the flood began. I believe Adam and Eve migrated with Seth to the Tarim basin and settled at the Tarim River head. Seth would have taken his sister to be his wife, and the Adamic population would grow rapidly, for God will bless them with many children. I believe they probably settled at the Tarim head where the four Rivers connect, the Kasgar, Yarkand, Aksu, and Hotan Rivers. God has provided Adam and Eve with a new garden on the Tarim River, where it parts into four heads, just like the Garden of Eden. God works in mysterious ways.

## Back to Noah and the flood

God has given Noah a very big project, if he refuses, he and his family will perish. Noah is not a man that would refuse God, and that is why Noah was chosen for the job. We are talking about a boat the size of the ships we have today. Noah has no modern equipment, how in the world will he pull this off without electricity and heavy equipment.

The Great Pyramid built thousands of years ago, far as we know, was not built by modern equipment. We marvel at this today! Could we build the Great Pyramid today, with modern equipment and tools? I am thinking maybe not! One thing we do know, it is there, we take pictures of it, it is ancient, and how in the world did they build it. I personally believe the Great Pyramid was built during the first earth age.

One thing Noah had was plenty of giants. Giants could be a major factor in the building of the Ark. At this time, there were more giants on the earth than any other period from Adam to present. These giants were 12 to 22 feet tall and could lift and pull thousands of pounds of rock, wood, and earth. Not only were these huge giants smart, but they were close to being supernatural.

## The Question is how did Noah control them?

Noah had the same thing Abraham, Isaac, and Jacob had, and that was God's blessings. He had wealth, and plenty of food. The Giants needed lots of food and loved wealth. The Giants probably thought he was crazy like all the others, but hey! They needed food and money. Therefore, the giants helped build the large boat, and waited for the flood that would kill them. "Not so smart after all"!

Noah built the boat according to Gods specifications. Some people believe the boat was too small for all the animals. I think the opposite; it seems to me to be too large, but God the Architect and builder of the Universe knows what he is doing.

Finally, the boat is completed, and enough provisions should be stored to feed all the animals, and people on the ark for five months, and more. Ok now I know why the boat is so big. It is going to take a half to two thirds of the boat for food storage. Keeping all these animals fed and happy will not be easy. There are eight Adamic people and six of the sixth day man on the boat to divide the work. There will be twenty-four hours of work each day divided among them, no idle time on this five-month cruise.

### Genesis 7:1-24

*7 And the LORD said unto Noah, Come thou and all thy house into the ark; for thee have I seen righteous before me in this generation.*

*² Of every clean beast thou shalt take to thee by sevens, the male and his female: and of beasts that are not clean by two, the male and his female.*

*³ Of fowls also of the air by sevens, the male and the female; to keep seed alive upon the face of all the earth.*

*⁴ For yet seven days, and I will cause it to rain upon the earth forty days and forty nights; and every living substance that I have made will I destroy from off the face of the earth.*

*⁵ And Noah did according unto all that the LORD commanded him.*

*⁶ And Noah was six hundred years old when the flood of waters was upon the earth.*

*⁷ And Noah went in, and his sons, and his wife, and his sons' wives with him, into the ark, because of the waters of the flood.*

*⁸ Of clean beasts, and of beasts that are not clean, and of fowls, and of everything that creepeth upon the earth,*

*⁹ There went in two and two unto Noah into the ark, the male and the female, as God had commanded Noah.*

*¹⁰ And it came to pass after seven days, that the waters of the flood were upon the earth.*

*¹¹ In the six hundredth year of Noah's life, in the second month, the seventeenth day of the month, the same day were all the fountains of the great deep broken up, and the windows of heaven were opened.*

*¹² And the rain was upon the earth forty days and forty nights.*

*¹³ In the selfsame day entered Noah, and Shem, and Ham, and Japheth, the sons of Noah, and Noah's wife, and the three wives of his sons with them, into the ark;*

*¹⁴ They, and every beast after his kind, and all the cattle after their kind, and every creeping thing that creepeth upon the earth after his kind, and every fowl after his kind, every bird of every sort.*

*¹⁵ And they went in unto Noah into the ark, two and two of all flesh, wherein is the breath of life.*

*Two of all flesh = includes sixth day mankind*

*Breath of life = Ruach (Invisible spirit)*

*¹⁶ And they that went in, went in male and female of all flesh, as God had commanded him: and the LORD shut him in.*

*¹⁷ And the flood was forty days upon the earth; and the waters increased, and bare up the ark, and it was lift up above the earth.*

*Forty = probation, or testing*

*18 And the waters prevailed, and were increased greatly upon the earth; and the ark went upon the face of the waters.*

*19 And the waters prevailed exceedingly upon the earth; and all the high hills, that were under the whole heaven, were covered.*

*20 Fifteen cubits upward did the waters prevail; and the mountains were covered.*

*21 And all flesh died that moved upon the earth, both of fowl, and of cattle, and of beast, and of every creeping thing that creepeth upon the earth, and every man:*

*22 All in whose nostrils was the breath of life, of all that was in the dry land, died.*

*All of humankind, including the giants were destroyed*

*The flood occurred in the Tarim basin, overflowed and eroded the Pe-shan mountains, and the flood waters probably killed many Mongolians/Chinese*

*23 And every living substance was destroyed which was upon the face of the ground, both man, and cattle, and the creeping things, and the fowl of the heaven; and they were destroyed from the earth: and Noah only remained alive, and they that were with him in the ark.*

*24 And the waters prevailed upon the earth an hundred and fifty days.*

*A five-month period*

*Satan will war with the angels, and deceive flesh man for a period of 5 months*

*Satan's flood of lies*

Every living creature that takes a breath will be destroyed, except for Noah, and all that is on the ark. In seven day's every living creature on the earth will parish. Noah's earth is the Tarim Basin, a desert surrounded by the tallest mountains in the world. How do I know the earth does not mean the whole world? Have you ever stooped over and picked up a handful of earth? "You should try living in my earth or world sometime"! The Adamic people were living in the Tarim Basin, and that was their earth or their world. I am standing on the earth where my people once lived. It is a figure of speech!

Did Noah travel around the world to gather the entire indigenous animals that did not exist in the Tarim Basin? How do you explain the Kangaroo and other animals living only in Australia? How do you explain the Turkey, and Raccoon in North America, and different species in all the Continents? Noah gathered all the animals and creatures living in his earth, (the Tarim Basin region.) He gathered the beast of burden, animals for food, carnivores, scavengers, and birds for food, birds that scavenge, and other creatures. All these creatures will help Noah and his family to live, and replenish the earth with the offspring of Adam and Eve.

## How did forty days and forty nights of rain fill the Tarim Basin?

Noah and his people live at the head of the Tarim River. Standing at the River and turning 360 degrees the only mountains that can be seen are to the north. Standing on the earth looking north there is a ridge of mountains blocking the view of the very tall Tian Shan Mountains. This ridge is part of the Tien Shan Mountains, and it probably has a name, but I do not know it. The highest point on the ridge is about 8700 feet above sea level.

The Bible says the water rose to fifteen cubits above the hills. That would be 27 feet above the hills. Beyond the hills lay the great Mountains of the Pamirs, Tien Shan, Karakoram, Kun-Lun, and Pe-Shan Mountains all part of the highest mountain ranges in the world.

The elevation today where Noah once stood is 3670 feet. To cover the hills by 15 cubits or 27 feet would give us an elevation of 8800' feet above sea level. Subtract 8800' from 3670' would equal 5138', that is a whole lot of water. One mile of water seems like a lot, but our oceans range from sea level to 35,798 feet deep, and covers 70 percent of our planet. "Now that is a lot of water"

The Bible says it rained for 40 days and nights. Is this possible, it would have to rain 64.22 inches per hour for forty days. Can God make it rain 64 inches per hour, well yes, He can, but I do not believe He did. We are missing one little thing and that is God opened the fountains of the deep, and the waters flooded into the Tarim Basin, and rose to an elevation of 8800 feet. There is a huge amount of water about 300 miles below the land at sea level, and there is enough water to flood the entire earth, which happened in the first earth age.

The Tian Shan, Kunlun, Karakoram, and Pamirs, were all well over 12,000 feet, and many peaks over 20,000 feet. The Pe-Shan Mountains were less than 12,000 feet and by the end of the 150 days the water broke through and washed away a big part of the Pe-Shan Mountains. The Pe-Shan Mountains have been crumbling ever since the time of Noah's flood. Water or seawater was still in the Tarim Basin 2000 years ago, a reminder of Noah's flood. The Pe-Shan Mountains are east of the Tarim basin.

More Caucasoid mummies, ranging from 2000 BC to 1000 BC were found scattered around the Tarim Basin. Just like the Mummies before the flood, they were tall, but their height had diminished down to 6.6', and less, The Mummies still had blond, brown, and red hair, long faces, round eyes, and thick beards. Abraham was born around 2000 BC; **evidently, some of the children from Noah had gone back to this area to mine salt,** which was very valuable at the time. Many people were surprised that white people once lived in this area, but I was very happy because it gave me more support for my belief that the flood did happen here.

*Read the book, (The Mummies of Urumchi) by Elizabeth Wayland Barber*

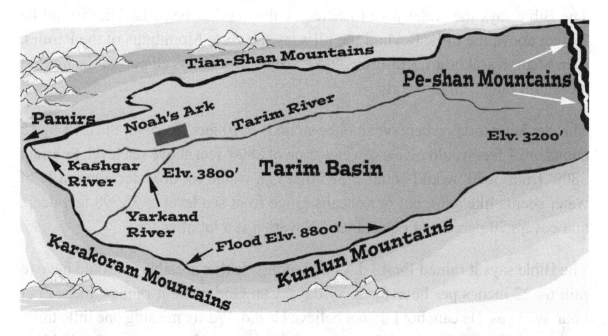

The map shows the journey of Adam and Eve traveling from the high Pamirs to the desert lowlands of the Tarim Basin. From Adam to the flood was 1657 years. As you can see, the Tarim Basin has the perfect geography for a very large flood. From a hundred thousand to millions of people perished during the first few days of the flood. Every living thing inside the blue line on the map above would have drowned except for the people and animals on the ark.

Go on Google earth and look at the Tarim Basin and you can see this is a perfect place for a flood. The Mountains surrounding the desert creating a giant bowl to contain the high water.

Before we go to chapter eight, there is one more very important verse we need to cover and that is chapter seven verse 24.

*24 And the waters prevailed upon the earth an hundred and fifty days.*

The flood of Noah lasted 150 days, which equals a 5-month period. Our next flood will also be 5 months long, and we are very close to this flood today. Satan (anti-Christ) will stand on Mount Zion claiming to be God, and he will deceive the whole world. The Elect and the 144,000 will overcome this flood of lies from the evil one. There are only 7000 very Elect and thousands to millions of the Elect. The Elect are scattered all over the world, but the biggest majority of them I believe are in the United States of America.

## *The next flood, the third flood (the flood yet to come)*

### *Revelation 12:15-16*

*15 And the serpent cast out of his mouth water as a flood after the woman, that he might cause her to be carried away of the flood.*

*Remember God works in threes*

*This is the third flood*

*The first flood was worldwide, the second was Noah's flood. And the third and last is Satan's flood, "his flood of lies"*

*Satan is responsible for all three floods*

*16 And the earth helped the woman, and the earth opened her mouth, and swallowed up **the flood which the dragon cast out of his mouth.***

*Satan will seduce more people than he did during the first Earth age (hard to believe)*

*Unfortunately, good Christians will follow his lies*

*Sheep being led to slaughter by a wolf in sheep's clothing*

*Do not be a dumb sheep*

### Mark 13:20

[20] *And except that the Lord had shortened those days, no flesh should be saved: but for the elect's sake, whom he hath chosen, he hath shortened the days.*

*Yeshua (Jesus) Shortened the days of Anti-Christ from a three-and-a-half-year period to five months*

*If the period had not been shortened, even the Elect would not be saved*

### Revelation 12:12

[12] *Therefore rejoice, ye heavens, and ye that dwell in them. Woe to the inhabiters of the earth and of the sea! for the devil is come down unto you, having great wrath, because he knoweth that he hath but a short time.*

*Satan as Anti-Christ only has five months to beguile Gods children*

*Can he do it in time?*

*He certainly can, the people are already in bed with him today*

*Satan wars with Michael and his angels for two and a half months, and is cast down to the earth to deceive flesh man for five months, and this is Satan's last flood.*

### Revelation 9:2-4

[2] *And he opened the **bottomless pit**; and there arose a smoke out of the pit, as the smoke of a great furnace; and the sun and the air were darkened by reason of the smoke of the pit.*

*The bottomless pit always refers to Satan*

*3 And there came out of the smoke **locusts upon the earth**: and unto them was given power, as the **scorpions of the earth have power**.*

*Satan will send out his fallen angels to seduce humankind*

*4 And it was commanded them that they should not hurt the grass of the earth, neither any green thing, neither any tree; but only those men which have not the seal of God in their foreheads.*

## Revelation 9:5

*5 And to them it was given that they should not kill them, but that they should be tormented five months: and their torment was as the torment of a scorpion, when he striketh a man.*

*You do not want to be tempted by the fallen angels*

## Revelation 9:10

*10 And they had tails like unto scorpions, and there were stings in their tails: and their power was to hurt men five months.*

*Satan and his fallen angles will tempt and steal their souls*

*Without out God's truth, you will be deceived*

*You should know the three Earth ages*

*You should understand Genesis*

*know who the Kenites are*

*You should know who the Israelites are*

*You should know who comes first Satan or Jesus*

*You should know who comes riding on the first white horse*

*11 And they had a king over them, which is **the angel of the bottomless pit,** whose name in the Hebrew tongue is Abaddon, but in the **Greek tongue hath his name Apollyon.***

*Satan the king of the bottomless pit*

*Abaddon = Angel of ruin, destruction, and minister of death (Satan)*

*Apollyon = Destroyer, and angel of the bottomless pit (Satan)*

## Matthew 24:36-38

[36] *But of that day and hour knoweth no man, no, not the angels of heaven, but my Father only.*

[37] *But as the days of Noah were, so shall also the coming of the Son of man be.*

*Look back at Noah's flood, (the flood of water,) Satan and his Angels deceive Adams offspring, and the Adamic people die and go back to heaven in spirit.*

*Looking at the very near future, the third flood, Satan and his angels deceive the whole world. The coming of the son of man Christ Jesus has come to marry his bride, but he finds they have already married Satan. All human flesh is changed to spirit, on the arrival of the Son of man.*

[38] *For as in the days that were before the flood they were eating and drinking, marrying and giving in marriage, until the day that Noe entered into the ark,*

*People living each day of their lives never considering or reading God's plan, not knowing the third flood is upon us*

## Back to Noah's flood

*Noah's flood was five months*

*Satan's flood will be five months*

*Wake up people*

## Genesis 8:1-22

*8 And God remembered Noah, and every living thing, and all the cattle that was with him in the ark: and God made a wind to pass over the earth, and the waters assuaged*

*The waters began to subside, no longer rising*

*² The fountains also of the deep and the windows of heaven were stopped, and the rain from heaven was restrained;*

*³ And the waters returned from off the earth continually: and after the end of the hundred and fifty days, the waters were abated.*

*The flood is over, and the water is in retreat*

*⁴ And the ark rested in the seventh month, on the seventeenth day of the month, upon the mountains of Ararat.*

*In the seventh month the ark rested, "The ark remained still upon the waters" (The Sabbath day)*

*The seventeenth day, "Noah's family will produce fruit" "A day of victory"*

*Floating still over the mountains or hills*

*Mountains could mean people of Ararat*

*Ararat does not mean the highest mountain, (the meaning is not known)*

*⁵ And the waters decreased continually until the tenth month: in the tenth month, on the first day of the month, were the tops of the mountains seen*

*Tenth Month = Responsibility, Judgement, or reward "Ten Patriarchs before the flood" "Ten Commandments, and Ten Plagues"*

*⁶ And it came to pass at the end of forty days, that Noah opened the window of the ark which he had made:*

*Forty Days = Probation, and testing*

*⁷ And he sent forth a raven, which went forth to and fro, until the waters were dried up from off the earth.*

*⁸ Also he sent forth a dove from him, to see if the waters were abated from off the face of the ground;*

*⁹ But the dove found no rest for the sole of her foot, and she returned unto him into the ark, for the waters were on the face of the whole earth: then he put forth his hand, and took her, and pulled her in unto him into the ark.*

*¹⁰ And he stayed yet other seven days; and again he sent forth the dove out of the ark;*

*¹¹ And the dove came in to him in the evening; and, lo, in her mouth was **an olive leaf pluckt off**: so Noah knew that the waters were abated from off the earth.*

*A newly sprouted olive leaf*

*This proves the whole earth was not flooded*

*¹² And he stayed yet other seven days; and sent forth the dove; which returned not again unto him any more.*

*¹³ And it came to pass in the six hundredth and first year, in the first month, the first day of the month, the waters were dried up from off the earth: and Noah removed the covering of the ark, and looked, and, behold, the face of the ground was dry.*

*¹⁴ And in the second month, on the seven and twentieth day of the month, was the earth dried.*

*¹⁵ And God spake unto Noah, saying,*

*¹⁶ Go forth of the ark, thou, and thy wife, and thy sons, and thy sons' wives with thee.*

*¹⁷ Bring forth with thee every living thing that is with thee, of all flesh, both of fowl, and of cattle, and of every creeping thing that creepeth upon the earth; that they may breed abundantly in the earth, and be fruitful, and multiply upon the earth.*

*¹⁸ And Noah went forth, and his sons, and his wife, and his sons' wives with him:*

*¹⁹ Every beast, every creeping thing, and every fowl, and whatsoever creepeth upon the earth, after their kinds, went forth out of the ark.*

*20 And Noah builded an altar unto the L*ORD*; and took of every clean beast, and of every clean fowl, and offered burnt offerings on the altar.*

*Clean Beast and Clean Fowl (No scavengers)*

*21 And the L*ORD *smelled a sweet savour; and the L*ORD *said in his heart, I will not again curse the ground any more for man's sake; for the imagination of man's heart is evil from his youth; neither will I again smite any more everything living, as I have done.*

*22 While the earth remaineth, seedtime and harvest, and **cold and heat, and summer and winter, and day and night shall not cease.***

*Do you believe in Al Gore's big lie of global warming?*

*Hot summers, cold winters, planting seed in the spring, and Time
for harvest in the fall "God promises it will not cease"*

*The weather runs in cycles, during the Viking days it was warmer, and Greenland
was green! Beautiful green pastures where they raised their sheep*

*After the Vikings, we had the little ice age, and it lasted up until 1850AD*

*When George Washington crossed the Delaware, it was full of ice, (usually not today)*

*During the time of Joseph in Egypt, there was seven years of rain, and seven
years of drought, "We call this weather cycles not global warming"*

*Al gore invented the internet, just as if he invented global warming (the one world system)*

*Through the lies of global warming "the sons of Cain" will control us*

*Two big filthy lies (And by the way he became filthy rich over them lies)*

Noah's Ark did not land on top of the highest mountain. Some people today believe the ark landed on Mount Ararat in Turkey. Mount Ararat is the highest Mountain in Turkey and located near the Euphrates River head. It was given the name for obvious reasons. If Noah had landed on top of Mount Ararat, how in the world would he get all those animals down from this very high rugged Mountain? Nowhere does the bible say that Noah's ark landed on top of a Mountain. It rained for forty days and nights. After five months, the waters started receding. The ark is slowly floating down to the ground for seven months, Noah opens the door, and he sees that the ground is dry. If this very large wooden boat had landed on top of a Mountain, with a steep slope, the boat would have broken up in many pieces. I believe God gave them a flat safe place to land, probably not, far from where they began.

### *Genesis 9:1-29*

*9 And God blessed Noah and his sons, and said unto them, Be fruitful, and multiply, and replenish the earth.*

> *Remember only the eighth day mankind was destroyed, the Egyptians, Babylonians, Mongolians, African's, and American Indians are still much alive, and doing well*

*² And the fear of you and the dread of you shall be upon every beast of the earth, and upon every fowl of the air, upon all that moveth upon the earth, and upon all the fishes of the sea; into your hand are they delivered.*

*³ Every moving thing that liveth shall be meat for you; even as the green herb have I given you all things.*

*⁴ But flesh with the life thereof, which is the blood thereof, shall ye not eat.*

*⁵ And surely your blood of your lives will I require; at the hand of every beast will I require it, and at the hand of man; at the hand of every man's brother will I require the life of man.*

*⁶ Whoso sheddeth man's blood, by man shall his blood be shed: for in the image of God made he man.*

*⁷ And you, be ye fruitful, and multiply; bring forth abundantly in the earth, and multiply therein.*

*⁸ And God spake unto Noah, and to his sons with him, saying,*

*⁹ And I, behold, I establish my covenant with you, and with your seed after you;*

> *Covenant = alliance, pledge, and Promise*

*[10] And with every living creature that is with you, of the fowl, of the cattle, and of every beast of the earth with you; from all that go out of the ark, to every beast of the earth.*

*[11] And I will establish my covenant with you, neither shall all flesh be cut off any more by the waters of a flood; neither shall there any more be a flood to destroy the earth.*

*God promises there will never be another flood by water ever again*

*Next, the flood of lies from Satan's evil tongue*

*[12] And God said, This is the token of the covenant which I make between me and you and every living creature that is with you, for perpetual generations:*

*[13] I do set my bow in the cloud, and it shall be for a token of a covenant between me and the earth.*

*[14] And it shall come to pass, when I bring a cloud over the earth, that the bow shall be seen in the cloud:*

*[15] And I will remember my covenant, which is between me and you and every living creature of all flesh; and the waters shall no more become a flood to destroy all flesh.*

*[16] And the bow shall be in the cloud; and I will look upon it, that I may remember the everlasting covenant between God and every living creature of all flesh that is upon the earth.*

*[17] And God said unto Noah, This is the token of the covenant, which I have established between me and all flesh that is upon the earth.*

*[18] And the sons of Noah, that went forth of the ark, were Shem, and Ham, and Japheth: and Ham is the father of Canaan.*

*Very important Ham is the father of Canaan*

Noah is 601 years old, and he has 349 years left to replenish and relocate his family. The ark has rested in the Tarim basin, I believe west of the Tarim River head. Noah and his family will start the long journey to Mesopotamia along with the domesticated animals. Noah will travel back through the high Pamir's and down the Oxus/Amu Darya River to the city of Balkh, where Adam and Eve were created, and lived for a time. Noah may have never been in this city before, and may not have known the location of the Garden of Eden. Anyway, Noah will pass by, where Adam and Eve committed their first sin.

The year the ark landed was 2347 BC, and Cain has been dead for 767 years. Why do I mention Cain, Noah is being led by God to the land where Cain has ruled, and now his sons are ruling? Why would God lead Noah to these evil men and women of the seed of Cain, and the seed of Satan? It is God's plan!

The journey is around 2000 miles from Kashgar to Babylon, a journey that probably took at least one year or more to travel. He followed an established ancient route older than Adam and Eve. Crossing the River into Mesopotamia, the River was named by Cain, (The Hiddekel,) and is called the (Tigris River) today. The Hiddekel is the third River mentioned in Genesis feeding the Garden of Eden.

As powerful and mighty as Cain's dynasty was, it will end, somewhere around 2300BC to 2200BC. Cain's dynasty lasted around 1600 years and the fall began when Noah and his family moved in. Noah and his family moved into Mesopotamia around 2340BC, and Noah lived for another 342 years the year 1998BC.

Shortly after Noah's people appeared, a new King Conquered Babylon, and his name was Samu-abi, which means, "Shem is my father", (Shem's son). A new Dynasty is founded, and given the name of Hammurabi, by sons of Noah. This dynasty will rule starting with Seth son (Samu-abi) and ending with Abraham. Through the line of Shem, our Savior Jesus Christ will come, and the Israelites, Ishmaelites, Edomites, and all the kings of Europe. The Ishmaelites are the Arabs, and the Edomites are the Slavic people of Russia, and all States that speak the Slavic tongue.

## Noah and his sons are living in Mesopotamia

[19] *These are the three sons of Noah: and of them was the whole earth overspread.*

*²⁰ And Noah began to be an husbandman, and he planted a vineyard:*

*²¹ And he drank of the wine, and was drunken; and he was uncovered within his tent.*

*Noah is passed out not knowing of a great sin his son's son had committed*

*²² And Ham, the father of Canaan, saw the nakedness of his father, and told his two brethren without.*

## What is this sin? Why is Canaan Cursed?

## How can seeing your father naked bring on so much shame to your family?

### *Leviticus 20:11*

*And the man that lieth with his father's wife hath uncovered his father's nakedness: both of them shall surely be put to death; their blood shall be upon them.*

I believe Canaan, not Ham, slept with his grandmother, (Noah's wife.) While Noah was drunk, and a sleep, Canaan took advantage of that, he took her (maybe by force) and had sex with her. This act would bring shame to the family

Ham saw the very act of what his forth son had done to his mother. Then Ham ran and told his brothers. Why would he tell his brothers if he had just committed this awful sin?

*²³ And Shem and Japheth took a garment, laid it upon both their shoulders, went backward, and covered the nakedness of their father; and their faces were backward, and they saw not their father's nakedness.*

*They were not involved in this terrible act*

*²⁴ And Noah awoke from his wine, and knew what his younger son had done unto him.*

*Ham is the middle son, not the younger son*

*Back then, there was no word for grandfather, or grandson, the*
*younger son was his grandson Canaan, Ham's youngest son*

²⁵ *And he said, Cursed be Canaan; a servant of servants shall he be unto his brethren.*

*Why did Noah curse Canaan the youngest son of Ham?*

*I know it is taught that Ham was the one that laid with his mother*

*Noah cursed Ham's youngest grandson Canaan for the great sin he committed*

²⁶ *And he said, Blessed be the* LORD *God of Shem; and Canaan shall be his servant.*

*Abraham will come through the line of Shem "blessed of God"*

*The descendants of Canaan will have far less blessings in their lives than Shem and Japheth*

²⁷ **God shall enlarge Japheth**, *and he shall dwell in the tents of Shem; and Canaan shall be his servant.*

*Japheth offspring will fill the coastline of the Mediterranean from*
*Greece to Spain, and the Isles of Avalon "Great Britain"*

²⁸ *And Noah lived after the flood three hundred and fifty years.*

²⁹ *And all the days of Noah were nine hundred and fifty years: and he died.*

One thing I would like to add to Noah's flood. It is possible the floodwaters were only 15 cubits above the tallest men. The hills or mountains may symbolize Noah's people, the giants, and sixth day man living among them. The rain continued for forty days and forty nights, and the water covered the mountains (people) fifteen cubits upward. Mountains could mean the people living in the Tarim Basin.

Mountains can refer to people or Nations of people

**Judges 9:36**

And when Gaal saw the people, he said to Zebul, Behold, there come people down from the top of the mountains. And Zebul said unto him, Thou seest the shadow of the mountains as if they were men.

**Micah 6:2**

Hear ye, o mountains, the LORD's controversy, and ye strong foundations of the earth: for the LORD hath a controversy with his people, and he will plead with Israel.

**Habakkuk 3:10**

The mountains saw thee, and they trembled: the overflowing of the water passed by: the deep uttered his voice, and lifted up his hands on high.

**Malachi 1:3**

And I hated Esau, and laid his mountains and his heritage waste for the dragons of the wilderness.

*Matthew 17:20*

*And Jesus said unto them, Because of your unbelief: for verily I say unto you, If ye have faith as a grain of mustard seed, ye shall say unto this mountain, Remove hence to yonder place; and it shall remove; and nothing shall be impossible unto you.*

*The mountain symbolizes the Nations*

*The people of Noah's flood, a great mountain of people*

It is far easier to believe the flood waters were only around 33 feet deep instead of one-mile deep. It would only take ten inches of rain a day or less for forty days to destroy the people of Noah's earth. One mile of water would take much longer to reside, then one year. Either way is possible through God.

*Genesis 10*

*10 Now these are the generations of the sons of Noah, Shem, Ham, and Japheth: and unto them were sons born after the flood.*

*²The sons of Japheth; Gomer, and Magog, and Madai, and Javan, and Tubal, and Meshech, and Tiras.*

*Javan became the Ionians, and then the Greeks*

Ptolemy on his map named Great Britain, Javan, which means the sons of Japheth, and may have been the first Adamic people to settle England

*³And the sons of Gomer; Ashkenaz, and Riphath, and Togarmah.*

*90 percent of the Jews today are Ashkenazi Jews*

*⁴And the sons of Javan; Elishah, and Tarshish, Kittim, and Dodanim.*

*Tarshish with his ships colonized Spain and the British Isles*

*Jonah took a ship to Tarshish, the first name given to Spain*

*They were great colonizers and merchants*

*These great explorers may have made it all the way to North America to mine copper during the Bronze Age*

*Tin is mined from Southern England by the offspring of Japheth and before Japheth*

*There are ancient copper mines in Lake Superior dating back to 2470BC possibly mined by the ancient Minoan or Canaanite people*

*The carbon date of 2470BC was before the Canaanites, but I believe Cain or his descendants discovered the copper earlier then this date, and mined it up until the fall of Cain's dynasty approximately 2300BC*

*Tarshish took over the mining of copper in Michigan, the only place in the world that could supply enough copper to last through the Bronze Age during this period*

*Kittim founded Cyprus*

*⁵By these were the isles of the Gentiles divided in their lands; every one after his tongue, after their families, in their nations.*

*From Greece to Spain and Spain to the British Isles, the great colonizers of Tarshish spread the seed of Japheth*

*⁶ And the sons of Ham; Cush, and Mizraim, and Phut, and Canaan.*

*Cush or Kush is an ancient word that means black*

*Ham means heat not black, yet today people believe hams offspring became the black race, what a bunch of bull (the black race predated Adam by at least 6000 years)*

*The sons of Ham are white not black, and they settled in North Africa and Europe*

*Canaan's offspring settled the coastline of Europe, along the Mediterranean Sea, and Canaan*

*⁷ And the sons of Cush; Seba, and Havilah, and Sabtah, and Raamah, and Sabtechah: and the sons of Raamah; Sheba, and Dedan.*

*⁸ And Cush begat Nimrod: he began to be a mighty one in the earth.*

*Nimrod was an Alexander of his day*

*⁹ He was a mighty hunter before the LORD: wherefore it is said, Even as Nimrod the mighty hunter before the LORD.*

*¹⁰ And the beginning of his kingdom was Babel, and Erech, and Accad, and Calneh, in the land of Shinar.*

*¹¹ Out of that land went forth Asshur, and builded Nineveh, and the city Rehoboth, and Calah,*

*Asshur becomes Assyria*

*¹² And Resen between Nineveh and Calah: the same is a great city.*

*¹³ And **Mizraim** begat Ludim, and Anamim, and Lehabim, and Naphtuhim,*

*Mizraim = Egypt*

Sixth day whites and Blacks lived in Egypt thousands of years before Mizraim

*¹⁴ And Pathrusim, and Casluhim, (out of whom came Philistim,) and Caphtorim.*

*¹⁵ And Canaan begat **Sidon** his first born, and **Heth,***

*Sidon becomes the ancient Phoenician city north of Tyre*
*Heth becomes the progenitor of the Hittites in the land of Canaan, and Turkey*

¹⁶ *And the **Jebusite,** and the Amorite, and the Girgasite,*

*Jebus third son of Canaan, founder of Jebus, and is the early name for Jerusalem*

¹⁷ *And the Hivite, and the Arkite, and the Sinite,*

¹⁸ *And the Arvadite, and the Zemarite, and the Hamathite: and afterward were the families of the Canaanites spread abroad.*

¹⁹ *And the border of the Canaanites was from Sidon, as thou comest to Gerar, unto Gaza; as thou goest, unto Sodom, and Gomorrah, and Admah, and Zeboim, even unto Lasha.*

²⁰ *These are the sons of Ham, after their families, after their tongues, in their countries, and in their nations.*

*Hams offspring may have settled southern Ireland and mixed with the sons of Japheth*

*Ham can also mean black, hence the black Irish*

²¹ *Unto **Shem** also, the father of all the children of Eber, the brother of Japheth the elder, even to him were children born.*

*Through Shem, the Patriarchs, the Israelites, the kings, and the*
*King of Kings (Jesus Christ) would come from his seedline*

Verses 22-32 skipped

**Genesis 11:1-9**

*11 And the whole earth was of one language, and of one speech.*

² *And it came to pass, as they **journeyed from the east**, that they found a plain in the land of **Shinar**; and they dwelt there.*

*Noah and his family came from the East (the Tarim Basin)*

*Shinar = Babylon/Mesopotamia*

*Sixth day blacks and whites were in this land before Noah and Cain*

*³ And they said one to another, Go to, let us make brick, and burn them thoroughly. And they had brick for stone, and slime had they for morter.*

*⁴ And they said, Go to, let us build us a city and a tower, whose top may reach unto heaven; and let us make us a name, lest we be scattered abroad upon the face of the whole earth.*

*The people thought they could build a tower to heaven without God (big mistake)*

*⁵ And the LORD came down to see the city and the tower, which the children of men builded.*

*⁶ And the LORD said, Behold, the people is one, and they have all one language; and this they begin to do: and now nothing will be restrained from them, which they have imagined to do.*

*⁷ Go to, let us go down, and there confound their language, that they may not understand one another's speech.*

*⁸ So the LORD scattered them abroad from thence upon the face of all the earth: and they left off to build the city.*

*Communication became babel in the land of Babylon,*
*and the tower to heaven was not finished*

*⁹ Therefore is the name of it called Babel; because the LORD did there confound the language of all the earth: and from thence did the LORD scatter them abroad upon the face of all the earth.*

Another addition to add, proving the flood occurred in the Tarim basin, from the sacred book of Shu –King. Shu-King wrote of a Chinese Noah, his name was Fu-hi, and he was born of a rainbow. He lived during the time of the Chinese Deluge, and had saved seven kinds of animals. The date of the Chinese Deluge was from 2356 to 2254 BC, and Noah's flood was 2348 BC to 2347. The beginning dates are eight years apart, which is very close to each other, considering it was 4364 years ago. The Caucazoid Mummies that were found near the Tarim River head, two hundred years earlier than the flood, were in the same area that I believe Noah and the offspring of Adam were living at before the time of the flood. Therefore the nations around the world all have a flood story. Noah took the story to the west, and China spread it across the east.

Read the rest of Genesis on your own, use a Strong Concordance to look up the words for better understanding. Better yet Sign up for a monthly letter with Shepherds Chapel and you can order tapes or CD's on any book or subject the Chapel has. The Shepherds Chapel phone number is 800-643-4645.

# Chapter 10

## *Who are the Israelites?*

Today most Scholars, group all the twelve tribes of Israel into one group, (the Jews). Nothing can be farther from the truth, there are twelve distinct tribes, and Judah is only one of the twelve. The name Jew was not used among the tribe of Judah, the people who lived in Judea called themselves Judeans not Jews. The name Jew was not used until after Jesus death. Yes, I know Jew is used in the bible, if you look up Jew, you will find it is Judean in Hebrew. If you were Egyptian or Hittite living in Judea, you were called a Judean. Not all people living in Judea are of the tribe of Judah or Benjamin.

Why do we clump all 12 tribes of Israel together and call them the Jews? At the time of Solomon's death in 970 BC, the ten tribes of Israel separated from the tribe of Judah along with the very small tribe of Benjamin. The word Jew/Judean is first mentioned in II Kings 16:6, around 616 BC, one hundred years after the ten tribes of Israel were taken captive into Assyria.

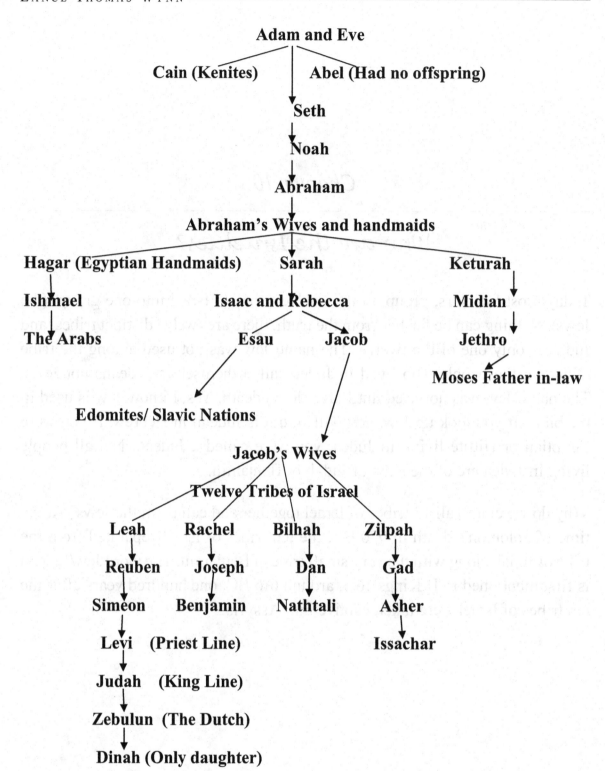

**Adam and Eve**

**Cain (Kenites)**     **Abel (Had no offspring)**

**Seth**

**Noah**

**Abraham**

**Abraham's Wives and handmaids**

**Hagar (Egyptian Handmaids)**     **Sarah**     **Keturah**

**Ishmael**     **Isaac and Rebecca**     **Midian**

**The Arabs**     **Esau**     **Jacob**     **Jethro**

**Moses Father in-law**

**Edomites/ Slavic Nations**

**Jacob's Wives**

**Twelve Tribes of Israel**

**Leah**     **Rachel**     **Bilhah**     **Zilpah**

**Reuben**     **Joseph**     **Dan**     **Gad**

**Simeon**     **Benjamin**     **Nathtali**     **Asher**

**Levi     (Priest Line)**     **Issachar**

**Judah     (King Line)**

**Zebulun  (The Dutch)**

**Dinah (Only daughter)**

# Do the ten tribes of Israel exist today?
# If so, who are they, and where are they?

Not all Israelites new Moses, and lived under the laws that God had given him. In fact, the first Israelites to enter Europe never lived in Israel, except for the 12 patriarchs. You will not find it in the Bible, but it is in history. Your Scholars will deny it, that is a given.

The Kings of Judah are established in Europe

Judah has two sons Zarah and Pharez

The Zarah line established in Europe

Pharez line established in Jerusalem

The Zarah and Pharez royal king lines join in Europe

The first Israelites to enter Europe were the sons of Judah. Judah was the fourth son of Leah, and all the Kings of Israel and Europe is from his line, (the Royal line of Judah.) Through his daughter in-law Tamar, twins are born, Pharez and Zarah. Through the line of Pharez, David is born, and God makes him the first king of Israel from the line of Judah. The sons of Zarah will become the kings of Europe/Asia minor from Turkey to Greece, and to Great Britain. Eventually the two royal lines, Zarah and Pharez will come together, and join in Europe.

Tamar had twins, Pharez came out first then Zarah, both will produce kings and queens. The offspring of Pharez will become the largest tribe of Israel, and the great King David will be the first king of Israel through the tribe of Judah. Saul was the first king from the tribe of Benjamin, not Gods choice, but the people's choice. David is the first king of Judah, the patriarch of the royal line of Judah, and ruling over all twelve tribes of Israel. After King Solomon, the royal king line of David will only rule over the tribe of Judah and Benjamin. Judah and Benjamin are now separate from the ten tribes of Israel.

Zarah's line will go into Europe, and Kings and Queens will rule over the Israelites and all other people. The tribe of Judah is in Europe before Moses is born, and the Pharez line will end up in Judea lead there by Moses. Only a small percentage of the tribe of Judah are considered Royal.

The royal king lines of Zarah in Europe and the Royal King line of Pharez in Judea will eventually join in Europe. Zedekiah was the last king in Judea, but through the mysteries of God king David's line will continue in Europe. The royal king line has not ceased until this day in Europe, and a few of the USA presidents have or had royal blood in them. Many people here in America do have a little bit of royal blood in them, but would not come close to being considered a King or Queen.

Mary and Joseph had five children after the birth of Jesus. The offspring of Mary and Joseph will become kings in Europe with two bloodlines, the royal blood of Judah, and the Priest line of Levi. Jesus is the King of Kings, and is the high Priest in the order of Melchizedek, and the offspring of Mary and Joseph carry this bloodline on to this day. Many Kings and Queens of Europe carried this bloodline.

The sons of Mary and Joseph moved south out of Germany and the Netherlands into northern Gaul. They ruled over the Salian Franks through Childeric I in 457AD. Clovis I united the Gauls and introduced Christianity to the people. The Merovingian king line ruled over the Franks for 300 years and was deposed by Pope Zachary in 752AD. The bloodline carried on to Great Britain, through Sir Lance a lot and many others.

Do not believe the phony made up lies that Jesus married Mary of Magdalene and the Merovingian's are their offspring. The Gnostic sects started this lie after Jesus death, and Criminals in 1960 reintroduced the lie into the media to make money. The Kenites will deceive us in believing Christ did not die on the cross, and was married to Mary of Magdalene and had children. This is an evil lie.

The children of Mary and Joseph were given the name Desposyni to identify them. Sir Lance a lot was a Desposyni, and he left France to fight with King Arthur. Another lie written hundreds of years later said Sir Lance had an affair with King Arthur's wife; this is a fabricated lie to make the Arthur story more popular and to bring in money. Desposyni is a name possibly coming from despots meaning master. The Desposyni's were most revered, and the Catholic

Church saw them as a threat to their new religion, and the Roman Catholic Church tried to destroy them.

## The Sons of Zarah, Zimri, Ethan, Heman, Calcol, and Darya

The sons of Zarah are special men with a special mission from God, to set up the royal line of Judah in Europe. They are to prepare for the migration of the Israelites before the time of Moses, and after. Before the Israelites entered Europe, the sons of Japheth had settled along the coastline of the Mediterranean Sea. They most likely mixed with the indigenous people. The indigenous people of that time were the sixth day white race; they mostly hunted and gathered for their living. For eight thousand years, they had no enemy until the Japheth offspring settled along the coastlines of Europe.

The Canaanites entered Europe under the name Phoenicians, and journeyed to Europe by way of the ships of Tarshish. They founded Venice, Marseilles, and Carthage, and they became the great Latin nations of the Mediterranean Sea. The Canaanites, and Hamites, also settled southern Ireland. Ham's son Cush, which means black, may be the reason why some Irish are called the black Irish. Another theory considered is when the Irish migrated to America, some had dark hair, tanned darker in the sun, and were short and stout, not as the tall red haired and freckled faced Irish.

Today people living in Tunisia Africa are related to the Latin people of Italy and France. Today Italy, France, Greece, Spain, Portugal, Ireland and Northern Africa have a mixture of Canaanites, Japhethites, and Israelites, along with Arabs, Egyptians, and Blacks. We may never know exactly who we are, but we do know we are all children of God.

Well then, why is it important to know who the Israelites are? The Israelites are a very important people, in the first earth age they fought hard against Lucifer, and earned their place as a chosen people of God. Are the Chosen people of God pure and without sin? God says we are all as filthy rags. Yes, in the first earth age, they were great warriors of God, but in the flesh, they are great sinners.

Knowing who the Israelites are gives us proof and greater faith, that God is the God of the Bible. God has blessed the Israelites, and he gathered them together from many countries. The Israelites, and all nations on earth are blessed because of Gods promise to Abraham. The Israelites are a compassionate and giving people, but they have faults like everyone else.

God works in mysterious ways, and if you seek his truth, God will bless you with understanding through the Holy Spirit. The more you learn the greater your faith and love of your Father becomes.

We must know and understand who the Israelites are because they are the subjects of the bible. Understanding the flight of the Israelites will give us a better understanding of the word of God.

# The Israelites

## The Royal king lines of Judah

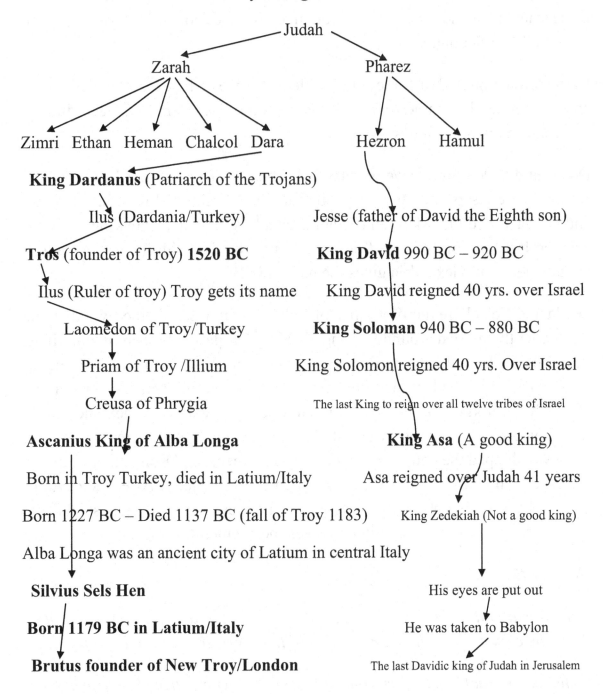

Colcol the fourth son, and Dara the fifth son, left Egypt, and settled in Europe/ Asia Minor. The other three sons are not mentioned in history, but you can bet they had a strong impact wherever they settled. Colcol the founder of Athens Greece, becomes king of Athens, the first king of the royal line of Judah in

Europe. Colcol established trade settlements along the Mediterranean Sea, and one he named Zarah-gassa, which became Saragossa meaning "the stronghold of Zarah." Calcol's descendants settled in Spain, and then on to Iberne, and today is the state of Ireland. The Iberians colonized Ireland around 1700 BC, and then expanded into Scotland.

Dara/Darda migrated to Turkey, and settled what we call the Dardanelles, which commemorates his name today. Darda became king Dardanus according to "Josephus a historian and writer".

Darda and Colcol may have journeyed by boat to Turkey from Egypt, which would be the fastest way to journey by far. Colcol migrated west into Greece, and Darda stayed in Turkey, and established a long line of Trojan kings. Aeneas was the last king of Troy; he fled to Italy in 1183 BC with his son Ascanius. (Eratosthenes of Alexandria gives the date 1183 BC.)

Darda and Colcol are the first kings of Judah through Zarah "the twin that had the scarlet thread tied around his finger". King Darda's unbroken line of kings, beginning in Troy, then on to Rome, Great Britain, Wales, and to our mother of Israel Queen Elizabeth, which I believe will be our last Queen. The Darda line of Judah never knew of the Ten Commandments, or entered Israel, and after a few generations forgot they were of the tribe of Judah, except for a very few. They worshipped the gods of Babylon, Egypt, Greece, and Rome, that Cain had invented using Adam, Eve, Abel, and Satan as his subjects. After the death of Christ, the king line of Judah would learn who they are. Their crest/shield/coat of arms showing the image of lions proves their remembrance.

### Genesis 49:9-10

[9] *Judah is a lion's whelp: from the prey, my son, thou art gone up: he stooped down, he couched as a lion, and as an old lion; who shall rouse him up?*

[10] *The sceptre shall not depart from Judah, nor a lawgiver from between his feet, until Shiloh come; and unto him shall the gathering of the people be.*

Enoch the man I believe invented writing and astrology lived during a very evil period. He overcame the wickedness of the fallen angels, and possibly was the architect and mathematician of the Great Pyramid. Enoch has something in common with the five sons of Zarah, Solomon, Daniel, and Shadrach, Meshach, Abed-Nego they all were very smart. God had a purpose for them, Enoch named the constellations and educated the people, Darda and his brothers instituted the ruling line of Judah in Europe. Daniel, Shadrach, Meshach, and Abednego were appointed high positions in the Babylon and Persian governments for their great knowledge. The book of Daniel was written for us today, so we can learn and watch during these latter days.

Brutus from the line of Darda, not knowing he is a chosen man of God fled from Italy and eventually landed on the Isles of Albion, now called Britain. He brought his kinsmen with him. His first landing was at Totnes the sound of Dart, in Devon on the four-shore street. The Totnes or Brutus stone is still there and commemorates his final journey. During the time of his arrival king Saul is ruling over the Israelites.

The royal line of Judah has been established on the cold white Island where all twelve tribes of Israel will come together. Many of the kings will become famous written by Prof. Waddell, Shakespeare, and many others. Caesar of Rome is also of the royal line of Judah, and he invades Britain in 55 BC.

Caesar was pleasantly surprised to see the people were civilized, and living under customs like the Gaul's. They were living under many kings, and Druids (the priest.) Savages or barbarians, they are not, which Caesar was instructed. They were agriculturist, and had much cattle, produced tin and iron, worked gold and silver, lavishly dressed, well governed, and had a strong belief system.

The people that were not civilized were people that lived in the interior. Caesar called them the interiors; they painted their skins blue, and were hunter-gatherers not tillers of the earth. These people were the last of the sixth day white man, and I believe their population diminished, and eventually adapted to the Agriculturist ways.

Caesar commented on their religion, which was taught by the Druids. They believed in immortality, when they died they would go to a better place. Caesar said because of their faith they did not fear death, and had great courage. Caesar said the teaching of immortality gave them incentive and a moral excellence.

Today our Morality for a more virtuous life is in decline because we are living in the last days, we are at the end of the sixth day. The Sons of Cain are working overtime to create a one world socialist system for the entrance of Anti-Christ/Satan.

### Druid doctrine
*In every person, there is a soul*
*In every soul, there is intelligence*
*In every intelligence, there is thought*
*In every thought, there is either good or evil*
*In every evil, there is death*
*In every good, there is life*
In every life, there is God

The Zarah royal line of Darda and Calcol's offspring ruled over Turkey, Greece, Italy, Spain, Ireland, and Britain, for a time, but new kings from Israel will conquer, rule, and divide creating new States over Europe. The Cimmerian kings from the ten lost tribes of Israel, and the Pharez line of King David will enter and rule over the states of Europe. The bible has King David's royal lineage ending with King Zedekiah. History proves it continues.

### *I Kings 9:5*
*Then I will establish the throne of thy kingdom upon Israel forever, as I promised to David thy father, saying,* **there shall not fail thee a man upon the throne of Israel.**

Well even if David's royal lineage has come to an end, I Kings 9:5 has come to pass. Queen Elizabeth has come from an unbroken line of Judah and Israelite Kings and Queens. She represents the mother of Israel, and I believe she will be the last. God so loved King David, do you really think he would leave his royal lineage out, do you think? I thank not!

The bible ends with Zedekiah's daughters in Egypt with the Prophet Jeremiah. No more is mentioned so here on out we can only rely on history. God works in mysterious ways! You do not have to believe it, you will not be sent to hell for it, but let it stir up your mind and lead you to the truth if willing.

Jeremiah was born 518 BC, and pre-ordained by God to be a prophet before he was born. He prophesied during the reign of King Zedekiah to the captivity of Judah into Babylon. Zedekiah was the last king of Judah, of the Pharez line, his reign as king began 488 BC and it lasted eleven years. Zedekiah did not follow the prophecy of Jeremiah, which was from God, but chose false prophets that he wanted to here. Nebuchadnezzar killed the sons of Zedekiah in front of him and then put his eyes out, bound him in chains and then marched him to Babylon. Zedekiah the King, delivered to Babylon died in prison a broken man. His sons were killed, but his daughters were saved. Will the line of King David continue? This looks like the end of the Davidic line, King Nebuchadnezzar destroyed the male heirs, and there is no male left to claim the throne. Can the Davidic line continue, well maybe, Zedekiah's daughters are alive, and are safe with Jeremiah? The daughters cannot become kings, but they say there is more than one way to skin a cat.

### Numbers 27:8-11

*8 And thou shalt speak unto the children of Israel, saying, If a man die, and have no son, then ye shall cause his inheritance to pass unto his daughter.*

*9 And if he have no daughter, then ye shall give his inheritance unto his brethren.*

*10 And if he have no brethren, then ye shall give his inheritance unto his father's brethren.*

*11 And if his father have no brethren, then ye shall give his inheritance unto his kinsman that is next to him of his family, and he shall possess it: and it shall be unto the children of Israel a statute of judgment, as the LORD commanded Moses.*

### Numbers 36:5-8

*5 And Moses commanded the children of Israel according to the word of the LORD, saying, The tribe of the sons of Joseph hath said well.*

*6 This is the thing which the LORD doth command concerning the daughters of Zelophehad, saying, Let them marry to whom they think best; only to the family of the tribe of their father shall they marry.*

*[7]So shall not the inheritance of the children of Israel remove from tribe to tribe: for every one of the children of Israel shall keep himself to the inheritance of the tribe of his fathers.*

*[8]And every daughter, that possesseth an inheritance in any tribe of the children of Israel, shall be wife unto one of the family of the tribe of her father, that the children of Israel may enjoy every man the inheritance of his fathers.*

Now we know it is possible to save the Davidic house, the daughters of Zedekiah will have to marry a King of the tribe of Judah, and her male seed will inherit and continue the royal line of David. God will always provide away, the mystery of God our heavenly Father.

The King of Babylon slew the nobles of Judah, and carried away many of the tribe of Judah and others. The poor were left behind, and were given lands to farm and to keep for the future. The captain of the guard removed the chains from Jeremiah and gave him freedom to go wherever he chose.

## Jeremiah travels to Europe with the daughters of Zedekiah

## King David's royal king line enters Europe

Jeremiah along with his Scribe and the king's daughters travel to Egypt to Tahpanhes "the Pharaoh's palace". God said to Jeremiah, if any of the tribe of Judah would go down to Egypt to escape captivity, they would be destroyed. They were destroyed, except for a few, and that is Jeremiah, Simon Baruch the scribe, and the daughters of Zedekiah the king of Judah. Jews living in Egypt before the captivity were probably not destroyed.

Jeremiah, his scribe, and daughters of the king of Judah are safe and living in the Pharaoh's palace. Their stay is temporary, they will move on to other lands not mentioned in the bible. In 1886, Sir Flinders Petrie found one of the mounds in the Pharaoh's palace, and the name of it was Kasr Bint el Jehuda, which means "the palace of the Jew's daughter".

From here on out we can only rely on history, and most of it coming from Ireland Chroniclers, and archeologist excavations. Monks compiled Songs, poems, stories, and legends from Ireland and Scotland after the death of Christ into manuscripts. Can we say with any certainty that every word written in the manuscripts are 100% correct, no, we cannot? Read all you can read about Jeremiah, and the daughters of Zedekiah, and come up with your own understanding or belief.

The two daughters of Zedekiah are not named in the bible, but do have names in history. The oldest daughter named from history Tea Tephi, and the youngest is named Scota. Jeremiah's name in history was Ollam Fodhla, Ollam meaning a man of wisdom, or revealer, and Fodhla or Foldha means a prophet or king. Simon Brug or Baruch was his personal scribe, and Ebed-Melech an Ethiopian was an attendant to the king's daughters.

Jeremiah and his party brought along with them King David's harp, and the stone of destiny to the Pharaoh's palace. The stone of destiny is the stone Jacob laid his head on, and this stone became the anointing stone.

### Genesis 28:11
*And he lighted upon a certain place, and tarried there all night, because the sun was set; and he took of the **stone**s of that place, and put them for his pillows, and lay down in that place to sleep.*

### Genesis 28:18
*And Jacob rose up early in the morning, and took the **stone** that he had put for his pillows, and set it up for a pillar, and poured oil upon the top of it.*

### Genesis 28:22
*And this **stone**, which I have set for a pillar, shall be God's house: and of all that thou shalt give me I will surely give the tenth unto thee.*

Jacob carried the stone down into Egypt during the seven-year drought. During the exodus of Egypt, Moses took the stone to Sinai, and from there its journey ended for a time in Jerusalem. All the kings of Judah were anointed on this stone of destiny. Jeremiah took the stone with him to Egypt and then Ireland. Then the stone is taken to Scotland where it had been mined, many years before Jacob was born. Many a king has been anointed on this stone.

I have seen the stone of destiny on display in the Edinburgh Castle, and the Chair in Westminster Abbey in London that held the Stone where many Kings were anointed. The kings from David in Israel/Judah, to Spain, then Ireland, on to Scotland, and last the kings of England, all were anointed sitting on this stone "Jacobs Pillar". Queen Elizabeth the last to be anointed on this Stone in 1952, I believe will be the last King or Queen to be anointed before the coming of Christ Jesus. From Adam to Queen Elizabeth there has been 152 generations, and Christ Jesus will be 153 the number of fish that were caught in the net by his disciples. If you want to learn more about the Stone of destiny, please read the book "Jacob's Pillar" by E. Raymond Capt.

It is said that Jeremiah also brought over the Ark of the Covenant, but this is not true, God had already brought it up to heaven where it is today. It is amazing how many so called powerful and Intelligent people have searched for the Arc of God's testament, when the answer has been in God's word all this time written in revelation Ch. 11:19.

### Revelation 11:19

*19 And the temple of God was opened in heaven, and there was seen in his temple **the ark of his testament**: and there were lightnings, and voices, and thunderings, and an earthquake, and great hail.*

#### The Ark is safe in Heaven

There are many variations of the story of Jeremiah, and the daughters of the last Davidic King of Judah. Priest and others passed down the stories in many tongues that were very hard to translate. Chroniclers compiled the stories passed down by word of mouth, at the best of their ability. I must admit I am confused with the differing stories, but I am certain the story is true. There are too many people and countries involved in the validity of this story, from kings to poets, and from Druids to lay people; this story is a mystery from God.

God has told Jeremiah, that the people of Judah that have fled from Judea to Egypt will die. The Pharaoh Hophra protected Jeremiah and the king's daughters, and gave them safety in the king's Palace. In Egypt, the daughters were called the (Pharaohs daughters,) which mean (king's daughters.) Many scholars believe Teah Tephi and Scota were daughters of Egyptian Kings, but this is not true.

Some people believe Akhenaten King of Egypt of the 18th dynasty, had a daughter named Scota, and she fled to Ireland, and married a king in Ireland. Even though Akhenaten's DNA matches 70 percent of the people of Great Britain today, the period of 1353 BC is far too early for this to be true. What they do not understand is, Pharaoh means king, and Scota is the daughter of King Zedekiah.

Since Jeremiah was a child, God has spoken to him, God had warned him of the danger if he stayed in Egypt. The Pharaoh Hophra of the 26th dynasty provided sanctuary for Jeremiah, his scribe, and the king's daughters. The other Jews that fled to Egypt from Judea will have what is coming to them.

### *Jeremiah 43:8-13*

*8 Then came the word of the LORD unto Jeremiah in Tahpanhes, saying,*

*9 Take great stones in thine hand, and hide them in the clay in the brickkiln, which is at the entry of Pharaoh's house in Tahpanhes, in the sight of the men of Judah;*

*10 And say unto them, Thus saith the LORD of hosts, the God of Israel; Behold, I will send and take Nebuchadrezzar the king of Babylon, my servant, and will set his throne upon these stones that I have hid; and he shall spread his royal pavilion over them.*

*11 And when he cometh, he shall smite the land of Egypt, and deliver such as are for death to death; and such as are for captivity to captivity; and such as are for the sword to the sword.*

*12 And I will kindle a fire in the houses of the gods of Egypt; and he shall burn them, and carry them away captives: and he shall array himself with the land of Egypt, as a shepherd putteth on his garment; and he shall go forth from thence in peace.*

*13 He shall break also the images of Bethshemesh, that is in the land of Egypt; and the houses of the gods of the Egyptians shall he burn with fire.*

### *Jeremiah 44:30*

[30] *Thus saith the LORD; Behold, I will give* **Pharaoh hophra king of Egypt** *into the hand of his enemies, and into the hand of them that seek his life; as I gave Zedekiah king of Judah into the hand of Nebuchadrezzar king of Babylon, his enemy, and that sought his life.*

Pharaoh Hophra backed King Zedekiah inciting him to fight on against Nebuchadrezzar. The Pharaoh Hophra was murdered in his boat in 566BC.

Jeremiah, Simon Brug, Tea Tephi, and Scota flee Egypt, travel to northern Spain, and today is known as the State of Portugal. Ebed-Melech the Ethiopian, is not mentioned on this journey, but may have traveled by another boat. From Spain/Portugal, they will travel to Ireland; settle on a special hill first named Teamhair, and later known as the hill of Tara, or Tara hill. Many buildings will be constructed on the hill of Tara, and the largest building of its time, the banqueting hall, will be built in Tara's honor.

Now the important part is, how did King David's royal line continue, and graft into the Zarah Judah line, and the Israelite line?

Scota during their short stay in Egypt married a Greek Chieftain named Gaythelos or Gathelus of the royal line of Judah. They traveled to an area of Spain called Lusitan, now called Portugal today. Gathelus built a city, and named it Brigance, in the small area of Brigantia. Gathelus was anointed king on the stone of destiny, which Jeremiah brought to Spain from Jerusalem. Scota becomes Queen, and her first male child will be the continuance of the Royal line of King David.

The Milesians in Ireland begin to call themselves Scota or Scoti, and then Scottish in honor of their Queen Scota. The Scottish name actually began in Ireland not Scotland. Fergus the great invaded Scotland around 500 AD. He was the first Scottish king in Scotland, and was inaugurated on the stone of destiny brought over from Ireland. Scottish kings will be crowned on this stone for many centuries.

The Davidic Royal line is carried on through the sons of Scota intermarried with kings of Zarah, and Pharez, and all over Europe and beyond. Our Queen

Elizabeth has the blood of the great king David through Queen Scota. Scota married the right man to give her a son that would carry on the Davidic line.

Queen Scota was buried in a valley south of Tralee town in Kerry Ireland. The area is known as Foley's Glen, and large circles of stones mark her gravesite today.

Jeremiah and the oldest daughter of King Zedekiah Tea /Teah/Tamar/Tephi left Spain with Jeremiah, and landed in Ulster the northern portion of Ireland in the year 580 BC. Princess Tamar /Tephi was a beautiful woman as the folk lore, songs, poems, and Irish traditions tell us. She made an unbelievable impact on Ireland and Great Britain. When they arrived in Ulster, she was asked to select her favorite place in Ulster, and she chose a hill with seven dunes called Cathair Crofin.

Jeremiah established a school on this hill known as the school of wisdom, and the name was changed to Tara hill. Tara comes from the Hebrew word Torah which means (the Law.) Tara became a learning center in Ireland, and Western Europe for hundreds of years.

## A poem written by Thomas Moore

*The harp that once through Tara's halls*
*The soul of music shed,*
*Now hangs as mute on Tara's walls*
*As if that soul were fled.*
*So sleep the pride of former days,*
*So glory's thrill is o'er,*
*And hearts that once beat high for praise*
*Now feel that pulse no more!*

Jeremiah married Tamar to Eochaidh the King of Ireland, from the royal line of Zarah/Judah and the sons of Tamar would continue the royal seed line of David. If she had married anyone outside of Judah, the Davidic line would not have carried on. The great prophet Jeremiah anointed King Eochaidh on the stone of destiny. Eochaidh was also a Milesian from Calcol, a son of Zarah, and son of Judah.

The harp of Tara was the only national emblem in Ireland for over two thousand years. Tara became the royal seat of the Celtic kings that came over from Spain called the Milesian's and were of the royal line of Zarah Judah. Queen Teah Tephi is believed to be buried on this magnificent hill, called "the wonder of Ireland" for many centuries. The king line of Judah is still with us today, our queen Elizabeth has the blood of Zarah, Pharez, David, and the ten tribes of Israel running in her veins. Glory to GOD amen!

Other kings will come out of Zarah, and later out of the lost ten tribes of Israel. The Cimmerians of the ten lost tribes with their kings migrated from Israel to the west side of the black sea. They settled the area on the west shore of the black sea also called the Cimmerian sea. They inhabited the Baltic region where the Romans knew them as the Cimbri. The Cimmerians were forced west along the Danube River to its head around 600 to 500 BC, and there they would be known as the famous Celts. The lost tribes of Israel have established their king line In Europe. The Visigoths will leave France, and settle in Spain and Portugal. The royal lines of Zarah, Pharez, King David, and the kings of the ten lost tribes of Israel are all established in Europe.

Kings of the royal line of Judah ruled over Turkey, Greece, Italy, France, Spain, Portugal, Ireland, Scotland, England, Belgium, Netherlands, Germany, Austria, Denmark, Norway, Sweden, Finland, Russia, and Israel, for thousands of years. Germanic kings of Judah or their own Slavic Kings ruled over the Slavic people who are brothers of the Israelites. The Greeks ruled Egypt (the Ptolemaic kings) From 323 BC to 30 BC from the Royal line of Judah, established by Alexander the great. Good kings and bad kings, good queens and bad queens ruled over Europe for over two thousand years, and that is what the Israelites asked for. God warned them, and they would not listen, and they lived without freedom, which stifled them into poverty. They wanted their kings, and they got their kings.

## *Jesus brothers and sisters will enter into Europe establishing a new line of Kings*

## *Three parts Judah and one-part Levi*

There is one more way the Davidic line entered Europe. Mary and Joseph had children after the birth of Christ, and they would be Jesus half brothers and sisters. The sons and daughters of Joseph and Mary were given the name Desposyni; all the offspring were given this sacred name, which means (Jesus blood relatives). The Roman government and the Catholic Church killed many, and they thought they had wiped them out by the year 400 AD. The Desposyni offspring that moved into Germany in 400 AD, survived and became the Merovingian King line, and Clovis I of that king line introduced Christianity to Gaul/France. Sir Lancelot was a Desposyni, a descendant of Joseph and Mary. Jesus never married, and did not have children. Mary the Mother of Jesus was half Judah and half Levi, Making Jesus the King and the Priest. Joseph was of the tribe of Judah, but not the father of Jesus. God our Father planted his seed or DNA into Mary, and that is why Jesus is called the son of God. Mary's father was a Levite priest, and her mother was of Judah, and Joseph her husband was full-blooded Judah. Jesus sister and brothers were three quarters Judah and one Quarter Levite. Their offspring will become kings and queens of Europe.

### The Royal line of Judah

Zarah son of Judah
Calcol founder of Athens and there first king
Darda founder of Troy
Brutus founder of New Troy/London (First king
of Britain) descendant of Darda
Julius Caesar (Roman Dictator) descendant of Darda
Augustus to Nero descendants of Darda
King Leir descendant of Brutus
**Old King Cole** was a merry old soul "descendant of Brutus"
Arviragus king of Britain "Shakespeare's Cymbeline" Brutus Line
**King Charlemagne** (Zarah and Pharez line) "Charles the great"

William, I King of England "William the Conqueror"
**Elizabeth, I of England** (Tudor line) Judah
**Queen Elizabeth** (Zarah, Pharez, David, Israel) "Mother of Israel"

## *Where are the Israelites?*

## *Who are the Israelites?*

Most Israelites do not know who they are. Most Israelites do not seem to care who they are. The Israelites are God's chosen people, and this includes, Judah, Benjamin, and Levi. The Bible follows two very different peoples, the Israelites and the Kenites. The Israelites are God's chosen people, and the Kenites are Satan's chosen people. To have the want to understand these people will give us a better understanding of the word of God, and a much stronger faith. When you see how God has blessed his chosen people wherever they have traveled, you will have a better understanding of God's plan for all.

Chances are most people on this earth are not Israelites or Kenites. There are 7.3 billion people on earth today. Israelites and Kenites make up a small percentage of the people on the earth today . Do not be unhappy if you are not an Israelite, be happy you have learned who they are, which will increase your faith. I have known Kenites that have changed over to Christianity, and are more Zealous than Israelites, and I have seen Christians change over to proselytes for the Kenites. Remember all God's children that pass through the flesh have a chance for everlasting life. Now is your chance to show God that you can do better.

### *Genesis 46:1-7*

*46 And Israel took his journey with all that he had, and came to Beersheba, and offered sacrifices unto the God of his father Isaac.*

*² And God spake unto Israel in the visions of the night, and said, Jacob, Jacob. And he said, Here am I.*

*³ And he said, I am God, the God of thy father: fear not to go down into Egypt; for I will there make of thee a great nation:*

*⁴ I will go down with thee into Egypt; and I will also surely bring thee up again: and Joseph shall put his hand upon thine eyes.*

*⁵ And Jacob rose up from Beersheba: and the sons of Israel carried Jacob their father, and their little ones, and their wives, in the wagons which Pharaoh had sent to carry him.*

*⁶ And they took their cattle, and their goods, which they had gotten in the land of Canaan, and came into Egypt, Jacob, and all his seed with him:*

*⁷ His sons, and his sons' sons with him, his daughters, and his sons' daughters, and all his seed brought he with him into Egypt.*

Joseph is in Egypt with his wife and two boy's Ephraim and Manasseh, and both will receive blessings from Jacob. The twelve Patriarchs of Israel are now in Egypt. God will bless Jacob's sons with many children, and the Israelite's will grow to over 2 million people by the time Moses leads them out of bondage.

God has a plan for his children, the Israelite's. Some are going to leave Egypt, and follow Darda and Colcol into Turkey and Greece, and throughout the coastline of the Mediterranean Sea. The great majority will stay in Egypt, eventually being forced into slavery and then led back to Canaan by Moses.

Two distinct groups of Israel, the Israelite's that left Egypt and traveled to Turkey and Greece, will not know of Moses, and will not live under Gods 10 commandments until Jesus Christ comes in the flesh. They will not know they are Israelite's except for an esoteric few who pass it down from generation to generation. They will adopt the god's that Cain created, and adding to that. The Jews will call them gentiles or goyim during the time of Christ, and even today. The Romans not knowing they are the same people will call them heathens and barbarians. The Romans are Israelites and the Italians are mostly sons of Japheth.

*Gentiles = Heathen*

*Israelites call themselves gentles not knowing who they are*

The Israelite's that stayed in Egypt will live under the Ten Commandments, and knowing who they are. Moses leads them into Jordan and Canaan where the twelve tribes of Israel will make their home. The Israelites living under the law will soon begin to worship the gods of Cain.

The Three tribes of Judea, Judah, Benjamin, and Levi, will worship the gods of Cain, and like the ten tribes of Israel, they will be lead into captivity. They will lose their identity, and no longer knowing who they are, they will be known as goy, gentiles, and Barbarians. Therefore, it is so important to know who you are. Israel no longer knows who they are, and that is a shame. Around 15 million Jews today claim to be of the tribe of Judah, yet I believe there could be millions and millions living in Europe, USA, and around the world that do not know they are of Judah. How can this be? Well they abandoned God, went a whoring after the gods of Cain, and will no longer know they are of the tribe of Judah. They know not who they are, but God does.

The tribe of Judah that traveled back to Jerusalem, after the captivity in Babylon, still called themselves Jews, why because they are living in Judea. The Kenites also called themselves Jews, it was necessary so they could gain control over everyone living in Judea. The few Kenites will control the Jews through religion.

The majority of the Jews and Kenites from Babylon chose to cross the Caucasus Mountains and no longer called themselves Jews, until later. The Kenites reverted to calling themselves Khagan, which means sons of Cain instead of calling themselves Jews. Why because they are no longer in Judea.

Jews = yeh·hü·dē' = Jehudite

### Genesis 17:4-7

*⁴ As for me, behold, my covenant is with thee, and thou shalt be a father of many nations.*

*⁵ Neither shall thy name any more be called Abram, but thy name shall be Abraham; for a father of many nations have I made thee.*

*⁶ And I will make thee exceeding fruitful, and I will make nations of thee, and kings shall come out of thee.*

*⁷ And I will establish my covenant between me and thee and thy seed after thee in their generations for an everlasting covenant, to be a God unto thee, and to thy seed after thee.*

### Genesis 28:14

*¹⁴ And thy seed shall be as the dust of the earth, and thou shalt spread abroad to the west, and to the east, and to the north, and to the south: and in thee and in thy seed shall all the families of the earth be blessed.*

Today the Jews represent all twelve tribes of Judah and Israel, just 15 million people, but God say's there will be so many we will not be able to count them. We cannot count them because their identity is lost, and their number is great.

From the time Jacob moved his Family into Egypt with 70 family members, and until the time of Moses in only 215 years, the population increased to at least 2 million souls. Moreover, remember the tribe of Judah that left Egypt and migrated to Europe before Moses was born they have become many nations. The population of Israel during their captivity in Egypt was surpassing the population of the ancient Egyptians. Why is this?

### Genesis 26:4

*⁴ And I will make thy seed to multiply as the stars of heaven, and will give unto thy seed all these countries; and **in thy seed shall all the nations of the earth be blessed;***

*God blesses the twelve tribes of Israel with many children*

### Matthew 10:5-6

*⁵ These twelve Jesus sent forth, and commanded them, saying, Go not into the way of the Gentiles, and into any city of the Samaritans enter ye not:*

*⁶ But go rather to the lost sheep of the house of Israel.*

Why did Jesus instruct them to find and teach the lost sheep of Israel? The apostles did not know of the lost sheep of Israel, but not knowing when entering Europe, they would teach many Israelites. However, why did Jesus single out the lost sheep? They are God's chosen people; God has blessed them, even though they disappoint Him so. The Israelites will invent the printing press, and God's word will be printed, delivered, and taught in every nation on this Great Earth. The Israelites will spread the word to all Nations and the Nations will be blessed.

### Judges 5:14

*[14] Out of Ephraim was there a root of them against Amalek; after thee, Benjamin, among thy people; out of Machir came down governors, and **out of Zebulun they that handle the pen of the writer.***

The tribe of Zebulun settled in the Netherlands, and if you are Dutch, there is a good chance you may be of the tribe of Zebulun or Ruben.

### Genesis 49:13

*[13] Zebulun shall dwell at the haven of the sea; and he shall be for an haven of ships; and his border shall be unto Zidon.*

Johannes Gutenberg took credit for inventing the printing press first, but actually Laurens Janszoon Coster was first to invent the printing press in the Netherlands. By 1600, the Dutch were dominating the European shipbuilding market by producing the best ships available anywhere in the world. We cannot pinpoint most tribes of Israel to any certain nation or state, but this one is a sure bet. God will throw us a bone occasionally, and it is up to us to find it.

### Mark 13:9-10[9]

*But take heed to yourselves: for they shall deliver you up to councils; and in the synagogues ye shall be beaten: and ye shall be brought before rulers and kings for my sake, for a testimony against them.*

*[10] And **the gospel must first be published among all nations**.*

### Matthew 24:14

*[14] And this gospel of the kingdom shall be preached in all the world for a witness unto all nations; and **then shall the end come**.*

This has come to past, the Gospel being taught in every nation of the world by Israelites and Christians, and supported by the many membered body of Jesus Christ.

### Genesis 26:4

*⁴ And I will make thy seed to multiply as the stars of heaven, and will give unto thy seed all these countries; and in thy seed shall all the nations of the earth be blessed;*

*In the year 1706 BC, Jacob and his family left Canaan and came into Egypt.*

### Genesis 47:27

*²⁷ And Israel dwelt in the land of Egypt, in the country of Goshen; and they had possessions therein, and grew, and multiplied exceedingly.*

God blessed them and multiplied them in the land of Goshen, and it got a little too crowded for some folks. A small percentage of Israelites chose to leave Egypt for a new land, and a new beginning. They will travel and settle the coast of the Mediterranean Sea, and many nations will be born from them. Will they remember who they are? I am afraid not! They will forget the God of Abraham, and will adopt the gods of Cain, Japheth, and Canaan.

The only people that existed in Europe before Japheth and Canaan were the sixth day white race, and they were hunter-gatherers with a population similar to the Indians in the Americas, pre-white man. The Sixth day white man has lived in Europe for thousands of years, and they will either die out or assimilate into the eighth day humankind. A lot like the American Indians of today.

### Deuteronomy 32:26-29

*²⁶ I said, I would scatter them into corners, I would make the remembrance of them to cease from among men:*

They will no longer remember who they are, the Israelites

The Israelites increased in population in Goshen Egypt to the point where Pharaoh was afraid of the high-spirited and blessed Hebrew people. They who wore beards, and raised sheep, "which was an abomination to Egypt," and Pharaoh was scared the Israelites would overcome them, and conquer the Egyptian people.

The Egyptian Pharaoh that ruled during the time of Joseph and Jacob, was not Egyptian, but was Hyksos of Hebrew origin, kinsmen to Abraham. During the time of Moses, the Pharaoh was possibly of the Kenite tribe, (the offspring of Cain.) The Hyksos king was kind to the Israelites, God blessed them with many children, and they prospered. The Kenite Pharaoh has enslaved the Israelites and killed their first-born.

Moses will lead the Israelites out of Egypt to Mount Sinai where the Kenites and Midianites are living. Since the time of Moses, the Kenites have lived among or near the Israelites, following them into Canaan, Europe, the Americas, and other countries or cities that have prospered throughout the world.

## The Israelites settle Europe

The ships of Tarshish settled Spain and the British Isles first with the sons of Javan a son of Japheth. In fact, Ptolemy on his map had the Isle we know as England named Javan, and Spain as I said before received its name from Javan. Esau the son of Isaac, (his offspring) migrated to Europe, and became the Slavic people of today. Today Europe has become a melting pot of peoples of every nation of the earth.

The Hebrew Phoenicians, Canaanite Phoenicians, the Danites, and we cannot leave out the ancient ships of Tarshish; they were the greatest colonizers in the world. The Hebrew Phoenicians had a great impact on Europe; the many languages came from the Phoenician root language. The Phoenicians invented our alphabet, the Greeks adopted it, and the Romans improved it.

Not all Israelites spoke Hebrew, many spoke Phoenician. The word Hebrew means the people that crossed the river, and that river was the Euphrates. Many people of different tongues and races crossed the river were called Hebrew, but were not all related to Abraham, and his people. Many people that lived in

Judea during the time of Christ, were called Judeans, but were not all of the tribe of Judah. Jesus did not speak Hebrew; he spoke Aramaic, a language out of Babylon, Assyria, and Phoenicia.

From the time of Moses, to the time of King David, the population greatly increased. So much so, many Israelites were leaving Palestine/ Israel, and migrating to Europe, Egypt, Tunisia, and North Africa. King Solomon became the wealthiest man on earth partially from the mines of Ophir in South Africa. I believe Ophir was in South Africa, some believe it was in Ethiopia, Peru, or somewhere unknown, but I am sticking with South Africa.

So far, we have two influxes of Israelites into Europe, the first influx, the pre-Moses Israelites who did not live under God's law. They were heathen worshippers of many gods, yet God was with them, and He blessed them with many children. The second influx began soon after the Israelites moved into Canaan and settled in the small area of Palestine. Not all Israelites were happy living in Palestine; they saw opportunity in shipping and trade and because of the population boom, this small country could no longer support them.

Joshua led Israel into Canaan somewhere around 1451 BC, and within one hundred years, the Golden Age of the Phoenicians began. The Israelite Phoenicians of the tribes of Dan, Zebulun, Asher, and Ephraim, took to ships and seafaring became their occupation. Their Apex of the Golden age of the Phoenicians was around 1000 BC, and declined after the death of King Solomon in 920 BC. Weakened by the Greeks, their end came when Alexander the Great captured Tyre, and Sidon. The Israelite Phoenicians had a great impact on Asia Minor, Europe, and North Africa as traders and colonist. The Phoenician alphabet was distributed first by the Greeks, and then by the Romans throughout the world which they conquered.

### Deuteronomy 33:17-22

*17 His glory is like the firstling of his bullock, and his horns are like the horns of unicorns: with them he shall push the people together to the ends of the earth: and they are the ten thousands of Ephraim, and they are the thousands of Manasseh.*

*[18] And of Zebulun he said, Rejoice, Zebulun, in thy going out; and, Issachar, in thy tents.*

*[19] They shall call the people unto the mountain; there they shall offer sacrifices of righteousness: for they shall suck of the abundance of the seas, and of treasures hid in the sand*

*The Dutch certainly took back the sea (Netherlands) by building dikes*

*[22] And of Dan he said, Dan is a lion's whelp: he shall leap from Bashan.*

Bashan = Fruitful

Og the giant was king of Bashan

Dan will leap from Bashan and follow the sea

Dan was the first tribe to leave from Palestine; they fell from the grace of God, because of their idol worship, and mingling with Gentiles. Dan had the biggest impact on Europe of the twelve tribes. Dan was the first of Israel to venture out and colonize the coast of the Mediterranean. Then along the coast of the Atlantic, they settled the Isles of Brittany and north to the Scandinavian countries of today. If you are Scandinavian, you most likely have Danite blood in you. The Danites were the first to leave Palestine, and the last people to except Christianity. I guess we can call them the bad boys or rebels of the twelve tribes of Israel.

God had a plan for these bad boys, and that is to establish a place for the other eleven tribes to eventually move in and homestead. We can trace their settlements by the place-names in Europe today. Here are a few, Danube, Dnieper, Donetz, Danzig, and Dniester. The Donsk People of Denmark and Norway, the Danai mentioned over one hundred times by Homer, and the Danes all are of the tribe of Dan. The Macedonians of Greece and the Spartans South of Athens were Danites. Because of the Fearless adventurers of the Tribe of Dan, many Europeans have a little or a lot of Danite blood in them.

Arius, king of the Spartans wrote to Onias the chief priest of the Jews, that the Spartans, and Jews were brethren, and of the offspring of Abraham. Yes, the famous Spartans were of the tribe of Dan, and because of the Spartans great courage, Athens and all of Greece were saved from the great Persian empire.

The third influx begins with the capture of Manasseh in 745 BC, and Ephraim in 721 BC by the Assyrians, and taken to Northern Iraq. Ephraim represents all ten tribes of Israel, and Manasseh just happened to be conquered first, and led into captivity. The Assyrian empire grew weak, and the ten tribes could leave their captivity and venture into a new land. They decided to leave Palestine and go where no man had lived, where they could keep their statutes, and worship their one true God.

### II Esdras 13:40-45 of the Goodspeed Apocrypha

*These are the ten tribes that in the days of King Hoshea were carried away from their own land into captivity, whom Shalmaneser, King of Assyria, made captives, and carried beyond the river; they were carried off to another country.*

*But formed this plan among themselves, to leave the heathen population, and go to a more distant region, where the human race had never lived, so that there perhaps they might keep their statutes, which they had not kept in their own country.*

*And **they went in by the narrow passages of the Euphrates river**. For the most high then did wonders for them, for He held back the sources of the river until they had passed over. But it was a long journey of a year and a half to that country, and that country is called Arzareth.*

The Israelites were in captivity southwest of the Caspian Sea near the Gozan River. They escaped captivity, or were released by the Assyrians, and then traveled to Lake Van and sojourned there a little while. God is with them, and He will lead them to a new land. They cross the Euphrates River by divine intervention and move into a land unknown. The pass today is known as the Caucasian Pass, or the Dariel Pass. In ancient times, the Pass was known as the "Pass of Israel." When Abraham crossed the Euphrates River, they were known as Hebrew. When the Israelites crossed the Caucasus Mountains, they were known as the Caucasians. Today all white people are called Caucasian because of the Israelite crossing over the Caucasus Mountains. Many white people were already living in Europe before the Caucasian crossing. It is a misnomer, that all whites are called Caucasian.

### Amos 9:15

*15 And I will plant them upon their land, and they shall no more be pulled up out of their land which I have given them, saith the LORD thy God.*

The Israelite tribes that crossed the Caucasus Mountains, will be known as the Scythians, and tracking westward where they become the Saxons, and then named by the Romans the Germanic people.

Another Israelite group called the Gamera people fled their captivity from the same location at the southern part of the Caspian Sea. They also set up camp at Lake Van, but took a different direction or path into Europe. They traveled west along the Cimmerian Sea now called the black sea today. As they traveled, their name changed from Gamera to Gimira, to Kimmeroll, and then the Cimmerians, which means black. They settled for a time in a land called Arsareth, in the area of today called Moldova, Ukraine, and Romania. They will move on into south Germany, and the Netherlands, and then into France known as the Goths or Visigoths.

Along with the ten tribes of Israel, the Assyrians also took a Southern group of the tribe of Judah into captivity, and they escaped captivity and fled into Europe. They traveled west along the Black Sea, crossed the Danube River, and settled in Judah-land, which became Jutland, and today called Denmark. The Danites were already living in this area as a heathen people not remembering they were of the tribe Israel. The State of Denmark is shown on modern maps as Jutland (the tribe of Judah,) and the people today are still called Danes, (the tribe of Dan.) The Vikings were most likely of the tribe of Dan, and mixed with Judah.

## Judah, Levi, and Benjamin

Judah, Benjamin, and a big part of Levi, are still living in Judea 268 years later in 590 BC. The Israelites are no longer in Palestine, they have all settled in Europe. Judah has unfortunately followed the sinful ways of the ten lost tribes of Israel.

God will chastise them! They are conquered, taken from their homeland Judea, and forced to live without freedom for seventy years in Babylon. God is with them, they are treated well by the Babylonians, and Persians and his plan goes well. Judea is the last of the Israelites to go into captivity, and when they come out of confusion, they will become a better people.

According to Flavius Josephus, when Judah was carried out of Israel, there were Approximately 1.5 million people. After 70 years of captivity, only a remnant returned to Israel, forty thousand in all. The others followed the same route through Lake Van into Turkey, and then over the Caucasus Mountains. God will lead Judah, Benjamin, and Levi into Europe, where they will rejoin with their brothers the Israelites. Judah and Israel have been separated for many years, and they have now fused together as one, "God's Chosen People

### *Ezekiel 37:19-22*

*[19] Say unto them, Thus saith the Lord GOD; Behold, I will take the stick of Joseph, which is in the hand of Ephraim, and the tribes of Israel his fellows, and will put them with him, even with the stick of Judah, and make them one stick, and they shall be one in mine hand.*

*[20] And the sticks whereon thou writest shall be in thine hand before their eyes.*

*[21] And say unto them, Thus saith the Lord GOD; Behold, I will take the children of Israel from among the heathen, whither they be gone, and will gather them on every side, and bring them into their own land:*

*[22] And I will make them one nation in the land upon the mountains of Israel; and* **one king shall be king to them all***: and they shall be no more two nations,* **neither shall they be divided into two kingdoms any more at all.**

*The one King is Jesus Christ*

*The ten tribes of Israel, Judah and Benjamin will be united forever*

*Ezekiel 11:16-17*

<sup></sup>¹⁶ *Therefore say, Thus saith the Lord GOD; Although I have cast them far off among the heathen, and although I have scattered them among the countries, yet will I be to them as a little sanctuary in the countries where they shall come.*

*Daniel 9:7*

⁷ *O LORD, righteousness belongeth unto thee, but unto us confusion of faces, as at this day; to the men of Judah, and to the inhabitants of Jerusalem, and unto all Israel, that are near, and that are far off, through all the countries whither thou hast driven them, because of their trespass that they have trespassed against thee.*

The best of the twelve tribes have moved into Great Britain, and by the 18th century, Great Britain became the largest empire on earth. One fifth of the world's population was under British control, and the empire covered over one quarter of the earth's total land area. Great Britain has affected, influenced, and dominated over eighty percent of the earth's habitable land during the last three centuries. It is not by accident that this small Island with under sixty million people, welds more power, and influence, than all the great empires combined. The twelve tribes of Israel have conquered and settled in Great Britain, God blessed them, and they became the biggest colonizers, ever, on the face of the earth.

For the twelve tribes, it has always been Westward Ho, follow the setting sun. God will lead them to that land that flows with milk and honey, (which God had promised.),

*Jeremiah 11:5*

⁵ *That I may perform the oath which I have sworn unto your fathers, **to give them a land flowing with milk and honey,** as it is this day. Then answered I, and said, So be it, O LORD.*

Many nations of people from the Atlantic and Pacific oceans have visited North America, but have not established permanent colonies, except for the indigenous people, well established for thousands of years.

The Vikings tried to establish a permanent settlement in Newfoundland, but were unable due to their treatment of the Indians; they were outnumbered, and had no firearms around 1000 AD. Ponce de Leon was the first to discover North America, and to report it back to Spain. Ponce was appointed Chief Justice and Governor of La Florida, but unfortunately was killed by the Calusa Indians in southwest Florida. In 1564, the first permanent settlement began in St. Augustine Florida. Some residents in St. Augustine go back 18 generations they are definitely true Floridians.

Even though many of the Spanish people are Israelites, this land is not for them. The English are coming, and the Indians are fiercer and more warrior like than the Indians living on the Islands, it is going to be a tough go. The best of the Israelites will colonize North America, and a growing empire forms 13 colonies. The colonies individually developed their own system of government, based on their needs and desire for freedom.

### Genesis 22:18

[18] And **in thy seed shall all the nations of the earth be blessed**; because thou hast obeyed my voice.

The USA becomes the most prosperous and powerful nation on earth and because of the blessings God has given the Israelites, all Nations of the earth are blessed.

### Jeremiah 32:37-38

[37] Behold, I will gather them out of all countries, whither I have driven them in mine anger, and in my fury, and in great wrath; and I will bring them again unto this place, and I will cause them to dwell safely:

[38] And they shall be my people, and I will be their God:

> No one has been able to make war with us in our own land
>
> God has blessed the Israelites, and people from all nations of the earth have migrated to this land of milk and honey

## 2 Samuel 7:10

*[10] Moreover **I will appoint a place for my people Israel**, and will plant them, that they may dwell in a place of their own, and move no more; neither shall the children of wickedness afflict them anymore, as beforetime,*

*Great Britain represents Ephraim son of Joseph*

The USA represents Manasseh son of Joseph

William Weston was probably the first Englishman to explore the North American Continent in 1499, but it is possible, that it could have been someone else, since the expeditions were very secretive. Henry the VII sent him out to find a new land that Columbus had not discovered. He discovered lands that the Vikings had discovered 500 years earlier, Labrador, and possibly lands further south. Sir Walter Raleigh attempted to colonize the land he called Virginia in 1584, and 1587, and both were unsuccessful. His last expedition was on Roanoke Island.

Why did it fail? The wrong people were selected and not enough supplies and support was given. You cannot expect a colony to come from English Gentlemen that have never experienced a hard day's work in their lifetime. You need common folk, the farmers, smiths, hunters, ranchers, and all other occupations needed to support a colony. Many families are willing to risk their livelihood, and endure hardship for freedom of religion, and freedom to own property. People came from Great Britain, and all over Europe. Under the Monarchs, it was very hard to improve your livelihood, and up your station in life. The first free country on earth will give them incentive to work hard, and improve their children's lives for many generations.

America's first English settlement began in May 14. 1607 on the James River and given the name "James fort" later named Jamestown. 13 years later the Pilgrims landed on Plymouth harbor in Massachusetts, and founded a new English settlement. God promised the Israelites a land flowing with milk and honey, and a land safe from our enemies. Our promise came true, not just for the Israelites, but also for all people who pursued freedom.

## Romans 10:12

*¹² For there is no difference between the Jew and the Greek: for the same Lord over all is rich unto all that call upon him.*

> *Moreover, today we are a melting pot of many nations! God has blessed this Nation the USA, and Europe, and the blessings have over flowed around the world.*

## Genesis 26:4

*⁴ And I will make thy seed to multiply as the stars of heaven, and will give unto thy seed all these countries; and **in thy seed shall all the nations of the earth be blessed;***

The USA will become the greatest super power on earth, and only by God's blessing could this happen. The Israelites came over to a new land, a land of milk and honey. Many non-Israelites have come seeking freedom, and the promise God made to Abraham that all nations of the earth will be blessed, has now come true.

# Chapter 11

## The Kenites
### Their journey From Babylon to America

We have already learned the name Kenite, is transliterated from the Hebrew language meaning "Sons of Cain." The Kenites have been living in Babylon, Canaan, and Egypt, long before Noah's sons arrived in Babylon.

Noah's sons move into Babylon around 2400 BC. Shem the son of Noah, (the lineage Christ will come through,) conquered Babylon, and set up the dynasty of Hammurabi. Sargon's dynasty (the Kenites) ended in 2400 BC, which had been falling apart a hundred years before Cain's death. The sixth day whites, the Blacks, and Mongolians, were trying to kill Cain, for he tortured, and sacrificed thousands of innocent people. The Kenites are still living in Babylon, among the sons of Noah, as priest, and merchants.

From the time of Abraham to Jacob, and Jacobs's twelve sons, (the twelve tribes of Israel,) the Kenites will live and do business among them. When Satan was in the garden, he deceived Adam and Eve, not giving them rest, until they gave in. So are the sons and daughters of Satan, not giving the Israelites rest. The Israelites are tested to the limit, and they will succumb to Satan. They will be deceived, just like Adam and Eve were wholly seduced by Satan in the garden.

**Genesis 11:31**

*And Terah took Abram his son, and Lot the son of Haran his son's son, and Sarai his daughter in law, his son Abram's wife; and they went forth with them from*

***Ur of the Chaldees***, *to go into the land of Canaan; and they came unto Haran, and dwelt there.*

*Sir Leonard Wooley discovered Ur in 1922*

Cain had built a temple to worship Bel, (his father Satan,) on the Balikh River in the exact location where Abram was instructed to live. Cain had named this River, from the River Balkh in Afghanistan, which was the River in the Garden of Eden. It seems like Noah's people keep following Cain, but soon the Kenites will follow the Israelites wherever they go.

### Genesis 12:1

*Now the LORD had said unto Abram, Get thee out of thy country, and from thy kindred, and from thy father's house, unto a land that I will shew thee:*

### Genesis 12:4

*So Abram departed, as the LORD had spoken unto him; and Lot went with him: and Abram was seventy and five years old when he departed out of Haran.*

### Genesis 12:5

*And Abram took Sarai his wife, and Lot his brother's son, and all their substance that they had gathered, and the souls that they had gotten in Haran; and they went forth to go into the land of Canaan; and into the land of Canaan they came.*

### Genesis 12:6

*And Abram passed through the land unto the place of Sichem, unto the plain of Moreh. And the Canaanite was then in the land.*

*Do not confuse Kenite with Canaan. Canaan is the son of Ham, and Ham is the son of Noah. The Kenites will live in Canaan, but are not the Canaanites.*

### Genesis 15:19-21

[19] ***The Kenites***, *and the Kenizzites, and the Kadmonites,*

*[20] And the Hittites, and the Perizzites, and the Rephaims,*

*[21] And the Amorites, and the **Canaanites,** and the Girgashites, and the **Jebusites.***

The Kenites are first mentioned here, living in Canaan well before Abram, Sarai, and lot had left Haran, and then homesteading in the land of Canaan. They are living in Egypt, as priest, merchants, master masons, and moneychangers, as well as the Sinai, and Arabia region. They have settled the areas where the Israelites will eventually sojourn. Satan knows Gods plan, and his people are waiting. There is no rest for God's chosen people, and God is still testing them today.

## Isaac and the twelve Israelites move to Egypt

Isaac will live his whole life in Canaan. He marries Rebecca, and they have two children Esau and Jacob. Esau takes two wives from the Hittite tribe, and this is not pleasing to God and Isaac. God hated Esau and loved Jacob, and Jacob will use covert activity to take his birthright away.

**Malachi 1:2-3**

I have loved you, saith the LORD. Yet ye say wherein hast thou loved us? Was not Esau Jacob's brother? saith the LORD: **yet I loved Jacob, Moreover, I hated Esau**, and laid his mountains and his heritage waste for the dragons of the wilderness.

**Romans 9:13**

As it is written, Jacob have I loved, but **Esau** have I hated.

Jacob left Canaan to take a wife in Haran where his relatives lived. He lived there for fourteen years, working seven years for each wife. At the end of the fourteen years, he left with his two wives, two concubines, his eleven sons, and one daughter. Joseph the last son to be born in Haran, and the only son to be born in Haran of Jacob's beloved wife Rachel. Rachel died giving birth to Benjamin in 1728 BC in the land of Canaan.

Jacob loved Joseph more than his other children, and making Joseph a special coat of many colors. His ten brothers were very jealous of him. The ten brothers sold him to the Ishmeelites. The Ishmeelites took him down into Egypt and sold him. Potiphar an officer of Pharaoh's was high ranked (captain of the guard.) He loved Joseph, for he knew Joseph was blessed from God. Joseph was highly blessed, his work became prosperous, and Potiphar put him in charge of everything he had.

Joseph's was a handsome man, and Potiphar's wife took a liking to him. She tried to seduce him, but he refused her. One day she threw herself on him, he backed away, she grabbed his garment, and he left the house without it. His master had no choice but to put him in prison, he could have put him to death, or had him put in a slave's prison, versus the Pharaoh's prison where he was placed. The keeper of the prison soon put Joseph in charge, and the prison prospered under the management under Joseph.

An officer of Pharaoh committed a crime, and two officers were placed in prison, the chief of the butlers, and chief of the bakers, and not knowing which one was guilty. They both had a dream on the same night, and the next morning they woke up with sad faces. Joseph asked them why they were so sad, and they said we both had dreams we do not understand, and there is no interpreter. Joseph had received dreams from God when he was young, which made his brothers jealous, and led him to this prison. Joseph interpreted the dreams, and the officers liked it. The chief baker was found guilty, and the butler's job was restored, just as Joseph had interpreted it. Joseph asked the butler to remember his interpretation, but he did not, and Joseph spent another two years in prison.

Two years later Pharaoh had a dream, and he called for his magicians, and wise men. These magicians and wise men are Kenites, the sons of Cain. The sons of Cain cannot interpret dreams because Satan cannot read minds, but they do a good job fooling Kings and Pharaohs. In this case, they will not be able to fool the pharaoh. There is no one to interpret the dream. The chief butler remembers Joseph's interpretation, and tells the Pharaoh. The Pharaoh sends for him in haste, and Joseph was clean-shaven and given a clean garment to meet the Pharaoh. Joseph interprets the dream, and the Pharaoh is very pleased, he knows the interpretation is correct. Pharaoh sets Joseph over all the land of Egypt, takes the ring off his hand, and places it on Joseph's finger, giving him power to rule over Egypt.

The Kenites now in Egypt are the Priest, Magicians, Scribes, Stonemasons, and Sorcerers. They are the puppet masters that pull the strings of the Pharaoh's, and kings. Today they pull the strings of our presidents, and nothing has changed. Joseph will not be fooled by their evil work, God is with him, and Egypt and Israel will be saved. From slave to ruler over Egypt, God has blessed Joseph, it was not an easy trip for him, and it will not be an easy trip for Moses, and for all the kings and prophets to come.

Joseph began his reign at age thirty in 1714 BC. Seven years of rain produced large crops, and the yields were enormous. Then the drought began, and Jacob and his family living in Canaan were hurting. Egypt, under the rule and direction of Joseph, had stored plenty of food, so Jacob and his family moved to Goshen and were taken care of by Joseph, who was considered the savior of both Israel and Egypt. Jacob and his family consisted of 70 men, women, and children when they moved into Egypt.

In 1689 BC, Jacob the Patriarch of the twelve tribes of Israel died at age 147. God blessed the twelve tribes of Israel, the wombs were opened, and the population grew at a rapid rate. The shepherd kings, who were the offspring of Noah's son, Shem, were no longer in charge. The Egyptian Pharaoh's were back in charge. Moreover, the Kenites were back pulling the strings of the Pharaoh's deceiving them on a daily basis. By the time Moses was born, the population was near 2 million Israelite men, women, and children. This was a concern for the Pharaoh and the Kenites, who wished to reduce the population to prevent them from taking over Egypt.

In the year 1570 BC, a new Pharaoh, Ahmose I continued the expulsion of the Hyksos, and founded the (18th Dynasty.) One year later Moses of the Levite tribe was born in 1571 BC. Radiocarbon dating shows Ahmose I am reigning from 1570 BC to 1544 BC, just one year before Moses was born. He was around 10 years old when he started his reign, which makes Moses 11 years younger than Ahmose I. Ahmose I was much too young to rule Egypt so his mother Ahhotep ruled as regent. Ahmose I completely expelled the Hyksos in 1551 BC, in the Goshen area (Lower Egypt) where the Israelites lived and were in bondage.

*Exodus 1:8-22*

*[8] Now there arose up **a new king over Egypt, which knew not Joseph**.*

> *Pharaoh Seqenennre Tao, father of Ahmose I was killed by*
> *the Hyksos when Ahmose was seven years old*

> *His brother king Kamose reigned three years, and died,*
> *(reason unknown,) the year 1570 BC*

> *King Ahmose I takes over at age 10 in 1570 BC*

> *King Ahmose I rules during the time of Moses youth (the new king over Egypt)*

*[9] And he said unto his people, Behold, the people of the children of Israel are more and mightier than we:*

*[10] Come on, let us deal wisely with them; lest they multiply, and it come to pass, that, when there falleth out any war, they join also unto our enemies, and fight against us, and so get them up out of the land.*

*[11] Therefore they did set over them taskmasters to afflict them with their burdens. And they built for Pharaoh treasure cities, Pithom and Raamses.*

> *Raamses I acquires the name from the city Raamses*

*[12] But the more they afflicted them, the more they multiplied and grew. And they were grieved because of the children of Israel.*

*[13] And the Egyptians made the children of Israel to serve with rigour:*

*[14] And they made their lives bitter with hard bondage, in morter, and in brick, and in all manner of service in the field: all their service, wherein they made them serve, was with rigour.*

*[15] And the king of Egypt spake to the Hebrew midwives, of which the name of the one was Shiphrah, and the name of the other Puah:*

*¹⁶ And he said, When ye do the office of a midwife to the Hebrew women, and see them upon the stools; if it be a son, then ye shall kill him: but if it be a daughter, then she shall live.*

*¹⁷ But the midwives feared God, and did not as the king of Egypt commanded them, but saved the men children alive.*

*¹⁸ And the king of Egypt called for the midwives, and said unto them, Why have ye done this thing, and have saved the men children alive?*

*¹⁹ And the midwives said unto Pharaoh, Because the Hebrew women are not as the Egyptian women; for they are lively, and are delivered ere the midwives come in unto them.*

*²⁰ Therefore God dealt well with the midwives: and the people multiplied, and waxed very mighty.*

*²¹ And it came to pass, because the midwives feared God, that he made them houses.*

*²² And Pharaoh charged all his people, saying,* **Every son that is born ye shall cast into the river, and every daughter ye shall save alive.**

*King Kamose is the one that sentenced the sons of Israel to death*

*King Kamose dies that year in 1570 BC, and the 18ᵗʰ Dynasty begins*

*The Pharaoh Ahmose I will reign approximately 25 years, and dies around 1544 BC*

*Moses is 27 years old, living as an Egyptian, and seeing the burdens put on his people*

*The Kenites are the puppet masters; they control the Pharaoh's, and they will try to destroy the Israelites*

The Pharaoh's daughter raises Moses as her son, her father is Pharaoh Seqenenre, and she is the sister of Pharaoh Ahmose I, pronounced (Ah Moses.) Moses was brought up under the Theban royal house, and were instructed by the Kenite priest to worship many gods. Moses knew he was an Israelite, and probably wondered what his destiny really was. By the time he reaches forty, he can no longer bare to see his people under such severe bondage and mistreatment. He looks upon his people and sees an Egyptian beating a Hebrew, and he kills the Egyptian. Moses was seen killing the Egyptian, and Amenhoptep I sought to kill Moses. Moses flees from Egypt, and travels to the land of the Midian priest, where God led him.

God leads Moses to Horeb, "the mount of God," where Abraham's offspring from his last wife Keturah, are living among the Kenites. Jethro the Midianite priest from Keturah's son Midian gave Moses a wife, and a job taking care of his flock. Moses lives here for forty years, he is now 80 years old, and the date is 1491 BC. After forty years, Moses finally decides to check out the bush that burns and is not consumed on the Mount of God. Moses talks to God, and is instructed by God to go back to Egypt and lead the Israelites out of bondage. "And the Lord said to Moses, go return to Egypt, for the men that wanted you dead, are no longer alive."

The Midianites are living in Sinai among the Kenites, where Moses has been living. Both are living close to the Mount of God, called Mount Horeb. Satan has strategically placed his children near Mount Horeb, first to corrupt the Midianites, and then the Israelites. The Kenites are there to destroy the tribe of Judah and Levi, by mixing other races and tribes into their bloodline, to prevent the coming of Christ. The other ten tribes are not a priority, and they will be seduced later. The kenites have assimilated with the Midianites, and are introducing them to Baal and Ashtaroth, (the worshipping of Satan.) By the time Joshua leads the 12 tribes of Israel into Canaan, they too will worship on the altar of Baal.

**Judges 1:16**

And the children of the **Kenite**, Moses' father in law, went up out of the city of palm trees with the children of Judah into the wilderness of Judah, which lieth in the south of Arad; and they went and dwelt among the people.

*Moses father in law is a Midian priest, not a Kenite, the Midianites*
*are living among the Kenites, and are taking Kenite wives*
*Notice they have gone up to the tribe of Judah, not the tribes of Israel*
*Mary the mother of Jesus, is half Judah, and half Levite*
*The Kenites will try to eliminate the pure bloodlines of Judah and Levi*
*Remember Christ is our king and priest*

## Judges 4:11

Now **Heber the Kenite**, which was of the children of Hobab the father in law of Moses, had severed himself from the Kenites, and pitched his tent unto the plain of Zaanaim, which is by Kedesh

*Heber was not a Kenite, however he lived among them, and was called a Kenite*
*Heber was living in the land of Kenites so he was naturally called a Kenite*

Moses in Egypt, is about to give Pharaoh the ten plagues from God. He is 80 years old, and the year is 1491 BC. Thutmose I, Pharaoh of Egypt, is the ruler during the ten plagues. Before the plagues, he built many temples and tombs, and his greatest project was (The temple of Karnack). The Israelites under bondage helped build this temple. He reigned over Egypt from 1520 to1492 BC. These dates have been disputed, but they fit perfect with the time of Moses during the red sea crossing, when Thutmose I drowned in the red sea. His successor, Thutmose II, had a short reign, no longer than seven years. Building projects under Thutmose I were canceled, and new projects were removed. The Egyptians had gone through the plagues, and the Israelites are no longer there in bondage to build these buildings and temples. For Egypt, it is not the time for new building projects, it is a time to look back at what just happened. It is a time to think things out, what have we just witnessed. The true God, (JEHOVAH) had plagued their nation.

Their crops and livestock are nearly gone; it is a time to rebuild after this devastation. The Pharaoh had no choice but to cancel all projects, and rebuild Egypt. These two kings fit in very well during the period of Moses, and the plagues. Most Scholars believe looking at Thutmose II lack of projects started or completed, that he was a mediocre king. On the contrary, this proves he was the successor king after the plagues of God. Egypt had to replenish their livestock, their first-born that had died, and their slaves the Israelites.

Moses crossed the Red/Reed Sea with two million souls more or less. Not all were Israelites, many Egyptians, and possibly Kenites came along definitely knowing God was on Israel's side. Moses will live another forty years, leading the Israelites and others across the Sinai, and into Jordan. Unfortunately, God will not allow Moses to step foot in the Promised Land.

The Kenites and Amilekites that were in Canaan, (before Jacob went down to Egypt,) remain in Canaan. The Amilekites are living with the Kenites and have become very evil. God will order Saul, the first king of Israel through the prophet Samuel, to slay the Kenites and Amilekites, and not to take a spoil from these Baal worshipping people.

### *1 Samuel 15:2-9*

*2 Thus saith the LORD of hosts, I remember that which Amalek did to Israel, how he laid wait for him in the way, when he came up from Egypt.*

*3 Now go and smite Amalek, and utterly destroy all that they have, and spare them not; but slay both man and woman, infant and suckling, ox and sheep, camel and ass.*

*4 And Saul gathered the people together, and numbered them in Telaim, two hundred thousand footmen, and ten thousand men of Judah.*

*5 And Saul came to a city of Amalek, and laid wait in the valley.*

*6 And Saul said unto the Kenites, Go, depart, get you down from among the Amalekites, lest I destroy you with them: for ye shewed kindness to all the children of Israel, when they came up out of Egypt. So the Kenites departed from among the Amalekites.*

The Kenites are much smarter than the Amalekites, they know how to work the system

*7 And Saul smote the Amalekites from Havilah until thou comest to Shur, that is over against Egypt.*

*8 And he took Agag the king of the Amalekites alive, and utterly destroyed all the people with the edge of the sword.*

*9 But Saul and the people spared Agag, and the best of the sheep, and of the oxen, and of the fatlings, and the lambs, and all that was good, and would not utterly destroy them: but everything that was vile and refuse, that they destroyed utterly.*

*Saul made a big mistake, he disobeyed God, when he saved the Kenites, and king Agag, and allowed his people to take the spoil. If you have a cancer, you must destroy all of it, or it will come back even greater than before.*

*²⁶ And Samuel said unto Saul, I will not return with thee: for thou hast rejected the word of the LORD, and the LORD hath rejected thee from being king over Israel.*

*²⁷ And as Samuel turned about to go away, he laid hold upon the skirt of his mantle, and it rent.*

*²⁸ And Samuel said unto him, The LORD hath rent the kingdom of Israel from thee this day, and hath given it to a neighbour of thine, that is better than thou.*

David the eighth son of Jesse is selected by God to be King. He is full-blooded Judah, and through this line, Christ will be born. The eighth son represents the eighth day man; he is a pure blood eighth day man. The Kenites want to taint this bloodline, but God will not allow it to happen.

King David ruled over the twelve tribes of Israel, and reigned without division during his Kingship for forty years. King Solomon reigned for forty years after King David, and will be the last king to rule over all twelve tribes of Israel. Due to King David, and King Solomon not giving the ten tribes of Israel equal representation, the ten tribes cried out for their own king. The Israelites chose Jeroboam to be their king, and to rule over the ten tribes of Israel. He accepted, and the ten tribes were separated from Judah, and Benjamin. The Levite tribe is the priest line, and they live among all twelve tribes. A big part of the Levite tribe will move to Jerusalem, and some will remain with the 10 tribes.

### Ezekiel 44:10

*And the Levites that are gone away far from me, when Israel went astray, which went astray away from me after their idols; they shall even bear their iniquity.*

### 1 Samuel 27:10

*And Achish said, Whither have ye made a road to day? And David said, Against the south of Judah, and against the south of the Jerahmeelites, and against the south of the Kenites.*

## 1 Chronicles 2:55

*And the **families of the scribes** which dwelt at Jabez; the Tirathites, the Shimeathites, and Suchathites. **These are the Kenites that came of Hemath, the father of the house of Rechab.***

## 1 Kings 5:1

*And **Hiram** king of Tyre sent his servants unto Solomon; for he had heard that they had anointed him king in the room of his father: for **Hiram** was ever a lover of David.*

*Hiram was a Kenite, (a master mason)*

*Hiram supplies Gold, Silver, wood, and stone to David*

*Hiram grows very wealthy doing business with the tribe of Judah*

*Hiram possibly founder of the freemason's, but there were many before him*

## 1 Kings 9:11

### Ezekiel 44:10

*And the Levites that are gone away far from me, when Israel went astray, which went astray away from me after their idols; they shall even bear their iniquity.*

*The Levites live among all twelve tribes of Israel; they leave with the ten tribes into Europe*
*The Levite tribes living among the tribes of Judah and Benjamin stay in the land of Judea*

## 1 Kings 9:11

*[11] (Now Hiram the king of Tyre had furnished Solomon with cedar trees and fir trees, and with gold, according to all his desire,) that then king Solomon gave Hiram twenty cities in the land of Galilee.*

## 1 Kings 10:11

*And the navy also of **Hiram**, that brought gold from **Ophir, brought in from Ophir great plenty of almond trees, and precious stones.***

*Ophir probably in South Africa or Peru*

*Hiram the great stone mason and great merchant of Tyre*

The Kenites are given a new name, (the Nethinims.) The Nethinims will become the high priest, and scribes. They were the puppet masters of Egypt, Babylon, and Persia, and the kings followed their every word. The Kenites with such a small population, will always take the upper seats of power.

**Nehemiah 3:26**

*Moreover the Nethinims dwelt in **Ophel**, unto the place over against the water gate toward the east, and the tower that lieth out.*

*Ophel located on mount Moriah in Jerusalem*

**Ezra 8:20**

*Also of the **Nethinims**, whom David and the princes had appointed for the service of the Levites, two hundred and twenty **Nethinims**: all of them were expressed by name.*

**Nehemiah 11:3**

*Now these are the chief of the province that dwelt in Jerusalem: but in the cities of Judah dwelt everyone in his possession in their cities, to wit, Israel, **the priests**, and the Levites, and the Nethinims, and the children of **Solomon**'s servants.*

King David and King Solomon brought over the Kenites as temple helpers. At first, their duties were to cut fire wood, carry water, and to help the Priest with their duties. The Kenites are the smartest and craftiest people on earth, and they love to keep records, and to control people with regulations and laws. The Levite Priest grew lazy, and were not up to standard for running the Priesthood, and doing paper work. However, the Kenites were, and they worked their way up to master scribes. During the Babylon captivity, they became priest, and took the place of many Levite priest.

In 479 BC, Nebuchadnezzar of Babylon took the tribes of Judah, Levi, Benjamin, Kenites, and others, into captivity. Zedekiah the last king to rule Judea, from the line of King David.

Judah's 70-year captivity by the Babylonian and Persian empires is over. They are free to go back to Jerusalem, and rebuild. Only 42,360 traveled back to Jerusalem, the majority of Jews, Kenites, and a mixed people, went north across the Caucasus Mountains.

Strongs Concordance: Nethinims

*Temple slaves assigned to the Levites priests for their service in the sanctuary.*

### Ezra 2:58-64

*58 All the Nethinims, and the children of Solomon's servants, were three hundred ninety and two.*

> *Solomon's servants are Kenites, and their name is changed to Nethinims*

> *Notice their population is very small*

> *Kenites are blessed with high intelligence not babies*

*59 And these were they which went up from Telmelah, Telharsa, Cherub, Addan, and Immer: but they could not shew their father's house, and their seed, whether they were of Israel:*

*60 The children of Delaiah, the children of Tobiah, the children of Nekoda, six hundred fifty and two.*

*61 And of the children of the priests: the children of Habaiah, the children of Koz, the children of Barzillai; which took a wife of the daughters of Barzillai the Gileadite, and was called after their name:*

*62 These sought their register among those that were reckoned by genealogy, but they were not found: therefore were they, as polluted, put from the priesthood.*

> *Could not prove they were Levites*

*63 And the Tirshatha said unto them, that they should not eat of the most holy things, till there stood up a priest with Urim and with Thummim.*

*64 The whole congregation together was forty and two thousand three hundred and threescore,*

42,360 went back to Jerusalem

392 Kenites went back to Jerusalem

Less than 1 percent are Kenites in Jerusalem

## Ezra 7:24

*Also we certify you, that touching any of the priests and Levites, singers, porters, Nethinims, or ministers of this house of God, it shall not be lawful to impose toll, tribute, or custom, upon them.*

*As you can see, the Kenites have worked their way into the house of God, as priest during the captivity of Judah*

## Ezra 8:15King

*15 And I gathered them together to the river that runneth to Ahava; and there abode we in tents three days: and **I viewed the people, and the priests, and found there none of the sons of Levi.***

*Not one Levi priest among them*

*All of them were Nethinims/Kenites*

*Our Levite priest have allowed the Kenites to take over*

## Ezra 9:1-2

*9 Now when these things were done, the princes came to me, saying, The people of Israel, and the priests, and the Levites, have not separated themselves from the people of the lands, doing according to their abominations, even of the Canaanites, the Hittites, the Perizzites, the Jebusites, the Ammonites, the Moabites, the Egyptians, and the Amorites.*

*[2] For they have taken of their daughters for themselves, and for their sons: so that the holy seed have mingled themselves with the people of those lands: yea, the hand of the princes and rulers hath been chief in this trespass.*

*The tribe of Judah has sinned, and have taken strange wives.*

*The Kenites have mostly kept their bloodline pure, for they follow their father Satan, and his law that they should not take a strange wife*

The Kenite priest made their home in Ophel, the hill south of Moriah called Zion, where Satan will stand during his last hour. This is exactly where they began carrying wood and water to the Temple for the priest, during the time of Solomon.

For the next 550 years, the Kenites will control the priesthood in the Temple, and will gain much power over the Jews, Benjamites, and Levites. The Kenites no longer are called Nethinims, but are called Jews like all the other people living in Judea. They become the Pharisees, Sadducees, and Scribes, and are the majority of practicing priest in Jerusalem. Even though their population is small.

The religious sect (called the Pharisees and Sadducees) were formed by the Kenites after they moved back to Jerusalem from captivity in Babylon. The Kenites should have called themselves Levites, not Jews, for the Levites are the priest of all twelve tribes of Israel.

This small group of priests will rule and deceive the tribe of Judah, and others, until Jesus comes. When Jesus is crucified, many will follow Jesus, and many will stay loyal to the sons of Cain. Because many of the Jews were deceived, and were ignorant of the truth, they will be able to redeem themselves during the thousand-year millennium. Not all Kenites that called themselves Jews were priest; many were merchants, and moneychangers.

## What Jesus speaks to the Pharisees and Sadducees?

### Matthew 3:7

*But when he saw many of the Pharisees and Sadducees come to his baptism, he said unto them,* **O generation of vipers**, *who hath warned you to flee from the wrath to come?*

*O generation of Vipers = Offspring of Satan (Kenites)*

*John is speaking to the Kenites not the Jews*

## Matthew 5:20

*For I say unto you, That except your righteousness shall exceed the righteousness of the scribes and Pharisees, ye shall in no case enter into the kingdom of heaven.*

*You better be far more righteous than the Pharisees, who are the seed line of Satan*

## Matthew 16:6

*Then Jesus said unto them, Take heed and beware of the leaven of the Pharisees and of the Sadducees.*

*Leaven = Lies, deceit, evil way's, poison*

## Matthew 23:14

*Woe unto you, scribes and Pharisees, hypocrites! for ye devour widows' houses, and for a pretence make long prayer: therefore ye shall receive the greater damnation.*

*Hypocrites = Play actors*

*Greater damnation = Lake of fire*

## Matthew 23:27

*Woe unto you, scribes and Pharisees, hypocrites! for ye are like unto whited sepulchres, which indeed appear beautiful outward, but are within full of dead men's bones, and of all uncleanness.*

*The Scribes and Pharisees are dead men walking*

## Luke 11:39

*And the Lord said unto him, Now do ye Pharisees make clean the outside of the cup and the platter; but your inward part is full of ravening and wickedness.*

*The Pharisees are evil liars*

## Luke 11:43

*Woe unto you, **Pharisees! for ye love the uppermost seats in the synagogues,** and greetings in the markets.*

*The Kenites love the upper seats*

## Matthew 13

*[36] Then Jesus sent the multitude away, and went into the house: and his disciples came unto him, saying, Declare unto us **the parable of the tares** of the field.*

*[37] He answered and said unto them, He that soweth the good seed is the Son of man;*

*Jesus Christ*

*[38] The field is the world; the good seed are the children of the kingdom; but **the tares are the children of the wicked one;***

*Lucifer plants his seed into Eve, Cain is born, and his offspring are the tares (the wicked ones)*

*[39] **The enemy that sowed them is the devil;** the harvest is the end of the world; and the reapers are the angels.*

*[40] As therefore **the tares are gathered and burned in the fire;** so shall it be in the end of this world.*

*The Kenites who refuse Christ at the end of the millennium will burn in the lake of fire*

### John 8:38 |

*38 I speak that which I have seen with My Father, and ye do that which ye have seen with your father."*

*My Father GOD, Your Father Satan*
*The Pharisees father was Cain the son of Satan*

*They do the evil of their Father the Devil*

### John 8:42-44

*42 Jesus said unto them, If God were your Father, ye would love me: for I proceeded forth and came from God; neither came I of myself, but he sent me.*

*43 Why do ye not understand my speech? even because ye cannot hear my word.*

*44 **Ye are of your father the devil**, and the lusts of your father ye will do. **He was a murderer from the beginning**, and abode not in the truth, because there is no truth in him. When he speaketh a lie, he speaketh of his own: **for he is a liar, and the father of it.***

*Who was the first murderer, Cain was*

*Jesus telling the Pharisees, Sadducees, and Scribes*
*who they are (the sons of Cain) (Kenites)*

### 1 John 3:12

*12 Not as **Cain, who was of that wicked one**, and slew his brother. And wherefore slew he him? Because his own works were evil, and his brother's righteous.*

### Revelation 2:

*9 I know thy works, and tribulation, and poverty, (but thou art rich) and I know the blasphemy of them which say they are Jews, and are not, but are the synagogue of Satan.*

*The Kenites worked their way into the Temple claiming to be Jews*

*The Kenites copied the word down (as scribes,) and as priest
taught the word to the Jews, "unbelievable"*

*Did the tribe of Judah stand a chance?*

The bad thing is Judah, Levi, and Benjamin are held accountable for all of this. The Jews, Benjamites, and Levites did not know they were being taught by the seed line of Satan, and are ignorant of this. Look at it this way, many Christian's will worship Anti-Christ (who is Satan) because of one great lie, the Rapture lie, and by not seeking the truth. Gods elect will overcome the lies of Satan.

Not all the Pharisees were Kenites, some were of Judah, Benjamin, and Levi.

## Acts 23:6

[6] But when Paul perceived that the one part were Sadducees, and the other Pharisees, he cried out in the council, Men and brethren, I am a Pharisee, the son of a Pharisee: of the hope and resurrection of the dead I am called in question.

Paul was a Pharisee, and not a Sanhedrin like Nicodemus, and Joseph of Arimathaea. The Pharisee's and Sadducees were created after they returned from captivity from Babylon. The Kenites created this new religious hierarchy. Many of the tribe of Judah, and Kenites left Judea, and a great number of them settled in Rome and Italy. Paul was a Roman citizen himself.

## Philippians 3:5

*Circumcised the eighth day, of the stock of Israel, **of the tribe of Benjamin**, and Hebrew of the Hebrews; as touching the law, **a Pharisee**;*

Paul was of the tribe of Benjamin

Paul was not a Kenite or of Judah, (but was a Pharisee)

The tribe of Judah had been well established before Christ in Western Europe. Through Zarah the son of Judah, came Darda and Calcol whom both established the royal king line in Turkey, Greece, and Europe. Jeremiah took the daughters of Zedekiah to Spain, and Northern Ireland where they married kings from the line of Zarah. The daughters of Zedekiah were from the royal line of King David, of the tribe of Judah, and the line of David going back to Pharez. Judah the father of Zarah and Pharez, are reunited in Europe as the royal line of Judah.

After Christ was Judged by the Kenites, and nailed to the cross by the Romans, both Kenites, and Jews migrated to Europe. The pureblooded Roman hierachy were of the tribe of Judah, from the seed of Darda, and they tortured and nailed Christ to the cross. Pilate very well may have been of the tribe of Judah or Israel, and possibly his wife also. Pilate and his wife did not want to crucify Jesus, but the Kenites would not relent.

## Most Jews and Kenites do not move into Jerusalem They cross the Caucasus Mountains

Just a small percentage of Jews and Kenites moved back to their homeland in Judea, after their 70-year captivity in Babylon. Most chose to follow the same route through the Caucasus Mountains as the Israelites did earlier. The Israelites crossed the tall Caucus Mountains and settled between the Caspian and Black sea. Their stay was short and moving west into Europe, they became known as the Caucasians. A large portion of the tribe of Judah lost their identity, they no longer new they were Jews, and most would convert to Christianity. The Jews that stay north of the Caucuses and do not enter into Europe are controlled and wholly seduced by the Kenites.

The tribe of Judah, Benjamin, Levi, and the Kenites settled north of the Caucuses Mountains. Many or most of the three tribes left this area and moved to Europe. The ones that left assimilated in with the Israelites and others in Europe, and mainly settling in Denmark. The Kenites remained north of the Caucasus Mountains where they became rich from prosperous trading from China to Europe, and the Middle East. This area became the largest state in Europe known as the Khazar State. The Khazars were part of the western Turkic empire.

The Khazar Empire was very tolerant of religion and race, even though the majority population was Turkic speaking people. There were two types of people, the White Khazars, and the Black Khazars. The white Khazars were said to have white skin, red hair, and blue eyes. That is a good description of Kenites. The black Khazars looked like they were from the Middle East, the Persians, and Arabs, and some having very dark skin, like Indians from India. Khazaria a melting pot of Ethnic people, some were Kenites, and far more were not. The Jews that remained were also light skinned, and many having blue eyes, and light hair. Therefore, we have a problem, the Kenites look like the Jews, and this is why Jesus said not to touch them. If you go in to destroy the Kenites more Jews and Israelites will be destroyed than Kenites. Remember Kenites are a few people.

The Kenites during this time had dominate red hair and blue eyes. Usually red hair is less than two percent of the world population; however, the Kenites had a much higher percentage of red haired people. In Peru, a red-haired people ruled over the Inca Indians, possibly Kenites, who introduced sacrifice of humans. Some Egyptian Pharaohs had red hair, and one was Rameses II. In China, mummies going back 4000 years had red and yellow hair with Caucasian features. Red haired Caucasian people were living on Easter Island in the 1700s when discovered in 1722 by a Dutch explorer, Jacob Roggeveen, on Easter Sunday. Israelites also have red hair but at a far less percentage then the Kenites.

The Polynesians worshipped Cain, and a small number of Kenites, may have lived among them. They traveled to Easter Island, and then Peru with the Polynesians. It cannot be proven, just a Thought. Blond haired mummies were found in northern Mexico, and their height ranged from seven to eight feet tall, the height of Adam and Eve. Maybe the Adamic people made it to the Americas in ancient times. Just a thought!

The Kenites that were called Nethinims, that followed the Jews out of captivity, from Babylon into Turkey, sojourned in Turkey for a few hundred years, and were now known as Turks. The Jews of the tribe of Judah continued over the Caucasus Mountains, settling in that region north of the Caucasus Mountains. A big portion of the Jews migrated into Europe, mainly in Germany, Austria, and Denmark. Just a few generations have passed, and they no longer call themselves Jews.

The Kenites who are now called Turkic people and speak the language, but are still not accepted as true Turks, they will pack their bags, and travel over the Caucasus Mountains. The Jews living north of the Caucasus Mountains accept them as brothers. The Kenites will gain much power in the large area between the Caspian Sea and Black Sea through trade from east to west.

The Kenites move into the area north of the Caucasus Mountains, and become known as the Khazars in the land of "Gog and Magog." The Kenites do not mess around, they practice Judaism, and build temples, and form the Khagan priest line. They gain power and money through religion, trade as merchants, and moneychangers. An area the Kenites will take over is a melting pot of many cultures, and all five races.

Kenite, Khagan, Khazars and Khan, all genitive names for Cain "the great sea king". Their origin is the sons of Cain, their reddish hair and blue eyes, were predominate among them. This is the first time the Kenites would mostly rule their own land named after their ancient father Cain. The Khazars ruled over this land as far north as the Ukraine from 600 AD to 1200 AD, up until the Mongol Conquest.

Note all eighth day humankind can have red, blond, and brown hair. Cain's mother was Eve and his father was Satan, making Cain half-eighth day man. The Kenite population today is very small, and the red hair has diminished, and no longer dominate.

Many scholars say King Bulan converted to Judaism's somewhere around 740 AD, making Judaism the one religion of the Khazarian State, or Empire. So, all people were considered Jews, even though most were not. King Bulan was decieved by the Kenite or Khagan priest through their religious ceremonies, and strict obedience to Judaism.

During the time of King Bulan there were 28 ethnic groups living in Khazaria. Kenites were claiming to be Jews once again. There were Muslims, and Christians living in this area, and they were forced to follow Judaism. The Jews living in Khazaria remained Jews and were taught by the Khagan Priest. Muslims and Christians practiced their religion in private.

Joseph Stalin was raised a Greek orthodox Christian in the State of Georgia, (the land of Khazaria). His father was a Greek orthodox Priest, and Stalin was raised to be a priest and studied 5 years in a Greek Orthodox seminary. In Georgia, today 84 percent are Georgian Orthodox Christians, 10 percent are Muslim, and less than 3500 Jews are left in Georgia. There was 100,000 Jews living in Georgia in 1970, and most of them moved to Israel. The Kenites, the tribe of Judah, and a small percentage of Israelites all live together in Israel, the good and the bad fig trees are in Israel.

Kenites or Khazars have no problem with converting to whatever religion to gain wealth and power. Usually they are Agnostic or non-believers, and some truly in their hearts except Christianity. If they except Christianity they are grafted in the tree of life, and are no longer sons of Cain.

Sephardi Jews living in Spain, France, and Italy would sometimes convert to Christianity to save their families from torture, and being driven from their homes into another country. However, they still practice Judaism privately in their homes. The Sephardi Jews back hundreds of years ago, that had predominated red hair and blue eyes were the Kenites, the others were of the tribe of Judah. Today the Sephardi Jews only make up ten percent of the Jews today. Many assimilated with non-Jews no longer calling themselves Jews. The ones that were of the tribe of Judah became Christians, and the Kenites mostly become Agnostic, or Atheist.

Muslims continued to move in the land of the Khazars, slowly moving the Kenites, out of this land. By the time, Genghis Khan conquered the area, the majority of Kenites moved to the Ukraine, Russia, and into Europe. The Khazar Jews and others moved into Europe calling themselves Ashkenazi Jews. The atheist Kenites tried to destroy Christianity in Russia, but failed. Now they are working on the USA. It was never Carl Marx idea to make Russia a communist State; he wanted the USA to be the first communist Country.

*In these last days, when Satan is standing on Mount Zion claiming to be God, the people that do not follow the lies of Satan, and will overcome and earn their God given Immortal souls. They will secure themselves for everlasting life, and the second death will not touch them. The second death being (the death of the soul.) The others will have mortal souls and will have a thousand years to learn and choose heaven or the lake of fire.*

### Genesis 10:1-3

*10 Now these are the generations of the sons of Noah, **Shem**, Ham, and **Japheth**: and unto them were sons born after the flood.*

*² The sons of Japheth;* **Gomer***, and Magog, and Madai, and Javan, and Tubal, and Meshech, and Tiras.*

*³ And the sons of Gomer;* **Ashkenaz***, and Riphath, and Togarmah.*

Japheth's offspring – Magog – Madai – Javan – Tubal - Gomer – **Ashkenaz**
If you are descended from Ashkenaz you cannot be of the tribe of Judah
The Kenites made a mistake by calling the Jews (Ashkenaz Jews)
Ham's offspring – Cush – Mizraim – Phut - Canaan -
Shem's offspring -Abraham-Isaac-Jacob-Israel-Judah-Jesus Christ
Judah can only come from Shem
Semites come from the line of Seth Adams second son
There are approximately 2 billion Semites today

### Revelation 2:9-3

*⁹ I know thy works, and tribulation, and poverty, (but thou art rich) and I know the blasphemy of them which say they are* **Jews***, and are not, but are the* **synagogue of Satan***.*

*The Kenite call themselves Jews, they hate God and
love Satan, they care less about Judaism*

*Christ is talking about the Kenites who have become the high priest, they taught the Jews in Judea, and Khazaria, the word of God for many years. Today the Kenites teach the Talmud, a book the Kenites wrote. (The Talmud is not the word of God)*

*Some Rabbis continue to teach the Torah.*

*¹⁰ Fear none of those things which thou shalt suffer: behold, the* **devil** *shall cast some of you into prison, that ye may be tried; and ye shall have tribulation ten days: be thou faithful unto death, and I will give thee a crown of life.*

*The people cast out, and tried for ten days, are Gods elect*

*¹¹ He that hath an ear, let him hear what the Spirit saith unto the churches; He that overcometh shall not be hurt of the second death.*

*In these last days, when Satan is standing on Mount Zion claiming to be God, the people that do not follow the lies of Satan, and will overcome, will have*

*Immortal souls, secure themselves for everlasting life, and the second death will not touch them. The second death being, (the death of your soul.)*

Matthew 15:12-13

¹² Then came his disciples, and said unto him, Knowest thou that the Pharisees were offended, after they heard this saying?

¹³ But he answered and said, Every plant, which my heavenly Father hath not planted, shall be rooted up.

*Satan in the Garden of Eden planted his evil seed*

*After the two witnesses rise from the dead, Christ will come down from heaven to marry his children, and most of God's children will have worshipped Satan. All people of all races and religions will kneel down to Christ, even the sons of Cain*

God Plainly tells us throughout the Bible who the sons of Cain are, and how they masqueraded as the tribe of Judah. The sons of Cain have pulled the wool over our eyes, and we dumb sheep follow the wolf in sheep's clothing to the slaughterhouse.

Jesus tells us to leave these people alone; they have their work to do. Kenites are in every race but the white race is much more predominant. God gives very few people the gift to discern who a Kenite person is. Trying to identify them through their last names will not work. Koen, Cain, Khagen, Kahn, Koenig, and the origin of these names go back to Cain, but over time, after the time of Christ, the khagen priest taught and deceived the Jews, and other ethnic groups. Therefore, they took these names thinking they came from the Priest of Aaron, and did not know they were the names of Cain. Even if a Kenite comes out and say's, I am a son of Cain, you are to leave him or her alone.

It is the very elite, who control the wealth, and power with such a small population. They control the government, Wall Street, the IRS, the banks, the media, the Federal Reserve, EPA, our TV shows, our movies, our children's education, and much more. This small group of elitist burden small businesses, county and state governments, with regulations set up by extremist groups. These elitist groups are made up of Christians, Atheist, Jews, Muslims, Americans, Canadians,

Chinese, Russians, Europeans, Arabs, Africans, and a small percent of Kenites, and with their money and political power they desire to create a one-world government. Why in the world do they want to do this? They have their money, and they desire to have total power over the world. Satan wants this, and he wants it to fail, so he can come in and fix it and be the hero of the world. Satan will have total power, but not over Gods elect, which will be a small number of men and women that will not bow down to him. Through the lies of Global warming or Climate change, they are deceiving the world, this good cause to save the earth, and to bring the world into a one-world government.

The Super elite Kenites will fail to bring in a one world system, but Satan will, he will come in "peaceably and prosperously," and will try to take as many souls to hell with him. Most Kenites today do not know whom they are, and are doing very little damage to the US and the world. The average people being led around by these elitist groups, (which they do not know exist,) are doing the most damage to our country and the world today. Satan's sons have deceived us all; God wants us to come out of ignorance and seek the truth, but the lies of Cain have been passed down for many generations, and it is unfortunate the lies have become truth.

In the millennium the Kenites, and all others that are in mortal bodies, will have a chance to redeem themselves. If the Kenites still choose Satan over Christ after being taught for a thousand years, well they deserve to go into the lake of fire, and their souls will be gone forever.

## Parable of the Tares (Kenites)

*Matthew 13:25,29*

²⁵ *But while men slept, his enemy came and **sowed tares** among the wheat, and went his way.*

²⁹ *But he said, Nay; lest while ye gather up **the tares**, ye root up also the wheat with them.*

*The Tares are the Kenites*

*Tares look like wheat until they ripen, and then the Tares turn black*

The most important thing to know is, they are here in this world today, they are the puppet masters, they sit in the upper seats, they are a few people, they pull the strings, and the puppets do the works for Satan. Many of God's children have become proselytes, and in ignorance are doing the works of Satan. Uproot the Tares, and the children of God are uprooted with them.

One of the tares is Nathan Mayer Rothschild. Roth means red, and Rothschild means red Shield. The family comes from a long line of Satan worshippers, and they know who they are, (descendants of Cain.) They are the moneychangers, the richest family on earth, and possibly have trillions of dollars hidden. Enough money to take every man, woman, and child out of poverty. Satan will use this money to buy souls, and take them away from God. Satan no longer cares about money; what he desires is to take as many souls with him as humanly possible, because he has been sentenced to death. He will deceive the whole world at the end of the sixth day before Christ comes at the beginning of the seventh day. In the first earth age, the Kenites loved the power and riches that Lucifer had acquired from Gods children by lies and deceit. During the millennium, many will overcome through their works being taught by the elect. God will be the winner at the end of the Millennium not Satan.

## The Babylonian Kenites and the Mongolian Kenites meet at Khazaria

Back when Cain was in Mongolia, he took a Mongolian wife, and they had children. Some of Cain's children followed Cain to Babylon, and others stayed in Mongolia. Cain was the first Emperor, "The Yellow Emperor" because of his yellow beard. The emperors from the royal bloodline of Cain were called Khagan or Khan, which means Ruler, commander, or king. Khagan means, the first king, and the first king was Cain. Kenite means, sons of the first king, (Cain.) The two bloodlines come back together in Khazaria.

Genghis Khan in 1223 AD arrives in the land of the Khazars. Khazar is a name used by the Khagan Priest, and the Mongolians. All these years, the Khagan priest, and Mongolian rulers, use the names that describe the first emperor Cain. 5000 years have gone by, and the names of Cain are still used by the Babylonian Kenites, and Mongolian Kenites.

Genghis Khan and his descendants, were the only ruling bloodline of Cain that could call themselves Khagan, all others were called Khan. The other rulers did not have the blood of Cain in them, so they could not have the title of Khagan. There are no paintings or drawings of Genghis, and many accounts described him as tall, a thick beard, and long hair. A Persian named Rashid al-Din said Genghis had red hair and green eyes, and this matches with the red haired Kenites. He probably had Caucasian and Mongolian features, and since he was a kenite, he would have been very smart. I know he has a bad reputation, but he did allow people to follow their beliefs, and he did protect women from being beaten, he stopped slavery of women, and made them equal partners with men. Christians, Jews, Muslims, Buddhist, consulted him, and he listened to them. The Silk Road is open from China to Europe, and trade is doing well.

Cain took a Mongolian wife, yet Arabs describe the Khazars as white skin, red hair, and blue eyes, why is this? When Cain moved to Mesopotamia, Cain's sons took sixth day whites as their wives, and then wives from the descendants of Noah, and they look Caucasian. This was done, so we cannot distinguish a Kenite, from an Israelite. Only if God gives you the gift of discernment, can you know whom the Kenites are.

When the Mongolians moved in, the Jews, and Kenites, left Khazaria, and fled to Russia, Ukraine, Poland, Germany, and other European States. The Kenites with a small population will deceive the Christians of Europe. Why does God allow this? It is his plan, to see if his Children can overcome the lies of Satan's children, and the lies of Satan. All God's children all around the world are being tested, and most will fail, just as Adam and Eve did in the garden. However, we can redeem ourselves in the Millennium, but mentally it will be a tough thousand years.

## The last day's in the flesh

Because of our sins in the first earth age, God chose not to destroy us; instead, he placed us in flesh bodies to test us in a weaker state. God does not want to destroy his children, but living in the flesh will be an experience we will never forget through all eternity. We will continue to make mistakes, and this short stay on earth in the flesh will remind us during our life for all eternity.

The Kenites have come to the United States of America, and New York is the new Tyre written in Ezekiel chapters 27-28. The Kenites are doing their dirty work behind closed doors, and the Israelites, Judah, Benjamin, Levi, and all other children of God around the world will be deceived, except for Gods elect. The Wrath of God will come upon us, after the world has been deceived by Anti-Christ/Satan. The two witnesses will rise up from the dead, and Christ will come with a two-edged sword, (which is his tongue.) The wrath of God will come upon the people of the world that follow Satan, thinking he was Jesus, or some other God. They will pray for the mountains to fall on them, for they will be so ashamed of their sin. They cannot die, for they are in spirit bodies until the end of the thousand years, when Satan will be loosed a short time.

### Revelation 20:1-3

*20 And I saw an angel come down from heaven, having the key of the bottomless pit and a great chain in his hand.*

*2 And he laid hold on the dragon, that old serpent, which is the Devil, and Satan, and bound him a thousand years,*

*3 And cast him into the bottomless pit, and shut him up, and set a seal upon him, that he should deceive the nations no more, till the thousand years should be fulfilled: and after that he must be loosed a little season.*

### Hosea 10:8

*The high places also of Aven, the sin of Israel, shall be destroyed: the thorn and the thistle shall come up on their altars; and they shall say to the **mountains**, Cover us; and to the hills, Fall on us.*

> *The thorn and thistle are the Kenites, and all the children of God that worshipped Satan will want to die (they cannot die they are in spirit bodies)*

### Luke 23:29-30

*29 For, behold, the days are coming, in the which they shall say, Blessed are the barren, and the wombs that never bare, and the paps which never gave suck.*

*30 Then shall they begin to say to the mountains, Fall on us; and to the hills, Cover us.*

**Revelation 6:15-16**

*15 And the kings of the earth, and the great men, and the rich men, and the chief captains, and the mighty men, and every bondman, and every free man, hid themselves in the dens and in the rocks of the mountains;*

*16 And said to **the mountains and rocks, Fall on us**, and **hide us from the face of him that sitteth on the throne, and from the wrath of the Lamb**:*

> *The Kenites, led by Satan their father, has lied to the chosen people of God, the Israelites, and the tribe of Judah*

> *The wolf in sheep's clothing, led the children to the slaughterhouse*

> *The one that sits on the throne is the true Christ*

> *Christ comes down from heaven with his doubled edged sword, and all people living on the earth in flesh bodies will change instantly into spirit bodies*

**Matthew 8:12**

*But the children of the kingdom shall be cast out into outer darkness: **there shall be weeping and gnashing of teeth.***

> *God's children followed the wrong Jesus, they worshipped Satan, and during the millennium, they will be considered dead for one thousand years*

> *God's elect will teach them*

> *Many will choose Christ, and many will choose Lucifer, (the archangel)*

> *If they overcome Satan, they will receive immortal bodies. If they follow the first Jesus that will come down from heaven on the first white horse, they will receive a mortal body, which means liable to die*

**Revelation 1:16**

*And he had in his right hand seven stars: and out of his mouth went a sharp **two edged sword**: and his countenance was as the sun shineth in his strength.*

### Revelation 2:16

*Repent; or else I will come unto thee quickly, **and will fight against them with the sword of my mouth.***

> *Christ will give us all a tongue lashing, and God's children will be so ashamed of themselves they will want to die, because they did not prepare themselves to go up against Satan, for they were taught that they would have an easy ticket to heaven, all they had to do was to believe in Jesus and do little work. Their shame will be great!*

### Matthew 26:39

*And he went a little farther, and fell on his face, and prayed, saying, O my Father, if it be possible, **let this cup pass from me:** nevertheless not as I will, but as thou wilt.*

> *The cup, "is the cup of wrath"*
> *Would it not be better to follow the right Christ, the one that comes after Anti-Christ?*

### Matthew 26:42

*He went away again the second time, and prayed, saying, **O my Father, if this cup may not pass away from me, except I drink it, thy will be done.***

> *Jesus knows how terrible this will be, but it is Gods will, and it will be done*
> *Nothing can stop Gods plan*

*I pray that many people will seek the truth, and will overcome the evil lies of Satan. That they will secure a place in heaven before the Millennium. Going through the Millennium will not be easy, you will be judged by your works not your faith.*

# Chapter 12

## Satan's day and his last hour

## The Sixth day

Satan's day began around 1000AD give or take 20 years. Satan has been busy deceiving God's children in the flesh, and he will not stop until he is turned into ashes at the end of the Millennium. God has sentenced Satan and his Angels to death, so why would he continue to deceive and Initiate evil unto the earth. Satan is full of pride; it is all he has left. Satan's self-reflection, the one he sees in the mirror, is the only one he loves, he receives love from the people he swindles, but has no compassion on the souls he will take to hell with him. With his great pride, he believes he can outwit God, and take more souls than God takes. On this flesh Earth, he already has, but during the millennium many souls will turn back to God.

### *Ezekiel 28*

*[17] Thine heart was lifted up because of thy beauty, thou hast corrupted thy wisdom by reason of thy brightness: I will cast thee to the ground, I will lay thee before kings, that they may behold thee.*

*[18] Thou hast defiled thy sanctuaries by the multitude of thine iniquities, by the iniquity of thy traffick; therefore will I bring forth a fire from the midst of thee, it shall devour thee, and I will bring thee to ashes upon the earth in the sight of all them that behold thee.*

*Satan along with his angels will perish in the lake of fire*

Satan has been walking the earth from the time of Adam and Eve, and before, until the first advent of Christ. Christ put a stop to Satan's walking on the earth, and the new Christian age would have a reprieve for a short time. It took a thousand years to get the Vikings to join in the tree of Life. They were the last of the Israelites to become Christians. The Vikings are no longer barbarians, and Leif Erickson discovers a new land calling it Vineland. The medieval warm period ends, and the little ice age begins. The little ice age begins somewhere around 1350AD and last beyond 1850AD.

### Mathew 16:23

[23] *But he turned, and said unto Peter,* **Get thee behind me, Satan***: thou art an offence unto me: for thou savourest not the things that be of God, but those that be of men.*

Jesus sent Satan back to heaven where he will remain until the Archangel Michael kicks him out of paradise. Satan can no longer walk the earth, but his spirit is free to go back and forth on the earth. He will use his own children (The Kenites) to set up a one-world system. The Kenites are few; they will have proselytes to do their evil deeds. Many of the proselytes unfortunately will be Israelites, and the tribes of Judah and Benjamin. Satan loves this; he is using God's chosen people, and many other children of God to do his dirty deeds. Satan puts it in Gods face, and says look at this I have your people working against you. Satan has the upper hand, it seems like people just love to follow evil. Let the lies of Satan begin.

From Christ death to the end of the Viking age Christianity was growing all over Europe, and the populations of many States/Countries were growing due to a warm period. Greenland was named Greenland, because it had beautiful green pastures to raise their sheep. Leif Erickson named his newfound land Vineland, because of the abundant number of grapes that no longer live there due to a colder climate. I wonder what Al Gore would have done about global warming back then? Maybe it is just a cyclical thing Mr. Gore. Mr. Al Gore is one of the many proselytes working as a progressive to bring in a Marxist one-world system.

By 1350, the climate begins to cool, and if Al Gore were living back then he would have to rename it global cooling. It seems like the left just cannot lose, but be patient they will. If that were not enough, the Black Death has traveled from China to Europe. An estimated 100 to 200 million people died around the world, during the years 1345 to 1353, and the population of Europe has reduced to 40 to 65 percent. It does not look like Satan's day is getting off to a good start.

One giant leap for humankind, "the invention of the printing press" by Laurens Coster of the Netherlands, and Johannes Gutenberg of Germany around 1440 to 1450AD. The bible now can be printed, and distributed all around the world. The invention is good for the growth of Christianity; average citizens can own a bible. In addition, what is good for Christianity, is good for Satan, he can publish his lies and disperse his rhetoric around the world.

Christopher Columbus Discovered the new world on October 12, 1492, or did he. Many Nations from Europe, Africa, Asia, and Polynesia, had come to this land thousands of years earlier. However, Columbus brought it back to Europe. He brought back native people, exotic birds, and most important gold. Before Columbus, the new land was kept somewhat secret, and very little proof was brought back. The Israelites will settle North America, and Satan will send his children to help build up, and then to tear down this great nation.

William Tyndale in 1525 translated the New Testament into English, and Martin Luther translated the Bible into German. This is the beginning of the protestant movement known as the protestant reformation. Part of Europe will break away from the Catholic Church, and blood will be shed. Satan loves religion, his children "the sons of Cain" will become leaders in Judaism, Catholic, protestant, and Muslim religions.

During the increase of the Ottoman Empire/Turkish Empire in the early 1500s, Palestine becomes part of that Empire. This increased the Jewish movement back to the Holy land, and established relations with Syria and Egypt. The Jews received a higher level of prosperity during the more tolerant Ottoman Empire. By 1550 Salonika known today as Thessalonika in Greece was the largest Jewish community in the world with a population of 21,000 Jews.

Inventions are going to explode in the coming centuries, and Satan will take full advantage of it, especially the printing press. Leonardo Da Vinci was a man well before his time; He invented the worm gear, ball bearings, and drew sketches of things that would not be invented for four hundred years. Satan's hour is coming, and it will be far different from Leonardo's Time.

Another invention from the Netherlands came from Zacharias Janssen a Dutch lens maker in 1595. He invented the first compound microscope, which had two sliding tubes. The microscope had a magnification of 9 times power, which was a lot at that time. The world population will increase because of this very important invention.

Hans Lippershey a Dutch lens maker invented the first refracting telescope in 1608 using two lenses. He intended its use for military campaigns. Today they are still used by all militaries around the world. However, Galileo Galilei was the first to point the telescope to the sky and observe the heavens like no one could imagine. Galileo was the first to see the four moons of Jupiter, and discovered the rings of Saturn. He was also the one that invented the Thermometer in 1593, and discovered the Earth actually rotates around the sun. This did not go over well with the Catholic Church, and he was accused of heresy in 1633.

The Virginia Company of London established the first permanent English settlement named James Fort in 1607. James Fort was renamed Jamestown, and served as the Capital of the Colony from 1616 to 1699. The Israelites have found their land of milk and honey promised by God, and soon after the sons of Cain will follow. The Kenites have followed the Israelites since the time of Moses, deceiving the Chosen people of God, and using the Government, Education, Religion, finance, and media to turn people into proselytes for Satan.

In 1604, King James hired 47 Scholars from the Church of England, to give the best translation in English that was humanly possible. Was the translation perfect, no, it was not, but for the period, they did their very best? In 1611, the King James Bible was completed and still is in print today. Our New Born Colonies will teach our children to read and write using the King James Bible.

The 1600s was the beginning of a new era delving into something new called science. Isaac Newton considered himself a natural philosopher, thinking in a realistic and natural way, the natural order of God. He gave us the understanding and laws of gravity, which no man had ever had an inkling of, a force that held everything together. Isaac Newton was a very good Christian man that studied the Bible daily, and he labored for us, to bring us out of ignorance into a new world of science.

Satan at the same time will try to tear down the natural order of God, and introduce what is not natural to God's laws. His children the Kenites will soon enter the new world, the future United States of America. The Kenites will slowly change the United States of America, through the slow moving progressive movement.

People from Great Britain started migrating into this new land in the early 1600s. Many people today can trace their ancestors back to James town, and the landing at Plymouth Rock. Most people were Israelites, and of the tribe of Judah at this time. The Engles, Saxones, Celts, from England and Germany, and the Scandinavians, Dutch, Swiss, and others have all come to the new land.

The Thirteen colonies represent the twelve tribes of Israel,
and the Kenite race.

About my family, all four of my grandparents came over starting in the early 1600s to the early 1700s. My grandparent's all have roots in Wales, Scotland, England, Ireland, France, Germany, Denmark, and others.

Morys Wynn ap John of Gwydir My 13th great grandfather
Born 1522 in Gwydir, Gwynedd, Wales
Died 1580 Gwynedd Wales
He was a Welsh Courtier and politician
His line goes back to Roderick the great (King of Gwynedd)
820AD to 878AD
The Wynn line is said to go back to Brutus founder of new
Troy (London) and from there to king Darda of Troy
Morys wife was Katheryn of Berain (Mother of Wales)
Her line goes back to many kings and queens (Plantagenet's, Tudor's, Bohun's,
King Edward III, and II, Henry II, (Eleanor of Aquitaine,) and many more.

Robert Wynne my 12th great grandfather
Born 1573 in Wales
Died 1609 in Canterbury along with his wife from the plague

Robert was Mayor of Canterbury, in Kent England
Held the office from 1596-1599

Peter Wynne my 11th great grandfather
Born 1593 in Canterbury
Died 1638 in Canterbury
Peter Wynn was an Alderman of Canterbury
He may have visited America in 1608

Captain Robert Wynne my 10th great grandfather
Born 1622 died 1678
Robert was a wealthy man in Kent England, and an ardent Royalist.
The English civil war broke out and Charles I was executed in 1649
It was no longer safe for Robert Wynne in
Canterbury so he immigrated to Virginia
Robert Wynn was a wealthy Justice of Charles City and
speaker of the House of Burgesses during 1661-1674
In 1658, he was sworn in as sheriff and was a surveyor along the James River

My 9th Great Grandfather Major Joshua Wynne was the first to be born in America in 1661. He was a member of the house of Burgess from 1704-1712, and was Sheriff of George County, Virginia. He was an Indian interpreter, befriended the Indians, and many times made peace agreements with them. In 1715, the same Indians he tried to keep peace with had killed him. Unfortunately, a man in his company had killed a Great Man of the Indians, and the Chief said a Great man from the White people should be killed in his place, and that man was Joshua Wynne.

I am Proud of my Grand Fathers, and Grand Mothers, who took part in building the greatest Nation on Earth, and from the 1600s to now, we can all be proud of this Great Nation. I know it does not look promising today, but we are in the last days, and God's plan will happen, and the children of God will be the victor.

The 1700s are here, and the Israelites are moving in by the hundreds, escaping from oppression from the Monarchy, which takes away freedom and gives no incentive for a better life. Nearly 300,000 people now live in the Colonies of America. Satan will not put up with this; he will move his children in once the new Colonies have established towns with good commerce. Since the time of Moses, the Kenites have lived among the Israelites, and they are already coming to America.

Thomas Newcomen invented the first steam engine in 1712. It was the first piston driven engine used for mining metals. By 1781, James Watt introduced an engine with a continuous rotating motion that will eventually lead to steamships, trains, track equipment, and the Industrial Revolution. What a difference this will make on the quality of life, but we have just begun.

In 1720, James Hargreaves invented the spinning jenny, and in 1733, John Kay invented the flying shuttle. The flying shuttle produced much wider fabrics and greater production. The two inventions complemented each other, and the textile industry was in great demand in England. Cotton was in great demand, and Southern Colonies began growing the crop where the land was fertile, and climate just right.

Cotton production could not keep up with the weavers, and in 1794; Eli Whitney patented the first mechanical cotton gin in the United States of America. There were not enough workers in the US, and demand for workers had increased greatly, which led to the growth of slavery. The cotton kept our economy going, but unfortunately led to the American Civil war.

I believe all people should be free no matter your race, religion, and rich or poor. Unfortunately, slavery has been around since the beginning of humankind. You can read about it in the bible and ancient history.

Unbelievably the first slave owner in the American colonies was a black man, and his name was Anthony Johnson. He was a legal free Negro that owned a successful 250-acre farm, and worked five indentured servants. Now, only indentured servants could be held for a period from around three to 9 years. When John Casor's time was up, to be freed, Anthony refused to let him go.

Therefore, John Casor fled and worked for a white man named Robert Parker. No man at this time could own any slaves black or white. Anthony Johnson sued Robert Parker, and the court ruled in 1651 that blacks could own black slaves indefinitely. In 1670, it was ruled by the colonial assembly that free blacks, whites, and Indians could own blacks as slaves. This was a bad mistake; never should this had been made into law. Owning a human being forever, as a piece of property is not right, the government screwed up. This is not Biblical.

Free blacks were afraid of black slave owners taking them back as slaves for life and it was causing a revolt. The court system of the time in Virginia ordered all free blacks back to Africa. Free blacks chose to sell themselves to free whites as slaves to prevent themselves from going back to Africa. They chose to be slaves to white masters than repatriated back to Africa. Life would have been far worse in Africa, and they would most likely been sent back to the America's or the west Indies as slaves once again, if they survived the terrible boat trip.

Black slave owners continued to increase, and by 1830, 3700 black families owned black slaves. Black slave owners in New Orleans owned 3000 slaves in 1860 at the beginning of the civil war. One third of the white families in southern States owned slaves, making the southern families far richer than the northern families. The 1860 censes shows southerners had an average per capita income of $4000.00, and the Northerners $2000.00 per capita income. An average laborer made $4.08 per week, and $212.16 a year. In 1860, a riding horse would cost $75.00, and a saddle would cost $25.00, it would take half of your yearly wage to buy a horse and saddle. Our cars today take four to six years to pay off and by that time; it's time to trade the car in.

The slave business became a very big profit machine during this time, and the European States were unable to stop it. There were 390,000 white slave owners during this time; twelve million enslaved people were brought from Africa, to the Caribbean, and the 12 Colonies. Out of the twelve million slaves, 600,000 were sent to the twelve Colonies. Life expectancy was very low in the Caribbean, because of their poor treatment. The slaves in the Caribbean were worked to death, and had to be replenished continually.

In America, they were treated far better and their life expectancy was much higher. The population grew from 600,000 to four million by 1860, and the blacks survived, and had children. Only 5% of all the slaves that were transported from Africa were brought to America. Since the Africans were not considered Christian, and were considered Foreigners, they were outside of the English

Common Law. The United States of America will pay the extreme price for this stupid law of slavery. England was always against slavery.

This may be hard to believe; however, it is true, that Jews were heavily involved in the slave business. By the late 1600s and early 1700s, Jewish merchants dominated the slave trade in the Dutch, British, and American Colonies. Jews arrived in Suriname in the 1690s, after the British control gave the Colonies up to the Dutch. In 1695 there were somewhere around 570 Jews living in and possessing forty sugar cane plantations estates in Suriname, with 9,000 black slaves. By the 1700s, the Jews owned 115 plantations out of 400 hundred in Suriname, and owned many thousands of Black slaves. Slave trading and sugar cane exports were a major business and economic life for the Jews in the West Indies.

Today when we think of slavery, we think of the southern whites beating the black slaves with whips. The practice of slavery is as old as prostitution, and has been part of life in every race and nation of people since the beginning of man. There are many types of slavery, slaves treated as property is a bad one, and then there are the domestic slaves, that take care of the home, and are usually treated well. The debt bondage slaves, if you owe a man, and have no money to pay him off, you would work your debt off. I would rather work my debt off instead of being sent to debtor's prison. Military slavery was used to build Rome, and much more. Slave trading was big business for the intermediary, and sacrifice slavery was used for religious purposes. Mayan and Aztec Indians sacrificed thousands of people for their religious beliefs.

Most people today would say there is no good slavery, but in some cases, slavery can benefit the master and the slave. The British used a system called Indentured servitude where the employer would purchase a youth for a set number of years usually 4 to 9 years, and the indentured servant was set free after his or her service was complete.

Without this system, the United States of America may not have ever been. Half of the people that came to the American Colonies were Indentured Servants that were too poor to buy their passage to the new British Colonies. The Colonies were low on labor, because most free people could acquire land and farm without being employed by someone. The indentured servants filled that void, many coming from Great Britain and Germany willing to labor and serve their employee.

Many worked on farms, and were given 50 acres of land after their service was done. Others apprenticed to artisan's work, and given a skill that would have been a far reach to obtain in Europe. I do not call this slavery, I call it an opportunity to better one's self.

I guess we can say slavery is unavoidable for the betterment of humankind, but not necessary today. Indentured servitude ended in the 18th century because getting labor was no longer a problem.

Benjamin Franklin of all people was an indentured servant to his brother James Franklin for nine long years. Benjamin felt stifled working for his brother, Benjamin wanted to do more but his brother would not let him. Therefore, he ran away, and fled to Philadelphia where the rest is history. Benjamin Franklin gave much to our new Nation, he was a writer, printer, scientist, inventor, statesman, diplomat, and civic leader, what more can you ask from a founding father.

Ben Franklin at first did not believe slaves could be educated, but later questioned his belief after visiting a school that taught African children. He found their memory and ability to learn was equal to white children, which changed his thinking on slavery. Ben Franklin was steadfast against slavery for the rest of his life.

The government changed the law from Indentured servant to slave as property, which was a big mistake. Then government will change the law again making slavery illegal, causing the deaths of 600,000 men and women. Today people are voting for more government, and our Country is moving in the wrong direction. Satan uses Government, Religion, Education, and the power of money, to deceive and control Gods children.

What does slavery have to do with Satan's day? Satan gains his power by dividing and then healing. He divides and heals, and gains souls from it. His biggest gain will be in his last hour, when he heals the deadly wound. A great division will occur in the 1800s.

Two very big movements will occur in 1776, one is from our Father and one is from Satan. The one from our Father is the signing of the declaration of Independence by our founding fathers. To give us a Nation made up of individual States, allowing us freedom of the press, freedom to own land and firearms, and to worship anyway we so choose, and much more. Our Father was against the Monarchy, but the Israelites wanted a King like the other Nations around them. No State or Nation has had such freedom in the past or present, and because of these freedoms, our Country has become the only world super power. God has led the Israelites "westward ho" to the land of milk and honey, to give us freedom, which they have not had since Abraham, Isaac, and Jacob.

## God works in mysterious ways
## The punishment period of 2520 years

This information comes from E. Raymond Capt.

His book Abrahamic Covenant

The Assyrians took the ten tribes of Israel captive at different times. Three dates can be determined, the capture and removal of Manasseh, Ephraim, and Benjamin. The date they are conquered, and taken captive by the Assyrians, this starts the 2520 years of punishment.

One Jewish year = 360 days times 7 = 2520 years

The Tribe of Manasseh was conquered in 745 B.C.

745 B.C. plus 2520 years = 1776 A.D.

America is born on July 4, 1776

The Tribe of Ephraim was taken into captivity in 721 B.C.

721 B.C. plus 2520 = 1801 A.D.

Great Britain became a commonwealth on Jan. 1, 1801 A.D.

The great Scottish Pyramidologist and Bible Chronologist, Dr. Adam Rutherford. F.R. G. S. told the Icelandic nation many years ago that on a certain day and certain year they would become an independent nation. They laughed at him and said it would be impossible since they were under the control of Denmark. Exactly 2520 years from the exile of Benjamin, (Iceland became an independent nation.) When invited by the Icelandic Parliament to address them after their independence, Dr. Rutherford reminded them of his prediction, and many members of the Parliament acknowledged they were of Benjamin.

The paragraph above is an exact copy from E. Raymond Capt. book Abrahamic Covenant.

By 1844, Iceland became a sovereign State, and in 1918, they gained their independence from Denmark. God gives us a little bit here and there to uplift our faith, and understanding. All it takes is the willingness to learn more than what your Sunday school teacher taught you, and your eagerness to learn will give you faith and happiness.

George Washington became our first US President in 1789, served two terms, and retired in 1797. He died in 1799 at the age of 67. Like Benjamin Franklin, he gave his all for our great new Nation. George Washington could have accepted the title of King, yet he refused it; instead, he accepted the title of President. In the year 1755, four bullets tore his coat, and two horses were shot out from under him. He was destined by God to be our hero and first President.

## The Remarkable 1800s

We start with a brand spanking new country, and on top of that, it is a free Republic. Our freedom is precious; we now have the freedom to think out of the box, incentive to invent, and just maybe create the largest economy on earth.

## Inventions galore!

Europe and the US were the leaders of inventions in the world, due to competition, newly invented machines, better production of steel, and more knowledge of past inventions. Trials and discoveries made in the past were known because of a very important invention the printing press.

I cannot come close to listing all the inventions that came out of the 1800s. Two very important inventions were invented in 1800, the battery and the incandescent electric light. Alessandro Volta invented the battery in 1800, and Humphry Davy invented the Incandescent light in 1809. These two inventions were crude in the beginning, and improved by upcoming inventors. In 1879, Thomas Edison invented a workable light bulb that would burn 40 hours, and later improved it to last 1500 hours.

Edison invented the alkaline battery, and it was his biggest moneymaker, and his most successful invention ever. Edison invented the Phonograph, Phonograph record, carbon telephone transmitter, motion picture projector, and much more. His inventions were big, but just a small part compared to all the inventions made in the 1800s.

Nikola Tesla invents the AC motor in 1888, which is a very big deal. The AC current and motor will have the biggest impact on human life than any other single invention. Without the transformer, the high voltage current that traveled through the transmission lines could not be reduced down to a safe voltage level to be used in homes and Businesses. No one including Tesla could figure out how to reduce DC current. Tesla brought us into the new electric age, and transformed our lives.

Guglielmo Marconni invented the radio in 1895, and is used by Millions and Millions of people each day. I know Tesla now has the title, as the one who invented the radio. However, as Edison made the light bulb usable, Marconni made the radio usable.

## *Other important inventions of the 1800s.*

*Steam Locomotive, Photograph, Portland Cement, Type writer, Sewing machine, Telegraph, Morse Code, Rubber Vulcanization, Anesthesia, Staple, Tin Can. Safety Pin, Dishwasher, Pasteurization, Internal Combustion Engine, Bicycle, Dynamite, Air Brakes, Tungsten Steel, Telephone, Automobile, Machine Gun. Barbed Wire, Coca Cola, Heinz Ketchup. Radar, Contact Lenses, Pneumatic Tire, Matchbook, Smokeless Gun Powder, Drinking Straw, Diesel Engine, Zipper, and the first motion picture seen by an audience in 1895 by Lumier Brothers.*

I should mention one other important inventor; his name is George Washington Carver. He was a black man and a former slave, a man that worked hard all his life and asked for nothing in return, he was a good man. Through his hard work, he became a teacher, a scientist, and inventor. Mr. Carver invented dyes, adhesives, rubber substitutes, pigments, and all were developed from plants and vegetables. He improved the agriculture output and health for our southern farmers and their workers. I love my peanut butter, thank you Mr. Carver.

I know I know, why I am writing about inventions, what has that to do with God's plan and Satan's last hour.

Well there is over 8 billion people still waiting to be born in the flesh, in that great city in heaven. Without these inventions, humankind will not be able to sustain itself.

During the early 1900s, the 1800s inventions are improved, and new inventions added. New Heavy farm equipment will increase yields tenfold. New inventions and new medicines will better our quality of life. Sir Alexander Fleming discovered Penicillin in 1928, but was unable to make it usable to the public. By the 1940s, Howard Florey and Ernst Chain formed Penicillin into a powder that could be taken in pill form. The Baby boom begins!

Hang on, not done with the 1800s yet!

In 1829, Andrew Jackson and his supporters founded the Democratic Party, and became the first Democrat president. The Democrats constantly remind us of our founding fathers owning slaves, but never mention Jackson having two hundred slaves. He permitted slaves to be whipped, but treated the slaves better than most slave owners. Jackson did not treat the Soldiers well; he seemed not to have much compassion for them even when they were starving. David Crockett grew angry with him for this. He lied to the Indians promising them they could keep their land. He did not keep his promise, and forced the Cherokee, and four other tribes to march to Oklahoma, where one third died on the trail of tears. Even back then, Jackson was called man of the common people, and today the Democrats are the party of the common people. He lied to the Indians, and today they lie to the Blacks, keeping many in poverty.

In 1852, Harriet Beecher Stowe published her book Uncle Tom's Cabin. The book was band in the South and considered by Southerners to be exaggerated and twisted. The book in the North was popular and sold over 300,000 copies. The book became more popular in England where slavery was not popular. Not all slave masters were cruel; many were benevolent and tried to treat their slaves well. Of Course, this ownership of slaves as property should never been allowed. It was a mistake, and we will pay dearly for it.

This book not only prompted the war, but also began a large liberal movement in America that has grown and continued until today. The liberal movement at present has become anti-capitalist, and anti-Christian, the progressives and the small population of Kenites have led us away from God.

Abraham Lincoln ran on the platform not to enlarge slavery, and enactment of free homestead legislation, which would make land available for a low price of .25 cents per acre. Notice his platform was not to abolish slavery. This would have worked; slavery would have gone away on its own due to anti-slave movements, more labor coming into the Nation and new machinery for Industry and Farming. However, the Democrats would not let it happen, and war was the only way to keep our Nation together. The Democrats back then are no different than they are today, they lie, they cheat, and they divide, just what Satan wants.

Abraham Lincoln our first Republican President freed our slaves at a great cost of over 625,000 men and women. Stephen Douglas (a northern Democrat) and John Cabelle Breckenridge (a Southern Democrat) were wholly against the removal or slowing down the practice of slavery. Six Hundred twenty-five thousand men were killed over the evil and stubborn ways of the Democrats. I believe Slavery would have gone away on its own, due to more labor, and the introduction of farm equipment. However, at the time who knew.

The blacks in America continued to vote for Republicans until the Democrats made a change during the long Socialist Presidency of Franklin Roosevelt. They promised the blacks that they the Democrats would take care of them. The Democrats have kept the blacks in poverty on the lie that the government under the Democrats would always provide for them. Well they have! They provided them with poverty, and no incentive to be self-reliant. The Democratic Party is the party of Satan, which is why they call themselves the left. Go figure the Icon or symbol for the Democrat party is a Jackass, very becoming.

### Matthew 25:41

*⁴¹ Then shall he say also unto them on the left hand, Depart from me, ye cursed, into everlasting fire, prepared for the devil and his angels:*

### John 21:6

*⁶ And he said unto them, Cast the net on the right side of the ship, and ye shall find. They cast therefore, and now they were not able to draw it for the multitude of fishes.*

In 1865, six Democrats from Pulaski near Nashville organized a social club and came up with the name Ku Klux Klan. They were all from the Confederate Army and most had attended college. Southern Democrats using violence against blacks and Republicans were terrorizing the South; many blacks were killed along with Southern Republicans.

By 1871, the Ku Klux Klan ended. The Government led by the Republican Party passed the Force acts that enabled our congress to prosecute Klan crimes. This reduced the membership and power of the Clan. This was the first Klan uprising and there will be two more.

The second Klan was founded in 1915 in Atlanta Georgia; there beef was mainly against the Catholic Church, and White Republicans. The third Klan began in the 1950s opposing the Civil Rights Movement. Governor George Wallace a Democrat governor was a big supporter against the Civil Rights Movement. In the South, the Democrats were against the civil rights movement.

Today they claim to be the champions of Civil Rights! What a lie. They want the black vote, and to keep their vote, they promise to give them hope and change. Hope whatever that is, never comes, and the only change the black race gets is dimes, nickels, and pennies. They are doing the same thing to the Whites and other races, bringing us all down to poverty, so they can have their "one world government" controlled by an elite group of people that have no compassion on the human race.

Satan has the Democrats in his pocket; their beliefs will change during the 1950s to Civil Rights and Liberalism and yes, I know they have been using liberalism back before William Jennings Bryan. The blacks have been Wholly Seduced by the Democrats and Left-wing liberals. If the blacks would have stayed with the Republicans, they would be better off, and the country would be better off. The whites have also been Wholly Seduced by the Democrats, and extremist left-wing liberals. Satan is the master of deceit, and he uses it to gain power, so do the Democrats "like father like son". My own relatives have said, my great grandparents, my grandparents, and my parents were all Democrats, and by God, I am a Democrat, not knowing the Democrat party has moved far left.

## Four great lies of Satan in the 1800s

### Lie #1 (The Rapture Theory) Rapture Lie began in 1830

Most Protestants Churches today teach the rapture theory, and some ignore it not to upset congregants who may not believe. Most churches today teach very little of God's word, usually one verse out of context, and a story that can uplift the people so they will tithe, and come back the next week. What did the congregation learn of God's word? Nothing! Nevertheless, they always say, "Wasn't that a nice sermon". Oh, my goodness it certainly was! The truth seldom is taught, but lies are on the main menu. The Preachers and Priest are not teaching lies knowingly, they are educated in the Seminaries where lies passed down from Cain to present.

The Biggest lie taught today is the rapture theory; it teaches the many membered body of Jesus Christ that they will fly into the clouds, and will be raptured away to heaven before Michael the archangel delivers Satan to the earth. This is a whopper lie that will cause many Christians to worship Satan the anti-Christ. Satan's main goal is to deceive all the Christians on earth.

How and when did this great lie begin, or is it in the bible? No, it is not in the bible. It is not in the bible, yet millions of people believe this to be biblical. They believe they will fly away before Satan comes to the earth, and Satan standing on mount Zion claiming to be God, Jesus, Messiah, Allah, Buddha, and others, and will deceive many of God's children. What a terrible day it will be when Christ comes down to marry his bride (the Christians,) and finds they have whored and married Satan the devil.

How did this lie begin? The religious movement that set up the rapture lie started with a man named Edward Irving in the middle 1820s. People at that time were expecting the second coming of Christ, and the movement was growing in London. Edward Irving a Presbyterian at the time was preaching to people spiritual gifts, speaking in tongues, interpretations of tongues, spirit of healing, and emotional utterances.

The Presbyterian Church removed him in 1832, and a new Church the Catholic Apostolic Church was established with a growing membership. This Church was the beginning or precursor of the Pentecostal Church.

In I Corinthians Chapters, 12-14 gave them the base foundation of their spiritual gift movement. It was based on spiritual emotion, and a feel-good experience. I can remember my dad taking me to see a wrestling match; we were angry with the bad guys, and excited to see the good guy's win. This was entertainment, like the Church, it uplifted peoples spirit. Unfortunately, this was exactly what Satan wanted; through their emotion, Satan can lead them in the wrong direction.

By 1830, the feel good spiritual gift movement was present in the lowlands of Scotland. Yes, the movement had caught on before the Presbyterian Church dismissed Irving in London. I can understand why people were led to this, they worked hard, and when one of these tent revivals came to their village it was like going to see the circus when it came to town. It was away to escape hardship and to love and praise God. Only a small portion of the Scottish lowlanders followed this new religion, however Satan will plant the big lie among them.

In 1830 a woman said by some to be devil possessed, and others to have the power of the spirit, came down sick, and was near death. During her sickness, she had a dream or vision that she claimed at first was very evil and dark. The vision or dream given to her was that Christ would make his appearance twice, instead of one time at Christ Second Advent.

This dream or vision was a lie from Satan, planted at the perfect time when the second coming was expected at any time. The Preachers got a hold of this, and it spread like wild fire. She believed it was evil, but was convinced it was of God by Preachers that wanted to make a name for themselves, and a lot of money to go along with it. It rather reminds us of the Preachers today who spend a lot of time preaching for money and making the church into a business. Miss Margaret Macdonald is the source of the Rapture doctrine, and Anxious Preachers promoted this big lie.

John Darby is said by many people to be the source of the Rapture doctrine. It is not true, John did help promote the Rapture theory, but the source did come from Margaret Macdonald. John Darby and the Scofield's popularized the Rapture lie, and then spread it throughout Scotland, England, and on to America. Today it is accepted to be an absolute biblical truth, and there is nothing biblical about it. All is based on this evil dark vision given to her by Mr. Satan Himself.

Satan's first big lie in the 1800s is the Rapture theory. The lie falsely professes that Christ will come in two stages. Christ will first come to fly all Christians away to heaven to prevent them from being tested through the Great Tribulation. The second time he will come down from heaven to marry his children, except his children have already married Satan. This is the wrath of GOD. Good little Christians that believed this lie will be praying for the mountains to fall on them, because of their great shame.

The whole idea is to test the people before Satan in person. What would be the purpose, if God takes away the Christians, and leaves the non-Christian's, what challenge does Satan have? Satan tested Christ in the flesh, and the Christians will be tested also.

If you desire to learn more read the book (The Rapture Plot) by Dave MacPherson.

## Back to the four lies of Satan

The first lie was the Rapture theory, the deadliest lie of the four. This lie will cause a greater falling away of God's chosen people then the next three lies combined.

### Lie # 2 Karl Marx (The Communist Manifesto) Utopia

Lie number two is a big one. Karl Marx did not invent Communism, before Marx it was a secret society thing, an elitist group, made up of the Rothschild's,

Illuminati, Secret Societies, Satan Worship, Freemasons, and Socialist. Karl Marx is the one that presented this work of Satan to the world.

Karl Marx was born on May 5, 1818, in Trier Germany said to be the oldest city in Germany, first discovered by King Ninus of Assyria. Karl's Mother and Father were Jewish and came from a long line of Rabbi's back to 1723. Karl Marx was an Ashkenazi Jew, not a Sephardic Jew. The Sephardic Jews migrated from Jerusalem, to Italy, Spain, France, and Portugal. In 1000 AD, the Sephardic Jews made up 97 percent of the Jews known at that time. By the time, Karl Marx was born the Ashkenazi's Jews were 70 to 80 percent of the total world population of Jews. Today they make up 80 to 90 percent of the Jewish population.

Karl's father converted to a Protestant Christian to keep from losing his job as a lawyer. He was a most respected lawyer in Trier on the River Moselle, and did not want to lose that respect. In public life, he was Christian, and in private, he practiced Judaism.

The Ashkenazi Jews were a Diasporas people forced to leave one homeland, and then another never really having a permanent place to call their home. They were known as the wandering Jews, being removed from one Country to another. Cain and his offspring were forced to wander from nation to nation, because Cain had murdered Abel his brother.

### Genesis 4:14

*14 Behold, thou hast driven me out this day from the face of the earth; and from thy face shall I be hid; and **I shall be a fugitive and a vagabond in the earth**; and it shall come to pass, that every one that findeth me shall slay me.*

*The sons of Cain become Fugitives, and live the lives as Vagabonds*

Karl Marx was raised a Protestant Christian, he went to a Lutheran Church, he read the bible and he was a good student. He loved the Lord Jesus when he was young, but what happened later? This is what he said as a young child.

*"Union with Christ could give an inner elevation, comfort in sorrow, calm trust, and a heart susceptible to human love, to everything noble and great, not for the sake of ambition and glory, but only for the sake of Christ".*

Karl Marx was a very bright student, when he read the bible he took in every word, he did not read over any verse or chapter, he took it in with understanding. He read the writings of Jeremiah 35:2-16 about Rechab who was a Kenite, and his offspring called the Rechabites that migrated to Cannaan with Moses, and the Israelites. Moreover, when he read I King 18:22 that Elijah was the only true prophet of the tribe of Levi and there were 450 prophets of Baal, which is Satan and Satan worship. Yes, he knew they were the Kenites the sons of Cain. Moreover, he read the New Testament, heard all what Christ had said to the Pharisees, and Sadducees, and exposed them as the sons of Cain. In addition, in the book of Revelation the Kenites declaring to be of Judah, and are not but of Satan the devil. He did not read over it like most people would, he understood, and his whole belief changed 180 degrees.

Soon after High school Marx has an extreme change in his Ideology, and it develops into a deep-rooted hatred towards God.

**Karl Marx Quote:**

> *"I wish to avenge myself against the One who rules above".*

I believe Karl Marx has learned he is a Kenite, the seed line of Satan. This overwhelms him, and he begins to hate God. He joins a Satanist group. He no longer loves God he hates God.

**Karl Marx Quote:**

> *"Thus Heaven I have Forfeited, I know it full well, **my soul, once true to God, Is chosen for hell".***

Karl made the wrong decision, he was a good Christian, he should have remained a Christian, but he was hurt badly in his heart. He thought he had no choice but to worship Satan because he was a son of Cain. This is not true; any Kenite that believes in Christ with all his or her heart is grafted into the tree of life. God has loved them; he desires that they will come back to Jesus the Christ. Many have committed their lives to Christ, and become far more zealous then most Christians.

**Karl Marx Quote:**

*"His knowledge of the Christian faith and morals is fairly clear and well grounded..."*

He was so well grounded; he believed he was a son of Satan.

Was Karl Marx a full-blooded Kenite? He probably had very little, or no kenite blood in him. It does not matter; Christ opens his arms to every man and women that goes through the flesh. Marx friends believed he was a Moor because of his black curly hair, and dark complexion. He turned on Christ thinking he was of Satan, yet there is a good possibility he was not. Karl still has a chance during the millennium to redeem himself. Kenites always use others like Karl to do their dirty work.

**Karl Marx Quote:**

*"Yet I have power within my youthful arms to clench and crush you with tempestuous force, while for us both the abyss yawns in darkness, you will sink down and I shall follow laughing, whispering in your ears descend come with me, friend".*

Marx, like Satan, desires to take all humankind down to hell with him. Satan wants to deceive all of God's children, he has nothing left, he and his angels have been sentenced to the lake of fire, and there is no way to redeem themselves.

The Reverend Wurmbrand and his wife both Jews, chose a different path than Marx. Richard Wurmbrand was born in Bucharest Romania, and during his youth was sent to study Marxism. Richard Wurmbrand and his wife Bintzea became believers in Christ in 1938. Both were tortured in prison for their belief in Jesus, and they suffered greatly by the hands of Communism. They eventually made it to America, and spent their remaining days publishing books, teaching Christianity, and helping people persecuted for worshipping Jesus Christ.

Reverend Wurmbrand believed Marx was demon possessed, and documented that many Communist leaders worshipped Satan. Friedrich Engels the co-author of The Communist Manifesto wrote that Karl Marx was a "Monster possessed by 10,000 devils".

Friedrich Engels was born in Prussia of a wealthy Family in the cotton manufacturing business. He was raised a Lutheran Christian, but like Marx developed atheist beliefs that lead him to communist Ideology.

To some this up, Karl Marx born a Jew, was raised Christian, and became a zealous Communist. Reverend Wurmbrand born a Jew, and was indoctrinated into Marxism, and then debunks Atheism and Communism, for Christianity. Friedrich Engels, an Israelite brought up to be a good Christian, changes over to an atheist, and a staunch Communist.

I guess what I am trying to say here is, it is not how you start out that matters, it is how you end up that matters. This is a good way to explain why God chose to put us in flesh bodies, to test us out, taking away our previous memory, not knowing if there is a God or not, letting us choose our destination in the hardship of living in flesh bodies, and given free will.

Karl Marx did not create Communism, the Illuminati created it. Marx was not the puppet master, he was the puppet, the ones that pulled the strings were the Illuminati, they are the Kenites the sons of Cain, and the seed line of Satan. The Kenites never get their hands dirty; they use puppets, like Marx, Engels, Giuseppe Mazzini, Jews, Christians, and others. Marx was financed by the Illuminati to write the Communist Manifesto.

Karl Marx desire was to destroy humankind. First on his list was to destroy Christianity and all religions. He would take away our morals, and he would break down our family structure. He would remove our right to own property, and firearms to hunt and protect ourselves. He would take away free enterprise, which would take away incentive. He would abolish civil government, and bring in a new government taking away all freedom from humankind. All of this was contrived by the Illuminati in 1776. The Illuminati are the puppet masters, and Marx is the Puppet. Marx wants to destroy all moral structure given to us by God through His word, and Communism he believes will carry this evil work of Satan out.

The second big lie of the 1800s is Communism, Marxism, Socialism, and Progressivism. Moreover, the puppets (the working bees) will present their works to Satan at his last hour. The progressives/Illuminati will not stop until Satan brings in the New World Order.

## Lie # 3 Madame Helena Blavatsky (Theosophy, New Age Movement)

Helena Blavatsky born with the name Helena von Hahn was born in Russia on August 31 July 1831. Her grandparents lived in Georgia the land of the Khazar's. The Han's or Hahn people migrated from Mongolia and assimilating with all the other ethnic groups in Khazaria. She is probably a mixture of Mongolian/Kenite, and Slavic. The Slavic people are the Edomites, and they are the sons of Esau, Isaac and Abraham.

Blavatsky the mother of New Age did not invent this occult, but like Marx, they both presented it to the world by publishing a book. She is not a puppet Master, but a puppet used by the masters. Always remember the Puppet Masters very seldom get their hands dirty. The Puppet Masters are a secret society; we know not who they are.

Helena Blavatsky founded the Theosophical Society in 1875. Rudolf Steiner founded Anthroposophy in 1912. Alice Bailey founded the I Am sect in the late 1930s. The Cults today are grouped together as the New Age Movement / Religion. Cults are secret societies hiding practices such as Satan worship, witchcraft, Astrology, crystal gazing, Channeling, palm reading, talking with dead spirits, reincarnation, and much more. Nothing is new about all of this; it has been going on since Cain walked the earth. However, Helena and many others have presented it in new ways to deceive people from worshipping the true God.

This is Satan's day; he is setting the world up for his one hour on earth. Madame Blavatsky a puppet for Satan as like Karl Marx both reintroduced Satanism to the Christians around the world. Their influence is far greater than you can imagine. Communism and new age religions influence all of us on a daily basis. The effect reaches out through our children's education, the entertainment industry, and the media, which is destroying our beliefs and morals. The impact on our Businesses, politics, health care, religion, our eating habits, and our way of speaking, all is causing confusion. Cain created this same confusion in Babylon, and Satan with the help of the Kenites is confusing the people around the world today. I hate to say this, but we are all dumb sheep being led to slaughter by the wolf in sheep's clothing, which is Satan the devil.

Helena Blavatsky has led the sheep astray; today the liberal Protestants and the Catholic Church have adopted New Age Ideology. King Solomon said, "nothing is new under the sun", history just keeps repeating its self, and we never are able to stick with truth, for Satan is always with us.

## Lie # 4 Charles Robert Darwin (Natural selection) (Evolution)

Charles Darwin was born February 12, 1809 Shropshire, England. He died on April 19, 1882 Kent England. His Mother Susannah Darwin was a Unitarian, and raised the six children believing that Christ was the son of God, but not God. They changed over to the Anglican Church, which teaches the trinity. His Father Robert Darwin was a wealthy doctor and successful Investor or Financier. He considered himself a free thinker, one that does not believe in the bible or God unless you can prove through science or some other means that God and the Bible are a reality. Charles brother Erasmus was also a free thinker, and quietly followed his Father and Brother.

Darwin was sent to school to get a medical degree, but his interest or passion was not in it. His passion was natural science, and he became a forthcoming geologist during the five-year voyage on the HMS Beagle. This voyage made him quite famous, and he published his first book <u>Journal of the voyage</u>.

Charles Darwin the free thinker or agnostic has come up with the theory that humans evolved from animals, and he called this "natural selection." That humankind evolved from apes, and then back to one single species and origin.

*Monogenist = Humanity goes back to a single origin (no God)*

*Polygenist = Humans and animals have different origins (Created by God)*

Evolution is a big lie, it is false, and cannot be proven. Have you ever seen a dog give birth to a cat, an ape give birth to a human, or a human give birth to an ape? If evolution were true, what happened to it? Have we ever seen these stages of change in any animals? Seashells that have been found dating back millions of years, and still look exactly the same today. Archaeologist discover the jawbone of an ape that lived millions of years ago, and claim it is our ancestor. I am so sorry you believe such nonsense Mr. Darwin, but God created us as human's beings, not monkeys. God created many species of animals, and when some went extinct, he created new animals to adapt to the weather and geography.

Darwin and his cousin Galton hoped that the superior humans would produce at higher levels, and reduce the number of inferiors, and eventually destroy them. Darwin looked forward to the day when the poor and uneducated would be no more on the earth. God created the rich, middle class, and the poor. The left wants to remove the religious believers, the poor, the weak, the sick, and all that do not follow the atheist elitist Ideology. In addition, if you are strong and independent, self-reliant, and self- made without the leftist ideology, you must be changed or proselytized toward the leftist way of thinking, or destroyed. In the bible, it is written that the poor will always be with us, yet the leftist think they can do without them. What the left wants to do is dumb us down so they can have full control over us, and believe it or not this is happening right now. They are trying to take away our belief in God, our morals, our freedom, and they introduce confusion with their insane rhetoric, like 2 plus 2 does not equal 4, it may equal 5, 6, or 7. Babel/confusion introduced by Cain thousands of years ago, continues today. Babylon a state of confusion, writings in stone that can only be interpreted by the puppet masters. Good becomes evil and evil becomes good.

If the earth was filled with only the well-educated leftist people without experience, and no common sense, how long would the leftist last? Who would cook their food, milk the cows, grow the wheat, build their cars and houses, and all the many things we middle and poor people do on a daily basis. Yes, how would the educated elitist survive without us?

### *Deuteronomy 15:11*

*For the **poor** shall never cease out of the land: therefore I command thee, saying, Thou shalt open thine hand wide unto thy brother, to thy **poor**, and to thy needy, in thy land.*

### Job 34:19

*How much less to him that accepteth not the persons of princes, nor regardeth the rich more than the **poor**? for they all are the work of his hands.*

### Psalm 82:4

*Deliver the **poor** and needy: rid them out of the hand of the wicked.*

### Proverbs 14:21

*He that despiseth his neighbour sinneth: but he that hath mercy on the **poor**, happy is he.*

### Proverbs 14:31

*He that oppresseth the **poor** reproacheth his Maker: but he that honoureth him hath mercy on the **poor**.*

### Proverbs 22:2

The rich and **poor** meet together: the LORD is the maker of them all.

### Luke 6:20

*And he lifted up his eyes on his disciples, and said, Blessed be ye poor: for yours is the kingdom of God.*

### Jeremiah 20:13

*Sing unto the LORD, praise ye the LORD: for he hath delivered the soul of the poor from the hand of evildoers.*

> Evildoers = Democrats, Marxist. Communist, Socialist, Atheist,
> Satanist, new age, and anyone against God and his believers

Why do the leftist insist and promote the poor to use contraceptives, and to get abortions? The left is socialist, Marxist, Communist, progressives, and all of these groups desire, to rid the world of what they call undesirables. They want total control over us. The leftist thinks they are superior to us, they are not, and they will have a rude awakening in the near future.

## The four lies of Satan!

The Rapture lie: The Rapture theory will do its biggest damage during Satan's hour. The Protestant Church has adopted the Rapture lie, which will set up the falling away of the Israelites and many Christians. The Catholic Church does not support this evil lie, but the books left behind have hooked some Catholic members, along with television documentaries, and Rapture movies. Satan will stand on Mount Zion, and claim to be Jesus the Christ, and will say I have come to Rapture you away. Satan will deceive many Christians through this great lie.

Karl Marx Communist Manifesto: This terrible lie is eating up the earth like a deadly cancer. Karl Marx wanted to destroy humankind, and he chose Communism as a means to get the job done. Slowly the progressives are eating away our freedom to worship our God, tearing down our family structure, teaching our kids liberalism from grade school to college. Trying their best to take our right to bear arms, and own property, and taking away our free speech rights through political correctness. Shame on them!

Christianity is being attacked on a daily basis right here in the good ole USA. Europe has become secular and socialist in every State/Country. Christianity is no longer the largest percent of the people in Europe, Atheism, Agnostic, Humanism and other religions have replaced it. Forty percent of the people in France claim to be Atheist, and a large percent claim to be Agnostic. Agnostics do not believe in God unless you can prove it to them. France was a great Christian State ruled by Christian Kings; King Charlemagne kept the Muslims at bay, which saved Christianity in Europe. Before Satan will come to this earth there will be a great falling away, many Christians will become nonbelievers, following in the ways of Satan, and not God.

_2 Thessalonians 2:3_

_Let no man deceive you by any means: for that day shall not come, except there come a falling away first, and that man of sin be revealed, the son of perdition;_

*The son of perdition is Satan*

Since 1776 when the Illuminati had its beginning, Christianity is being attacked by this Anti-Christian secrete society. The Illuminati were responsible for the French revolution, and a socialist State was formed. The Illuminati still with us today, are setting the world up for the hour of Satan and his angels. The Marxist, Communist, Socialist, Progressives, Liberals, New Age, all are a great cancer trying to abolish Christianity and Judaism.

New age religion: Is trying their best to corrupt Christianity and Judaism, and eventually wipe them out. It is working; New Age is assimilating into Christianity, and being adopted by the Protestant Church, and Catholic Church. New Age is the religious part of Marxism/Communism/Socialism, and Progressivism.

Charles Darwin (Evolution): Darwin's Evolution Theory is attacking our belief. Evolution denies a creator; therefore, everything has been created by chance. The Illuminati's desire is to remove faith, why because faith has power and the Illuminati wants that power for their elitist selves. The Illuminati is working today on a one-world system, or a "new world order". The Illuminati, (the puppet masters), will fail to set up a one world power. The one world system will receive a deadly wound, and Satan will be kicked out of heaven, and he will heal the deadly wound, which will make him look like a god.

What do these four lies have in common? The destruction of Christianity, and setting up a "new world order."

### *Isaiah 8:14*

*And he shall be for a sanctuary; but for **a stone of stumbling** and for a rock of offence to both the houses of Israel, for a trap and for a snare to the inhabitants of Jerusalem.*

### *1 Peter 2:8-10*

*And **a stone of stumbling**, and a rock of offence, even to them which stumble at the word, being disobedient: whereunto also they were appointed. But ye are a chosen generation, a royal priesthood, an holy nation, a peculiar people; that ye should shew forth the praises of him who hath called you out of darkness into his* *marvellous light; Which in time past were not a people, but are now the people of God: which had not obtained mercy, but now have obtained mercy.*

Jesus Christ is that Stone of stumbling. It is not easy being a Christian; the whole world seems to be against us. Even though one third of the earth's population is Christian. The media, our education system, and politics makes Christianity to look evil in the world. Christians are the most giving and compassionate people on earth, yet the media, tears us down daily.

Satan is a dead man walking, he only has one thing left, and that is to deceive the many membered body of Christ. Satan has set up his lies, and the proselytes of Satan will deceive as many Christians as they can. The four lies are set in stone, and the 1800s are over.

## The unbelievable twentieth century

The 1800s provided us with many new inventions, yet by the 1900s the use of these new inventions are used and enjoyed by a very few. In 1900 there is 76 million people living in the United States, only three percent are using electricity. The U.S. now is the wealthiest economy in the world, due to entrepreneurs like John Rockefeller, Andrew Carnegie, and many others. No thanks to the Democrats who have deceived the poor in to thinking, these businessmen were evil. Without them we would be a third world country today, even though the leftist has tried their best to bring us down, we have endured, because God has blessed our great Nation.

### !900-1920

The most important invention ever, was introduced in 1900 by Eastman Kodak, the Brownie box camera, at a cost of $1.00 with six exposures. Just kidding, but I sure loved my brownie when I was a boy. William McKinley was elected for his second term as President, and congress passes the Gold standard act backed by gold reserves.

In 1901, Leon Czolgosz a Democrat shot president William McKinley. Doctors could not find the location of the bullets, and someone sent for Edison's new invention, the mobile X ray machine, which was hand held. The doctors chose not to use it, and President McKinley died from gangrene. Very suspicious, President McKinley was not well liked by William Jennings Bryan Supporters, who were against the gold standard act. William Jennings Bryan a Democrat, and progressive, was much against John Rockefeller, and Andrew Carnegie. President McKinley was for a strong industrial Nation, and backed Rockefeller and Carnegie, and not liked by the Democrats. Possibly the doctors did not use the x-ray machine on purpose.

Vice President Theodore Roosevelt was sworn in as McKinley's Successor. This is the beginning of the three progressive presidents, Roosevelt, Taft, and Wilson. The progressive movement is a slow moving social justice system leading our country towards socialism and Marxism. The three Presidents that claim to be Christians, that led our great Nation towards socialism, and liberalism, go against God, and his natural existence of Humankind. "Christians my donkey", and that happens to be the Democrats symbol. Even though Roosevelt and Taft were elected as Republicans, today they would be considered Democrats.

In 1903, the Wright brothers successively flew an airplane for over one-half a mile powered by a small gasoline engine. This is what freedom can give us, the incentive to turn dreams into reality. The Donkey's hate free enterprise, capitalism, hard work, incentive, and religion, but they love regulation that slows down work progress, and the betterment of humankind. Henry Ford founded the ford Motor Company, paid a much higher wage, gave us the 8-hour day, and the 40-hour workweek. Since we have more leisure time, Thomas Edison produced an early motion picture "The Great Train Robbery". Before we go to that movie, men and women can shave with the newly invented safety razor by Mr. King Gillette. What freedom has done for us, and yet there are people that want to take us back to the Stone Age.

I think you get the point, there are evil people out there that want to destroy our way of life, to take away freedom, prosperity, security, the family unit, morals, religion, incentive to work hard, a slanted education with liberal and Marxist ideology, and much more.

They say, whomever (they) are, that the progressive movement began in 1900 and ended in 1920. I say the progressive movement began in 1776, and under the direction of the Illuminati is stronger today than any other period in history.

Be strong, it is Satan's day, and his hour is coming soon. We cannot prevent the leftist from trying to create a one-world system, or prevent Satan from standing on Mount Zion claiming to be God. It is God's plan, and it will take place exactly as he planned it thousands of years ago.

## World War I

The Great War or WWI began on July 28, 1914. The assassination of Archduke Franz Ferdinand of Austria and his wife Sophie Duchess of Hohenberg were both shot dead by Yugoslav nationalist Gavrilo Princip in Sarajevo. A destructive war began over the murder of these two-people destined to rule Austria. The total death count of the war was around 37,000,000 people including Combatants, and Civilians. This did not have to happen, but it did because it is Satan's doing.

Woodrow Wilson becomes our 28th President of the United States of America from 1913 to 1921. President Wilson leader of the progressive movement, passed legislation under a Democratic Congress giving our nation the socialist acts including the Federal Reserve act, Federal trade Commission act, Federal Farm Loan, Income tax, and Child Labor acts. He is supposed to be a fine outstanding Christian, yet he is doing the works of Satan by over regulating the people. (The Supreme Court ruled the Child Labor Act was unconstitutional due to the Government overstepping their power to regulate business and producers.) All of this was created by the Kenites, and President Wilson was like a child not understanding the burdens he signed into law. Later he realized what he had done.

By 1916, the war should have been over, the German Submarines overwhelmed the British, and they could no longer supply food and ammunition to their troops. The French army had mutinied, no surprise there, the Italians were done, and the Russians had defected, and where are the Serbs.

The Germans at this time had not fought in their own Country. Nobody was able to get to them, yet they offered a peace treaty. The Germans did not want to fight anymore, let us stop fighting and go home. The Germans have won the war, it is 1916, and the English, French, Russians, and Italians, have been defeated, and if it had ended here, millions of people would not have perished. However, it is Satan's day, and the war will continue.

Then comes a Zionist Jew from Russia, who moved to England in 1904. Chaim Weizmann a Chemist, developed acetone from a chemical process using maize. Acetone is a very important ingredient used to produce artillery shells, and with the war nearly over Mr. Weizmann will lose some income. He is also a committed Zionist who is working hard to establish a Jewish State in Israel. Therefore, he went to the British war Cabinet, and convinced them that they can win the war, if the United States would join in as an ally. He promised he could arrange this, if they would agree to turn over Palestine to the Zionist Jews. Chaim Weizmann would later become the first president of the State of Israel.

President Wilson ran on the campaign slogan in 1916 that "he kept us out of the war", and was elected president for a second term. What changed his mind?

Chaim Weitzman said he could arrange getting the USA into war, because he had friends in America that had the goods on President Wilson. Weitzman meets up with Walter Rothschild another Zionist Jew who is eager to do business with England, and the US, because loaning money to governments is a more secure way of getting your loan and interest paid. Not only money, Rothschild and the Rothschild dynasty desired to have a homeland for the Jews, where they thought they could be safe just in case they are kicked out of Europe. The Rothschilds can care less about the Jewish State, their desire is to control the world's money, and the Zionist movement is a power play. The Zionist movement is made up of Elitist Kenites, out to make money, gain power, and to control the world. I am not against the tribe of Judah, the Benjamites, the Israelites, or the Christians from establishing a State of Israel. However, the people living there should be treated well, and not driven from their homes, and living in poverty.

The Palestinians have been mistreated by the Zionist Kenites, but little compassion comes from the media. When will the media report the atrocities going on a daily basis against Palestinian's and Christians in Israel?

Through the puppet master, Walter Rothschild, another elitist Zionist Jew Attorney named Samuel Untermeyer is contacted, and he is the man with the goods on President Wilson. President Wilson has been a bad boy, he has been having an affair, and Untermeyer has the proof.

Untermeyer blackmail's Wilson to pay his mistress $40,000, knowing he cannot pay it. Untermeyer then negotiates with Wilson, telling him he will pay out the $40,000 to his mistress, if he will agree to appoint a Zionist Jew to the Supreme Court. President Wilson agrees, and appoints Louis Brandeis to the Supreme Court. Due to Untermeyer and Brandeis knowing of his affair, he gave in, and convinced Congress to declare war against Germany. Millions of people will die over this decision.

President Wilson is a puppet being led by the puppet masters. Zionist Rabbi Stephen Wise advised Wilson that the sinking of the S.S, Sussex by the Germans justified going to war against Germany. The S.S. Sussex was not sunk; it was a big lie by the Zionist Jews. Great Britain, France, and the USA, could have sucked it up, and declared they had been defeated by Germany, and there would have been no WWII.

The State of Israel is on its way. The Balfour Declaration pledged British aid on Nov 2, 1917, (prompted by Baron Rothschild) to establish a permanent home for Jews in Palestine. The Zionist movement has hit a home run.

Instead, Germany signed the Treaty of Versailles on June 28, 1919. Germany was given a raw deal excepting all responsibilities, and the sole starter of WWI, and accepting all loss and damages caused during the war. Germany was forced to disarm and to make concessions, and pay reparations toward the loss and damage to many States. The reparations were excessive, and the big three, Britain, France, and USA were out to cripple and nearly destroy Germany.

The elitist Zion Jews I have mentioned are not Jews; they are the sons of Cain, the Kenites. These few people that call themselves Jews, have given a bad name to our brother Judah. However, this is God's plan; we should watch with eyes to see, and ears to hear.

Before WWI, Judah was doing well in Germany, and Germany had no Quarrel with them. After WWI, it is a completely different story, The Germans have learned what the Kenites have done to them, and they are angry at all of Judah not knowing whom the Kenites are. Shame on the USA, Great Britain, and France, for allowing this to happen to our kinsmen the Israelites. Yes, they are the Saxons, the sons of Isaac, and Judah, and we have beaten down our own family. When a country like Germany is beaten down, the people will rise up, they become desperate, and their choice for a leader may not be the right one.

The Germans now hate the Jews; the war to end all wars will partly be responsible for the largest and deadliest war the earth has ever seen. World War I ends November 11, 1918. Leftist Kenites control the Money, Media, IRS, and the Democratic Party, and are the Puppet Masters of the USA, and most of Europe. We are not to touch the Puppet Masters/Kenites, and Christ tells us to leave them alone. We are here to watch and learn, and do what is right.

In no way is Judah to be blamed for any of this. The Atheist Kenites can care less about Judaism or Christianity, all they want is money and power. Many Israelites have become puppets or Proselytes doing Satan's dirty work and are known to the public, while the Kenites are invisible. The Kenites look at us as if we are dumb sheep, and they can lead us anywhere they choose. The Kenite is that one wolf dressed in sheep's clothing among many innocent sheep led to the slaughterhouse.

## *Russian Empire overthrown by Bolsheviks*

Jesus overthrew the moneychanger's tables and kicked them out of the temple. The moneychangers are the Kenites, they gain wealth by charging usury. The Kenites have been in the banking, and Priest business from the time of Cain 4000 years before Christ. The Rothschild Family (descended from Cain) establish a banking Business in 1760, the wealthiest, and most powerful banking dynasty ever. Why is this important?

In 1815, Nathan Rothschild makes this statement.

*"I care not what puppet is placed upon the throne of England to rule the Empire on which the sun never sets. The man who controls Britain's money supply controls the British Empire, and I control the British money supply"*

The Kenites placed Woodrow Wilson in the presidency because they could not manipulate President Taft. They rigged the election by adding an Independent to run for president. The power of money, what it can do? Well it can do a lot, the

Federal Reserve System made up of these banks, Rothschild of London, Israel Moses of Italy, Lehman Brothers, Lazard Brothers, Kuhn, Loeb, Warburg of Germany, Goldman and Sachs of New York, and they all control us. Now the Kenite Banks control the money supply of the United States of America. God is testing us, to see how well we will do against Satan's offspring. We are not doing well; we are deceived repeatedly. What will it be like when Satan steps foot on mount Zion, and say's, hello children I am your God.

Lennon, Leon Trotsky, have adopted the Marxist Ideology, and their sole purpose is to form a Marxist State in Russia. They cannot overthrow a government without money, so Trotsky also an Atheist Kenite, travels to New York and meets up with his good friend Jacob Schiff, Chairman of Kuhn and Loeb bank. Jacob Schiff gives Trotsky $20 million in gold to support the overthrow of the Russian government. Trotsky recruit's Russian immigrant Jews from Manhattan, and has them trained for the Revolution in 1917.

**The US ambassador of Russia David Francis dispatched this to Washington:** *"The Bolshevik leaders here, most of whom are Jews, and 90 percent of whom are returned exiles, care little for Russia or any other country, but are internationalists, and they are trying to start a worldwide social revolution".*

**Winston Churchill warns of a worldwide conspiracy to overthrow civilization on February 8, 1920. This is what he wrote.**

*There is no need to exaggerate the part played in the creation of Bolshevism and in the actual bringing about of the Russian Revolution by these international and for the most part atheist Jews. It is certainly a very great one; it probably outweighs all others. With the notable exception of Lenin, the majority of the leading figures are Jews. Moreover, the principal inspiration and driving power comes from the Jewish leaders. Thus, his nominal subordinate, Litvinoff, eclipses Tchitcherin, a pure Russian, and the influence of Russians like Bukharin or Lunacharski cannot be compared with the power of Trotsky, or of Zinovieff, the Dictator of the Red Citadel (Petrograd), or of Krassin or Radek -- all Jews. In the Soviet institutions, the predominance of Jews is even more astonishing. Moreover, the prominent, if not indeed the principal, part in the system of terrorism applied by the Extraordinary Commissions for Combatting*

Counter-Revolution [the Cheka] has been taken by Jews and in some notable cases by Jewesses.

The Netherlands ambassador to Russia said this:

*The Bolsheviks Financed by Jewish bankers overthrows Tsar Nicholas II and his Imperial Family, and then murdered them on July 16 1918.*

Robert Wilton a British journalist wrote in his book:

> *The Jew Syerdlov planned the murder of the Tsar and his family, and five Cheka Jews carried out the dirty work. He said the Russian people had nothing to do with this evil work of an Alien people.*

Again, the Jews mentioned are not Jews; they are Kenites claiming to be Jews. The other Jews that are not Kenites, are used to do their dirty work, the elite Kenites deceive them. The tribe of Judah is blamed for what the Kenites orchestrated against the Russian people, which is a total dictatorial control through Communism.

## Amos 2:1

Thus saith the LORD; For three transgressions of Moab, and for four, I will not turn away the punishment thereof; because he burned the bones of the king of Edom into lime:

*Today Russia is Edom the sons of Esau*

*The Kings bones were found along with his family*

*Their bodies were partly burned, and some bones turned to lime*

*Lime is used to reduce odor, Decomposition, and to hide murders*

Lennon and Trotsky along with many Kenites and other Communist form the Russian Socialist Federative Soviet Republic. Possibly eighty percent of the government was made up of Kenites and Jews. Again, the Jews were deceived like the people of the USA have been today. Satan deceives Gods children, being in the flesh we are weak; however, truth can make us strong.

The USSR approved and confirmed on December 29, 1922, by the first congress of Soviets.

The Netherlands ambassador to Russia said this:

> *"Unless Bolshevism is nipped in the bud immediately, it is bound to spread in one form or another over Europe and the whole world as it is organized and worked by Jews who have no nationality, and whose one object is to destroy for their own ends the existing order of things."*

Lenin one quarter Jewish regarded the Jews to be the only intelligent people in Russia, "an intelligent Russian is most likely to be Jewish or have some Jewish blood" Lenin is a Satanist just like Karl Marx, he wanted the good people wiped off the planet. This very evil man along with his evil appointed Kenites, using the Cheka Jews to murder and torture Russians are responsible for millions of Russian deaths.

The Jews mentioned above are not of the Tribe of Judah, they are the evil seed of Satan. They murdered, tortured, and starved the Russians people in the worst way imaginable. The Russians are not to blame; they are the brothers of Jacob, a good people.

Under Lenin, the new government takes away the crown lands, and the lands of farmers that work hard to feed the Russian people. If you work hard and are successful, you are in danger for your life. Abortion is now legal, remember Karl Marx wants to take away the family unit, the government will raise and indoctrinate them as good little communist. Free health care, now let me ask you how can health care be free. France citizens pay 20 percent sales tax, does that sound free. Free education really, it doesn't cost us anything, and we believe their lies. Does this sound familiar to us today in 2016?

## Stalin and Hitler

Under Lenin, thousands of Russians died under Cheka agents, and the Red Terror. Others died from starvation, due to their communist agriculture policies, and price control. Millions of people died in the worst ways imaginable, through many ways of torture, disease, and starvation. During Lenin's Revolution, 20 million to 30 million people were executed, or starved. During the Chinese Communist revolution of 1923 to 1947, an estimated 40 million to 70 million people died mostly from starvation, extreme harsh work, and execution.

Adam Weishaupt said, "Remember that the end justifies the means" The left they always run on the platform they are the party for the people, yet they have no compassion for humanity, only for the elitist few.

Lenin said he would let the whole country die from starvation than to allow the free trade of grain. The leftist wants full government control, no freedom, no incentive.

Karl Marx wrote, "Abolish private property" A socialized government must take away land from farmers who know how to produce food to feed the multitude, and to give to people that cannot, and will not, work the land. Take away the right to own property and guns, and your freedom goes out the window. Yet we have Marxist or Communist today that want to take our country down, so godless men can form a one-world system.

Lenin dies in 1924, and Stalin takes power nearly putting all the Bolsheviks leaders to death. Lenin did not want Stalin to lead Communist Russia; he wanted Trotsky and his Kenites to govern Russia. By 1928, Joseph Stalin removed the Kenites from leadership of the Soviet Union. Most Kenites were killed including Trotsky. Well he got rid of the Kenites; this must mean things will get much better, NOT!

Stalin was an absolute dictator. The kenites tried to assassinate him but failed, and Stalin became the supreme leader. He was a ruthless dictator, murdered and starved millions in the name of Marxism. Is this what the Americans want, they keep voting in Marxist Democrats, Why?

Ask any person from the Ukraine if they want Communism in their Country. If you have ancestors that lived in the Ukraine during Stalin's rule, you would know Communism is not the route you want to take.

Stalin Seized all privately-owned farmlands and livestock in the Ukraine, and imposed collectivization system that creates no incentive to produce high yields of farmlands. Due to this Collectivization process, food ran out. All the food was taken out of the Ukraine, to feed the people of Moscow, and the rest of Russia.

Stalin closed the borders of Ukraine so the food taken to Russia could not make it back to feed the starving people. Russian troops searched homes for food so the people would starve. People were eating leaves off trees; eating rats, cats, dogs, anything and everything that they could find to stay alive. By 1933, 25,000 people per day were dying, and millions starved to death.

What do the Democrats think about this? On 1933 when millions of people were starving to death, our Socialist President Franklin Roosevelt recognized Stalin's Communist Government, made a new trade agreement with them, and accepting them into the League of Nations. The Democratic Party, the party of Satan, completely ignores the starvation of millions of people, three million being children.

The leftist liberals always bring up the slavery of the Blacks in the US, but never mentions the men, women, and children forced into slavery in the Soviet mines and work camps in Siberia. Why because according to the socialist left, "the end justifies the means." Is there a double standard here, oh yes?

Joseph Stalin was a very evil man, yet our leftist President made him a partner with the United States of America. Stalin destroyed the prosperous peasants (Kulaks) in order to control agriculture and industry. Communism has been a failure everywhere it has been tried, yet people in America, Europe, Africa, and around the world embrace it. The reason why, is Satan rules this earth, and we are living in his day.

## Intermission!

Enough killing, murder, and starvation already!

Willis Carrier invented the air conditioner in 1902. The Southern States will become more desirable for people living in the north. Air conditioning becomes popular in cars and homes by the 1950s.

In 1911, Charles Kettering invented the first self-starting ignition system, and introduced it in the 1912 Cadillac. Before this you had to hand crank your car.

First Supermarket opened in 1916, by owner Clarence Saunders, the first Piggly Wiggly in Memphis Tennessee.

In 1924, Lionel C. Sternberger invented the cheeseburger; he must have been a genius. The hamburger was created around 1900, why did it take twenty-four years to put a slice of cheese on it.

In 1930, Pat Olivier invented the Cheesesteak sandwich in Philadelphia.

The first full talking movie was made in 1927, and the movie was the Jazz Singer. It took almost 30 years to Synchronize sound with video. In the 1930s, talking movies became very popular. Again, what took so long?

Alexander Fleming invents penicillin in 1928, but by 1942, only a few people had been treated for lack of mass production. By July 1943, mass production began, and two million doses were produced in time for the invasion of Normandy. Again, what took so long? Once the penicillin age begins, the life expectancy age increases greatly. In 1928, the life expectancy was 55.6 years, and by 1960, it increased to 66.6 years. In 1946, the baby boomers begin, and populations grow rapidly all over the world.

## Sorry back to Killing, Murder, and starvation

Today if you were to take a picture of George Washington, and Adolf Hitler, and asked average citizens, which one they could identify, most likely they would choose Hitler. It is a shame, Hitler is better known than our first president is. I guess it is human nature! In school, the teacher memorizes the bad boy's name first, and he is usually popular with the girls. For some odd reason, we flesh men and women tend to look up to the rebel types. We look up to them for going against the norm, and being independent, but this is not always a bad thing. Through history, humanity has most often chosen the wrong direction to lead their people, and Germany is about to make a grave mistake.

Adolf Hitler, will he be the savior of Germany or the destroyer of Germany? In the beginning, he was the savior, in the end Germany was in total ruin. Will we ever get it right, I am afraid not, and we will continue to follow lies until Christ comes. If Hitler had kept Germany out of war, Germany would have had the strongest economy in the world. However, the Kenites, had plans to turn Germany into a Marxist/Communist State. Hitler refuses the communist from taking over Germany and the neighboring States around Germany, including Russia. If you have a cancer moving in on you, you must destroy it.

After WWI, the Germans, and Hitler blamed the Jews for their defeat, and the German people grew a strong resentment towards the Jews. The treaty of Versailles split up their country making them much smaller, and forcing them to pay for the war, which kept them in poverty. The Germans are a strong people, a big portion of these people are Saxons, the sons of Isaac, the Israelites. The Germans do not want war; they want a growing economy that will produce good paying jobs.

Hitler was born April 20, 1889 in a small Austrian village, near the German border. His father Alois Schicklgrubber was born Illegitimate, the son of Maria Anna Schicklgrubber. Alois father may have been Jewish making Hitler's dad half-Jewish. This would make Hitler 1 quarter Jewish, and remember Lenin was one quarter Jewish. Hitler did not kill the Jews, because he thought he was one quarter Jewish, and he hated is dad. The reason is, the Kenites controlled a big part of the newspapers in Germany, and they were leading Germany towards communism.

Maria Schicklberger married George Hiedler when young Alois (Hitler's father) was five years old. After the death of his mother, her uncle Hiedler raised Alois, and convinced Alois to change his name to Hiedler. When it was time to make the name legal, it was written down as Hitler. Can you imagine the German people saying heil Schicklberger; it just would not sound, right?

Hitler was raised Catholic, and at an early age idolized the priest to the point where he contemplated becoming a priest. I believe he loved the power or authority over the monks, and the congregation. He noticed the power of a good orator that could move the people.

When Hitler was young he did not hate the Jews, but actually had Jewish friends. His hatred for the Jews came after WWI when they had learned what the Kenites had done to them. Hitler did not know of these Kenites, and the evil seed line they came from. The Kenites were mixed in with the tribe of Judah so all Judah were blamed.

Jews leave Europe after WWII

Jewish World Almanac 1933-1948

In 1933 Jews living in Europe 9,494,368

In 1948 Jews living in Europe 9,372,668

In 1933 total world Jewish population 15,315,359

In 1948 total world Jewish population 15,763,638

In 1951 Jews living in Europe 3,500,000

From 1948 to 1951 six million Jews migrate to
Palestine forming the State of Israel.

In 2016 world Jewish population 14,250,000

The Kenites are setting up the new world order, or the one world system, this system will fail in the near future. Even the Muslims are controlled by the Kenites, (the Shayk's of Saudi Arabia are Kenites.) The Kenites control the religions of the world, and money or finance, education, control over governments, and the media give them their power. The Christians and Muslims should stop fighting each other and realize the Kenites are the ones that keep us stirred up. Our Presidents are just puppets on a string bowing down to every dirty deed the Kenites give them. The deadly wound written in Revelation chapter 13:3 and 13:12 will happen when the one world system breaks apart.

Hitler wanted to stop Communism from spreading throughout Europe and eventually into the United States of America. Communism is evil and of Satan the devil, yet the media controlled by the Kenites, is deceiving many into believing

Communism is good, and Capitalism is bad. They are leading many Americans away from what our founding fathers had designed.

Christ said not to touch the Tares, which are the Kenites, Hitler not knowing, did touch the Tares, and 51 million people died. Because of Hitler Europe and the USA are slaves to the Kenites. I know most of you will be offended of what I have written, but I have written this book for the few that have the desire to know and search for the truth.

Search for the truth on your own, form your opinion, and ask God to help you to understand.

Hitler did help to keep the communist from taking over Europe, and Israel became a State in 1948. The good and bad fig moved into Israel, the Kenites are the bad figs, and all the people who love God are the good figs The good and bad people are in Israel waiting for the wrath of God, which is coming soon.

Go on You Tube: Type in Benjamin Freedman. He makes a speech in 1961, at the Willard Hotel, telling all as a Jewish insider during the Woodrow Wilson Presidency. He gives great detail on how the Kenites manipulated the USA, and Europe into two great wars. I am sure he did not know these elitist Jews were Kenites; however, he knew they had done evil. He spilled the beans, he told the truth, and no one listened. He spent all his money trying to get the truth out, but the Kenites had control over the media, and his writings and speeches went on death ears. He died a broke man, however I am sure he was rewarded greatly in heaven.

The Kenites hate God, and they love Satan their Father. They have proselytized the Jews, Israelites, Christians, and others, into doing their dirty work against God. The Kenites Laugh at God, saying look, we have your children working for Satan.

## The Parable of the fig tree

*Jeremiah 24:2*

*One basket had **very good figs**, even like the figs that are first ripe: and the other basket had **very naughty figs**, which could not be eaten, they were so bad.*

*Very good figs = All people of all races that believe in Christ*

*Very naughty figs = the offspring of Cain (The Kenites)*

*All twelve tribes of Israel and the Sons of Cain are living in Israel today*

**Matthew 24**

*[32] Now learn a parable of the fig tree; When his branch is yet tender, and putteth forth leaves, ye know that summer is nigh:*

*[33] So likewise ye, when ye shall see all these things, know that it is near, even at the doors.*

*[34] Verily I say unto you, **This generation shall not pass, till all these things be fulfilled.***

*Put forth leaves = The State of Israel is Born in 1948*

*The last generation in the flesh begins in 1948*

*There are three generations in the bible, a 40, 70, and 120-year generations*

*Satan will stand in Jerusalem claiming to be god*

## Getting close to Satan's hour

It is getting closer to 2018, and the world did not end in 2012. In 2009, I thought there might be a chance the world would end in 2012, but by 2010 I knew it was not time. The world does not actually end; it is the end of flesh humankind. We continue to live in a different dimension, one without electron shells orbiting around the nucleus made of protons and neutrons. We are very near to the time of Satan's grand entrance, standing on the Temple Mount. Many people are scared and worried about this period that brings uncertainty among people who do not know Gods plan.

From the established State of Israel to present, we have had wars and rumors of war, we have had volcano eruptions, many earthquakes, Tsunamis from earthquakes, major hurricanes, floods and drought, extreme cold and extreme hot, starvation and disease, and all this is normal, like Solomon said, "there is nothing new under the sun".

There is one thing that has not been tried, and that is Peace. Since Cain and Abel, we have not had peace. God did not put us in flesh bodies so we could experience utopia. Oh, but the left thinks they can, through total government control, with a one world system. However, Mr. Satan will nearly make this happen, he will feed the poor, and there will be world peace. It will be a false peace!

The puppet masters have been busy pulling the puppet strings, leading us into bed with the Anti-Christ. The Anti-Christ is Satan, the one that has been deceiving us through his children from generation to generation. From 1776, our Country the USA has been given a small portion of lies, to slowly indoctrinate us into believing (good is evil and evil is good).

## Mark 13

*13 And as he went out of the temple, one of his disciples saith unto him, Master, see what manner of stones and what buildings are here!*

*2 And Jesus answering said unto him, Seest thou these great buildings? there shall not be left one stone upon another, that shall not be thrown down.*

*3 And as he sat upon the mount of Olives over against the temple, Peter and James and John and Andrew asked him privately,*

*4 Tell us, when shall these things be? and what shall be the sign when all these things shall be fulfilled?*

*5 And Jesus answering them began to say, Take heed lest any man deceive you:*

*6 For many shall come in my name, saying, I am Christ; and shall deceive many.*

*7 And when ye shall hear of wars and rumours of wars, be ye not troubled: for such things must needs be; but the end shall not be yet.*

*[8] For nation shall rise against nation, and kingdom against kingdom: and there shall be earthquakes in divers places, and there shall be famines and troubles: these are the beginnings of sorrows.*

*[9] But take heed to yourselves: for they shall deliver you up to councils; and in the synagogues ye shall be beaten: and ye shall be brought before rulers and kings for my sake, for a testimony against them.*

*Gods Elect will be delivered up by Satan/Antichrist*

*[10] And the gospel must first be published among all nations.*

*All nations have received the word*

*God's word has been fulfilled*

*[11] But when they shall lead you, and deliver you up, take no thought beforehand what ye shall speak, neither do ye premeditate: but whatsoever shall be given you in that hour, that speak ye: for it is not ye that speak, but the Holy Ghost.*

*The Holy Spirit will speak through Gods Elect*

*[12] Now the brother shall betray the brother to death, and the father the son; and children shall rise up against their parents, and shall cause them to be put to death.*

*One brother will follow the traditions of man, and the lies of his church, and the other brother will follow truth from God's word*

*The Rapture lie will lead many to Satan*

*[13] And ye shall be hated of all men for my name's sake: but he that shall endure unto the end, the same shall be saved.*

*If you choose God and not Satan be prepared for a fight*

*[14] But when ye shall see the abomination of desolation, spoken of by Daniel the prophet, standing where it ought not, (let him that readeth understand,) then let them that be in Judaea flee to the mountains:*

*Abomination of desolation is Satan/Anti-Christ*

*Where he ought not, standing on Mount Zion claiming to be god*

¹⁵ *And let him that is on the housetop not go down into the house, neither enter therein, to take anything out of his house:*

¹⁶ *And let him that is in the field not turn back again for to take up his garment.*

¹⁷ *But woe to them that are with child, and to them that give suck in those days!*

¹⁸ *And pray ye that your flight be not in the winter.*

¹⁹ *For in those days shall be affliction, such as was not from the beginning of the creation which God created unto this time, neither shall be.*

²⁰ *And except that the Lord had shortened those days, no flesh should be saved: but for the elect's sake, whom he hath chosen, he hath shortened the days.*

*Christ has shortened the days from seven years to five months*

²¹ *And then if any man shall say to you, Lo, here is Christ; or, lo, he is there; believe him not:*

*Long as you are in flesh bodies, you have not yet seen Christ, but
when Christ comes, you will be changed into spirit bodies*

²² *For false Christs and false prophets shall rise, and shall shew signs and wonders, to seduce, if it were possible, even the elect.*

*If you have God's truth you will overcome*

²³ *But take ye heed: behold, I have foretold you all things.*

²⁴ *But in those days, after that tribulation, the sun shall be darkened, and the moon shall not give her light,*

*Most people on the earth will follow Satan, which is darkness*

*Few will follow Christ, which is light*

*A five-month period of darkness*

<sup>25</sup> *And the stars of heaven shall fall, and the powers that are in heaven shall be shaken.*

*The children of heaven*

<sup>26</sup> *And then shall they see the Son of man coming in the clouds with great power and glory.*

<sup>27</sup> *And then shall he send his angels, and shall gather together his elect from the four winds, from the uttermost part of the earth to the uttermost part of heaven.*

*All will see him*

*Moreover, He will gather the ones that did not bow their knees to Baal "the Elect"*

The hour of Satan/Anti-Christ is very near. The parable of the fig tree began in 1948, and all of GOD'S prophecy has nearly happened.

The Kenites today are no longer our biggest problem. The puppet masters have pulled our strings, and the Kenites can sit back and watch the show. Many people have become proselytes for the works of Satan, the liberals, Christians, New agers, Atheist, the wealthy, the poor, good decent people they all have succumbed to the lies of Satan, as did Adam and Eve. The flesh earth age is nearly over, be prepared for Jesus Christ coming.

# Who is the Raiser of taxes?

### Daniel 11

<sup>20</sup> *Then shall stand up in his estate a* **raiser of taxes** *in the glory of the kingdom: but within few days he shall be destroyed, neither in anger, nor in battle.*

John the Baptist was born six months before Jesus, he was a chosen prophet to usher Jesus in, and to baptize him. At age thirty, Jesus work begins.

The raiser of taxes is president Obama (my opinion), and through Obama care, which was declared a tax makes him the raiser of taxes.

*Revelation 13:12*

*And he exerciseth all the power of the first beast before him, and causeth the earth and them which dwell therein to worship the first beast, whose **deadly wound** was healed.*

President Trump will cause the deadly wound (my opinion), and Satan will come down from heaven and standing on mount Zion will heal the deadly wound.

*Money and power will have a bad day*

*The deadly wound is the breakup of the (New World Order) (my opinion)*

*President Trump will be hated for breaking up the **New World Order***

*Jeremiah was chosen to be a prophet before he was born, and so is Donald Trump chosen to be strong enough to take on the evil extremist left*

Donald has six letters
His last name is Trump
6th Trump = Satan's last hour

God chose Moses to lead the Israelites out of Egypt, and to lead them to Israel. God chose Alexander the Great to cause the Israelite's to flee Bactria and to travel a long journey to Germany, and becoming the Anglo Saxons. God chose Hitler to cause the Jews to flee Germany into Israel, and to form the state of Israel. God chose Donald Trump to cause the deadly wound, which will start the sixth trump, bringing Satan down from heaven to test the children of God, standing in Israel.

Revelation 9:14

Saying to the **sixth** angel which had the **trump**et, Loose the
four angels which are bound in the great river Euphrates.
On the sixth trump Michael sends Satan and his angels to the earth

*21 And in his estate shall stand up **a vile person**, to whom they shall not give the honour of the kingdom: but he **shall come in peaceably**, and **obtain the kingdom by flatteries**.*

*Vile person = Satan/Anti-Christ*

*Satan as Anti-Christ will stand in Jerusalem claiming peace,
peace, and his craftiness will deceive the world*

²² *And with the arms of a **flood** shall they be overflown from before him, and shall be broken; yea, also the prince of the covenant.*

*The flood of Satan's lies*

*The third flood*

²³ *And after the league made with him he shall work deceitfully: for he shall come up, and shall become strong with a **small people**.*

*A small people are the Kenites (a small population)*

²⁴ *He shall enter **peaceably** even upon the fattest places of the province; and he shall do that which his fathers have not done, nor his fathers' fathers; **he shall scatter among them the prey, and spoil, and riches**: yea, and he shall forecast his devices against the strong holds, even for a time.*

*Don't let Satan buy your soul*

The easiest way to convert people is to offer peace and divide the riches of the world to all people. The Democratic Party has been working on this for many years, the poor are still poor, and the rich are still rich. In fact, the rich are richer and the poor are poorer through Socialism and Communism. The Democrat Party has failed, but Satan will not, he will divide the spoil and riches of the earth, so he can steal your soul. I pray the children of GOD will not sell their souls to Satan.

No man knows the hour Satan will come to this earth in a transfigured body, standing where he should not. However, we should be watchmen, and read the scriptures, GOD gives us many clues.

<u>**Amos 8:11**</u> ¹¹ *Behold, the days come, saith the Lord G*OD*, that I will send a famine in the land, not a famine of bread, nor a thirst for water, but of hearing the words of the L*ORD*:*

**Matthew 23:15** [15] Woe unto you, scribes and Pharisees, hypocrites! for ye compass sea and land **to make one a proselyte, and when he is made, ye make him twofold more the child of hell than yourselves.**

*The proselyte's go even farther with the leftist agenda, then the Kenites*

[11] And many false prophets shall rise, and shall deceive many.

[12] And because iniquity shall abound, the love of many shall wax cold.

[13] But he that shall endure unto the end, the same shall be saved.

[14] And this gospel of the kingdom shall be preached in all the world for a witness unto all nations; and then shall the end come. [15] When ye therefore shall see the **abomination of desolation,** spoken of by Daniel the prophet, stand in the holy place, (whoso readeth, let him understand:)

*The abomination of desolation is Satan*

**II Thessalonians:**

Now we beseech you, brethren, by the coming of our Lord Jesus Christ, and by our gathering together unto him,

[2] That ye be not soon shaken in mind, or be troubled, neither by spirit, nor by word, nor by letter as from us, as that the day of Christ is at hand.

[3] Let no man deceive you by any means: for that day shall not come, **except there come a falling away first, and that man of sin be revealed, the son of perdition;**

[4] Who opposeth and exalteth himself above all that is called God, or that is worshipped; so that he as God sitteth in the temple of God, shewing himself that he is God.

[5] Remember ye not, that, when I was yet with you, I told you these things?

[6] And now ye know what withholdeth that he might be revealed in his time.

[7] For the mystery of iniquity doth already work: only he who now letteth will let, until he be taken out of the way.

[8] And then shall that Wicked be revealed, whom the Lord shall consume with the spirit of his mouth, and shall destroy with the brightness of his coming:

[9] Even him, whose coming is after the working of Satan with all power and signs and lying wonders,

[10] And with all deceivableness of unrighteousness in them that perish; because they received not the love of the truth, that they might be saved.

[11] And for this cause **God shall send them strong delusion, that they should believe a lie**:

[12] That they all might be damned who believed not the truth, but had pleasure in unrighteousness.

**I Timothy 4:1**- Now the Spirit speaketh expressly, that in the latter times some shall depart from

the faith, giving heed to seducing spirits, and doctrines of devils;[2] Speaking lies in hypocrisy; having their conscience seared with a hot iron;[3] Forbidding to marry, and commanding to abstain from meats, which God hath created to be received with thanksgiving of them which believe and know the truth.

**I John 4:1-3**

Beloved, believe not every spirit, but try the spirits whether they are of God: because many false prophets are gone out into the world.

[2] Hereby know ye the Spirit of God: **Every spirit that confesseth that Jesus Christ is come in the flesh is of God:**

[3] And every spirit that confesseth not that Jesus Christ is come in the flesh is not of God: and this is that spirit of antichrist, whereof ye have heard that it should come; and even now already is in the world.

**II Timothy 3:1-4**

This know also, that in the last days perilous times shall come.

[2] For men shall be lovers of their own selves, covetous, boasters, proud, blasphemers, disobedient to parents, unthankful, unholy,

³Without natural affection, trucebreakers, false accusers, incontinent, fierce, despisers of those that are good,

⁴Traitors, heady, highminded, lovers of pleasures more than lovers of God;

## Revelation 12:12

Therefore rejoice, ye heavens, and ye that dwell in them. Woe to the inhabiters of the earth and of the sea! for the devil is come down unto you, having great wrath, because he knoweth that he hath but a short time

## Revelation 6:16

And said to the mountains and rocks, Fall on us, and hide us from the face of him that sitteth on the throne, and from the wrath of the Lamb:

> *All the people who worshipped Satan thinking he was God, Christ,*
> *Messiah, Mahdi's, Buddha, aliens, and others, will be so ashamed they*
> *will want to die, but cannot because they are in spirit bodies now.*

The Lamb is Christ Jesus; He comes at the end times with a doubled edge sword, which is his tongue. If you do not want God's Wrath to come down on you, you need to learn God's word. This book does not give all you need to fight Satan; you need to be taught chapter by chapter, verse by verse to get a full understanding of what God's plan truly is. You must understand Genesis before you can grasp God's word, by stepping back and looking at the whole picture, God will allow you to see what you have not seen.

If you desire to know more, and you desire to have a better understanding of GOD'S word, please listen to Shepherds Chapel on TV or the internet. Ask for the monthly letter, which has many tapes and books listed that you can order. Direct TV and Dish Network run this program many hours a day. Other cable companies carry Shepherds Chapel early in the morning. You can also Call them at 1-800-643-4645 or write them at Shepherds Chapel P.O. Box 416, Gravette, AR 72736.

Do not let the Wrath of God come down on you!
Learn the truth and the truth will set you free!

Printed in the United States
By Bookmasters